AGENT OF INFLUENCE

Other books by Ian Adams

Fiction
Becoming Tania
Bad Faith
End Game in Paris
S. Portrait of a Spy

Non-fiction
The Real Poverty Report (co-author)
The Poverty Wall

Feature screenplays
Bad Faith

Stage plays
S. Portrait of a Spy (co-author)

Ian Adams

AGENT OF INFLUENCE

A True Story

101262

Stoddart

Published in 1999 by Stoddart Publishing Co. Limited
34 Lesmill Road, Toronto, Canada M3B 2T6
180 Varick Street, 9th Floor, New York, NY 10014

Distributed in Canada by General Distribution Services Ltd.
325 Humber College Blvd., Toronto, Canada M9W 7C3
Tel. (416) 213-1919 Fax (416) 213-1917
Email customer.service@ccmailgw.genpub.com

For information about U.S. publication and distribution of Stoddart Books,
contact 180 Varick Street, 9th Floor, New York, NY 10014

03 02 01 00 99 1 2 3 4 5

Canadian Cataloguing in Publication Data

Adams, Ian
Agent of influence: a true story
ISBN 0-7737-3123-7

1. Watkins, John, 1902–1964 — Death and burial. 2. Royal Canadian
Mounted Police. 3. United States. Central Intelligence Agency.
4. Espionage Soviet — Canada. 5. Canada — Foreign relations — United
States. 6. Ambassadors — Canada — Biography. 7. United States — Foreign
relations — Canada. 8. Spies — Canada — Biography. I. Title.

FC621.W37A62 1998   327.1247'071'092   C98-931462-6
F1034.3W37A62 1998

Jacket Design: Bill Douglas @ The Bang
Text Design: Tannice Goddard
Text Layout: Mary Bowness

Printed in Canada

*Stoddart Publishing gratefully acknowledges the Canada Council for the
Arts and the Ontario Arts Council for their support of its publishing program.*

To my sons, Shane and Riley,
and
for Graziano Marchese — one of the good guys

"The longest journey is the journey inward."
Dag Hammarskjöld,
Markings

The Main Characters

John Watkins, Canadian ambassador in Moscow
Jane Fletcher, inspector, RCMP Security Services
David Present, head of the RCMP's KGB desk
George Merleau, CIA officer
Murray Fletcher, intelligence officer, External Affairs
Anatoly Nikitin, alias Anatoly Gorsky, KGB officer
Oleg Gribanov, alias Alexei "Alyosha" Gorbunov, alias "Zoltan," KGB
    officer
Khamal Stoikov, Watkins' lover

Agent of Influence, an account of the interrogation and death of Ambassador John Watkins, is based on true events, declassified documents, and investigative reporting. Some of the characters in this book are wholly fictional; some are fictionalized composites of two or more real people. None of the characters represents a single real individual.

AGENT OF INFLUENCE

INFLUENCE

1

A NEEDLE PIERCES HIS BRAIN. The roar of the Moscow subway crashes in intermittent waves of sound through his head. The dank chill of the unheated car seeps into his bones. Dobryininskaia Station. Through the grime-covered glass, a crowded platform. Is that Akhundi's face turning away? The emergency light over the exit explodes into shards of red lightning . . . He opens his eyes.

Six inches from his face, the cream-coloured phone rings repeatedly, its red buttons flashing under the logo of the Windsor Hotel. He is not in Moscow but in Montreal. This finally must be the call from Mike, the call that has kept him waiting, chained to this hotel room, for the past three days. He shoots out an arm to snatch the phone from its cradle, and an excruciating pain detonates inside his chest wall. An electric current locks his hand in a spasm as he picks up the receiver. He can hear the metallic voice of the secretary from the PMO: "Mr. Ambassador? Hello, Mr. Watkins? Are you there, sir? This is the Prime Minister's Office . . . Hello?" But he can't bring the receiver to his ear. He tries to call out, but he can't even breathe. With his other hand he carefully feels for the small metal container under the pillow. He knows that if he accidentally pushes it off the edge of the bed he will be lost. Gasping for air, with awkward crab-like finger-movements, he inches the little silver tube out from under the pillow. Between his index finger and thumb he screws off the cap and lets the pills slip out onto the sheet. "Hello? Hello?" the tinny voice keeps inquiring. "Is anybody there? . . . Mr. Ambassador?" He manoeuvres one of the pills into his mouth and traps it under his tongue. He gropes for another pill from the pile on the sheet and successfully paws it between his lips. The open phone line clicks off in his hand. The female voice is followed by a long buzzing. Like a crane releasing a steel girder, his hand at the end of his still inflexible arm drops the receiver back into the cradle.

Watkins lies there, staring at the phone, waiting for the nitroglycerin to work, to lift the concrete slab off his chest. He reflects on the indignity of a body he can no longer rely on, a body that betrays him at the moment he is most in need. The room is cold from the window he left open before he fell asleep. Long white muslin curtains curl and float in the chilly draught. Beyond the window, thunder rolls in waves over the heavy grey air of the city.

GROMYKO — WHY, HE HAD WONDERED at the time, wasn't Molotov handling this? — turned from the tall window to read aloud in his excellent English another extract from the *New York Times*. Behind him, the view of Moscow was obscured by the cold spring rain that lashed against the curved panes. " 'The Russians are not to be trusted,' says Lester Pearson, Canada's usually more pro-Soviet minister of external affairs, at a press conference today." Then Gromyko, old war horse of the Stalin years, marched right up to where Watkins had been kept standing on the thick Bokhara carpet he had so often admired in previous, more amicable meetings and thrust the newspaper in the Canadian ambassador's face, glaring at him from a space of three inches. The closeness was nauseating, as the rotten odour of Gromyko's gum disease fouled the air between them. "Perhaps it's time for you to be more careful, Ambassador," Gromyko growled. "When a leader asks you to put personal loyalty above love for your country, you know he is ready to abandon you. A man with your talents should possibly be looking for other options." What a strange thing to say. But then, Gromyko already knew a great deal about betrayal. Was he making an offer or a threat?

And what was all this fuss about? It was nothing new. The U.S. media had always been hostile to the Canadian view of the world when it didn't coincide with theirs. So the papers had printed yet again an intentional misinterpretation of statements made by Mike at a press conference. Big deal! They did it all the time. The usual rot. Of course Mike had said no such thing. He had been there himself, and he had already told Molotov he could confirm that the newspaper account was false. Gromyko knew that he knew . . . God, what nonsense! But perhaps the Soviet foreign ministry didn't have the luxury of lashing out at the U.S. media, so it was the Canadians' turn to play the whipping boy. While he pondered Gromyko's bizarre counsel, he searched around for a reply to deflect the foreign minister's misdirected anger.

"*Druzhba druzhboi, a tabachok vroz'.*"

He knew that Gromyko had a weakness for translated aphorisms. The minister's bushy white eyebrows slowly separated. Thankfully he backed away, unable to maintain the absurdity of this clumsy attempt at intimidation. His stern face reluctantly gave way to a twisted smile. "Congratulations, Ambassador. Your fluency in Russian becomes more impressive on every occasion. So tell me, how would you say that in English?"

Watkins, relieved to get Gromyko at least temporarily distracted, took his time. "Literally it would be 'Friendship is friendship, except when it comes to tobacco.' But our proverbs are not as colourful as yours, so it would probably be translated more blandly as 'Friendship is friendship, but business is business.'"

"What are we going to do about these Americans?" Gromyko asked, relaxing his tone. "We ask them to collaborate with us in the exploration of space, and they challenge us to a race to the moon. What an enormous waste of money! Everyone knows putting a man on the moon is irrelevant. Perhaps they think, like the leaders of antiquity, that it will bring them closer to God."

"You may have something there, sir. Then, again, that could be America's greatest strength — the inability to see the world in any other way than they wish to see it."

Gromyko smiled broadly — unusual for such an icy man. "Have you ever lived in the United States, Ambassador?" Suddenly Gromyko the intellectual was curious, and Watkins thought he could detect a longing for the years when Gromyko had been the Soviet ambassador to the United Nations.

"Yes, sir. I studied there and worked in New York for more than ten years."

"Where did you study?"

"My earlier degrees were in languages — Latin, French, German. I wrote my doctorate in Scandinavian languages at Cornell University."

"What was your thesis?"

"The life and work of the Danish dramatist and novelist Gustav Weid. Obscure turn-of-the-century writer." Gromyko nodded. Watkins had never seen this side of the man before. Hoping to draw him out, he laughed and added: "I think, after my advisers, Dag Hammarskjöld was the only one in the world to read it."

That was definitely the wrong thing to say. Gromyko's face darkened. "He was a good man," he muttered; "such stupidity . . ." He broke off and turned away to the window. How much did Gromyko know about the circumstances of Dag's death? Watkins cursed himself for breaking that rare moment of another kind of communication. The foreign minister very definitely signalled that the session was over, but he turned back and whispered conspiratorially, "Don't forget my advice, Ambassador, before it's too late." Then he curtly waved to an aide to show Watkins out.

THE ANGINA PAIN begins to ebb away. Watkins swings his legs over the side of the bed and struggles to sit up. Why has he dreamed about

Dobryininskaia Station? Was that really Akhundi on the platform? It doesn't make sense. He never met him anywhere in Moscow. He breathes into the pain and, while he waits for the waves of vertigo to pass, he gazes around the room. A life lived in hotel rooms prepares one for solitary contemplation. He clears his voice and tries to speak out loud: "He loved Caesar, but he loved his country more." The words come out, but they sound weak, as if coming from a long way off. The Windsor is comfortable enough as hotels go, but he feels nostalgic for his room at the Lennox, his favourite Left Bank haunt. That hotel holds an ambiance that always makes him feel at home. Joyce had lived there, and also Camus from time to time, or so it is rumoured. But they were men who loved women and were probably seeking temporary sanctuary, whereas, for him, hotel rooms are his destiny.

He waits a few more minutes, then dials the front desk: "This is Ambassador Watkins. Please put me through to Ottawa. Yes, the number I have been calling all week." When the phone rings back, he is able to speak more normally, with his usual quiet authority and seriousness. It's the metal voice from the PMO again.

"Oh, yes, Mr. Ambassador, I was just trying to phone you. The prime minister wants you to know he's dreadfully sorry he didn't get back to you. He's having a hectic week — the flag business, you know — and he just left to fly out to Vancouver for a speaking engagement. He'll try to phone you from there — or at the latest when he gets back, before the Thanksgiving weekend."

Nothing to be said. He mutters his thanks and hangs up. At least the woman hasn't added to his humiliation by letting a tone of embarrassment or pity creep into her voice. He dials again, this time to External Affairs.

"This is Ambassador Watkins speaking. Please put me through to the minister." A moment of silence. The executive assistant hesitates: "Oh yes, of course, sir. One moment, please." He hears a quick, muffled conversation. "Putting you through now, Ambassador Watkins." The phone rings and rings. He finally hangs up and stares out at the grey Montreal skyline that blends into an even greyer October sky. He recognizes the old ploy. The *apparatchiks* frequently used it in the Kremlin. A trick to play on foreign diplomats who became a nuisance by aggressively calling the ministry too many times in one day: Plug them into the Siberia line, a phone no one will ever answer. He feels sad and betrayed. He never expected the same deception to be played on him in his own country.

AKHUNDI KISSED HIM on both cheeks and then Russian style, directly on the lips. He could taste the vodka and salted herring. The Uzbek's usually bemused eyes were still and sober. He did not smile. His familiar gold teeth were hidden behind a now serious mouth. "Maybe this is goodbye, John, and maybe not. But I have to warn you, you must be more careful. In future, you must do the choosing. Always remember: never trust the ones you allow to choose you because they will betray you."

"You chose me."

Akhundi flashed his gold teeth. "Yes, but that's different. You and I, we're both artists, poets. And when the KGB comes to me and tells me do this and do that, I will tell them to go fuck themselves and then fuck their mothers, because I am Akhundi, an Uzbek from Samarkand. And you know what? They will go away shaking their heads because, as they say in Moscow, *Zastav' duraka bogu molit'sia, on i lob rasshibiot* — "Make a fool pray to God, and he'll smash his forehead." But what they really mean to say is that you can't count on a dumb Uzbek to do anything right.

That's why he dreamed about Akhundi in Dobryininskaia Station. Akhundi used to ridicule the way the party bosses had made the Moscow subway system into an icon of Soviet culture. He layered the irony by mocking one of Leon Trotsky's famous speeches: "One cannot tell whether the Moscow subway will succeed in producing 'high' tragedy. But socialist art will revive tragedy. Without God, of course. The new art will be atheist. And it will also revive comedy, because the new Soviet man will laugh so hysterically at the future that he won't want to kill himself on the Moscow subway tracks."

WATKINS RETRIEVES a slim volume of poetry from the night table and moves slowly to a chair. He tenderly handles the Swedish edition of

Hammaskjöld's *Markings*. He opens it up and pauses yet again to read the hand-written note: "For my dear friend and colleague John — a mutual friend at the UN sent this to me and I immediately decided to pass it on to you, for I remember how well you and Dag spontaneously connected. Holding the book in my hand filled me with many warm memories of the times the three of us spent together, and also, of course, with a feeling of deep sadness. Mike." Watkins crumples the note and tosses it into the waste basket.

He selects a page and reads, in his heavy, dark voice: "Tomorrow we shall meet, Death and I . . ." Did you meet death, Dag, or did they bring it to you? And who did the serving: the CIA? Belgian mercenaries? Or was it the Cubans acting for the KGB?

"A long life!" Dag had raised his glass, he remembers, and they clinked in response. "I look forward to a long life, John. To the time when I'm older and all the unimportant details are forgotten, and the poetry will flow in simple words and pure images."

But that's not how it works, Dag. They lied to us about that. You didn't live long enough to find out. Because, my friend, the painful truth is that I can remember everything, often excruciatingly so. The trivial lives side by side with the most significant. The inexorable meetings of diplomats hang like David's tableaux in my memory, Akhundi strumming Uzbek folk songs on his strange lute-like instrument, the trees glittering with ice in the brilliant blue calm around Norval Station . . . It's all there, Dag, every gesture, every mood all the time, in every jagged detail. At sixty-two I remember everything as vividly as the moment it happened, and I think it's driving me crazy. Yet at the same time I savour every moment of it.

The phone rings again. He carefully puts down the book of poems and reaches for another Players, the last in the pack.

"Mr. Ambassador, this is the front desk. There's a gentleman asking for you downstairs. A Mr. Jenkins from Norval, Ontario."

Puzzled, Watkins tells the operator he'll be right down. He needs cigarettes anyway. He sorts through a sheaf of papers on the bureau. The pages, typed in Russian Cyrillic, are covered in red-inked hand-written English translations — the work of his last three days of waiting for the phone call from Mike. He puts the papers in order, then casually stuffs them into his suit pocket.

About to go out the door, he remembers the small metal container on the bed. He scoops the little pile of pills on the sheet back into the tube and puts one more pill under his tongue. There must be some coincidence or a bizarre mistake. Billie Jenkins has been dead more than ten years. Watkins has even been to his grave at Norval Station. He carefully tucks the container into an inside coat pocket as he pauses at the window. Thunder still rumbles continuously on the grey horizon, punctuated by short flashes of lightning. Dag, you should have been with us on the road south of Kharkov — there was a moment that called for a poem.

THE ELECTRICAL STORM backlit the rolling countryside and the long convoys of Gypsies half-blocking the Kharkov highway. The others in the car were impatient to return to Moscow, a full two days' drive. But, Dag, I was in no hurry to get back to the claustrophobic embassy. I kept thinking of excuses to distract them, to stop the car so we could at least get out and explore a bit. I was willing to forgo for several more days the tiresome task of combing through *Pravda* and the mind-numbing official releases, all of which said nothing, but had to be read in the endless search for clues to the internal workings of this closed Soviet society. Nor was I in a hurry to get back to the loneliness of my bleak two-room flat. But when I suggested we stop and chat with the Gypsies, my proposal fell on deaf ears.

I was surprised, Dag, to see so many caravans. In one group alone, a few miles from Kharkov, I counted more than two hundred Gypsies. Most were travelling in crude four-wheeled carts drawn by two or more horses, with lively spring colts running alongside. The carts were heaped high with rolls of quilts and swarms of children. I was especially drawn to some of the old bearded patriarchs. They looked handsome and dignified, their faces deeply lined from a lifetime of endurance. They had stories to tell — and I wanted to hear them. Again I said I would like to stop at one of the encampments where groups had stopped to build a fire and make some tea. But the others in the car pretended not to hear me.

I know you would have stopped at once, Dag. Unfortunately, these bureaucrats have no interests outside the constricted little lives they lead in Moscow. So strange, when you offer humans a breath of freedom, they often find it threatening. Here are these minor officials, living in this totalitarian state with all its restrictions on travel and casual conversation, and they are determined to race back to their little Moscow cells as fast as they can. The poem, as I see it, Dag, is exactly that: to compare the pathetic psychological acceptance of repression by my companions with the seeming freedom of the Gypsies on the road beside us.

"Even those things which are not forbidden are forbidden," an official of their foreign ministry once told me, in all seriousness, as I applied yet again for a travel permit to visit Georgia.

"I see," I said, "so everything is forbidden?"

"No," she replied testily, "only that which is forbidden. But not everything that is forbidden has to be written down as forbidden."

When I mentioned to Maxim, my chauffeur, that I was surprised to see the Gypsies travelling so freely, he became quite conversational for a change. He explained that the Soviet authorities had tried to organize the Gypsies into the Soviet social system. What he really meant was that the state had tried to force them into daily factory work. But the project had been a disaster and the bureaucrats had finally given up. "It was just like trying to make the Jews farm in Birobidjan," he said, falling back on that anti-Semitism that is so deep in Soviet culture. "It couldn't be done. The Jews spent all their time trading and driving hard bargains with each other and did no farming."

"They seem to have no problem with the farms they have created out of the desert in Israel."

"Oh yes," he replied. "I've heard that in Israel they are good fruit farmers — but that's different."

The Gypsies, he continued, lived mainly by stealing, although they made a pretense of mending pots and pans. Historically, there had always been large numbers of them in the Ukraine because, in that part of the country, people were rich, and generous, too. "In my own region, Tver, there have always been just a few Gypsies, but people dislike and fear them and never give them much."

When I asked Maxim if the Gypsies were required to send their children to school, he said no, they were always on the move. Now there, Dag, is perhaps another poem: victory over the totalitarian state by the weakest.

WATKINS EXITS the elevator and crosses the ornate lobby of the Windsor Hotel to the reception desk. The clerk looks around for the visitor. "Yes, Mr. Ambassador. He was here a moment ago — a Mr. Jenkins — said you knew him. Perhaps he just stepped out for a moment." Watkins shrugs and tells the clerk that if Mr. Jenkins reappears, he will be over at the newsstand buying cigarettes.

FOR A MOMENT Inspector Fletcher is seized by a dreadful panic, similar to what she experienced in the icy whirlpool when the powerful pull of the swirling water dragged her under one more time. But Fletcher is not in the river. She is seated in a deep brown leather armchair in the baroque lobby of the Windsor Hotel, having thirty seconds earlier slipped in through the side door, and has glanced up from her feigned reading of the *Montreal Gazette* to survey the activity just past the maze of monstrous sofas and chairs. Something has gone wrong. That fool Morissette, of all people, is following the ambassador much too closely. And O'Reilly and Davis here too? The whole surveillance crew she briefed only this morning has been replaced without her being informed. How on earth did Morissette get reassigned to her Watcher team? The guy doesn't have the IQ to pass a urine test. He's going to screw it all up, just the way he did this summer in the Scharansky business.

Fletcher forces herself once again to examine every face in the lobby. She scrutinizes them all — sitting, standing, pacing idly about — and compares them with her mental catalogue of faces from the "other side." It's one of her talents, this photographic memory — score sheets, schedules, faces, and names. No, she can't find anybody from the other side there. But they will likely send in one or possibly two of their support people from their Montreal consulate any moment now to do a quick walk-through of the lobby, the way they did back in July. By now their people must all know Morissette. If they see him here it will be all over — unless, of course, Merleau is right and this is a genuine Soviet rogue operation.

The panic Fletcher has experienced in nightmares is now overtaken by a fierce anger — the kind of rage she has felt often since the accident on the river, a rage that scares her in its intensity. It sends surges of energy up the back of her neck and across her scalp, electrifying her with the ominous sensation that she is about to lose control. Concentrate, she urges herself. Focus on the issue at hand.

The problem as she now sees it is how to get Morissette out of the lobby before Poliotov arrives, without tipping off the ambassador. Fletcher glances at her watch. Not feasible. There is no time left. Damn their arrogance at headquarters! Who made these last-second decisions to change her Watcher crew without even consulting her? What do those senior officers think they are doing? Such blatant demonstrations of primitive egotism. Why don't they just take their dicks out of their pants, wave them around in the air, and let the audience decide? Then everyone would understand what is really going on here, and we could all get on with the actual work.

She waits and watches. Morissette still trails like an obedient collie at the ambassador's heels as he makes his way across the pale-ochre tiles of the Windsor lobby floor to the cigarette kiosk. How incredibly stupid! And after she has extracted a specific agreement from Present never to let Morissette work on her assignments again. Never! Ferguson, the director of the Watchers, or whoever has recycled Morissette back on duty, is going to pay for this farce. With a surreptitious hand signal she tries to catch the attention of O'Reilly, dressed up like a workman, on the ladder. But O'Reilly, another participant in the Scharansky disaster, supposedly in place to photograph an anticipated exchange between Watkins and Poliotov, is not paying attention. His eyes are glued to two young women checking in at the front desk. Unbelievable! This is like watching a fatal accident about to happen. What feeble-mindedness! It's no wonder the only spies the RCMP have caught in twenty-five years are the ones who walked in the front door to give themselves up — and even these few volunteers had a hard time convincing the Force who

they were. If the public had the remotest idea how incredibly incompe-
tent these high-priced intelligence services really are . . .

Fletcher fights to control her anger. She focuses on Watkins buying
his carton of Players at the kiosk. This is the first time she has seen him
in person. Until now, her only knowledge of him has been information
abstracted from photos and tapes. But now her heart tightens. So this is
the surprise Murray told her to expect. She begins to understand why
from the start she felt so uncomfortable about this operation. It wasn't
just the counter-intelligence hypothesis, the dangerous gamble of trap-
ping the ambassador, that had seemed so suspect to her ears. It was
something more deeply intuitive . . . There it is again! All in the way the
ambassador turns and looks up, his glasses catching the many-pointed
reflections of the chandeliers. His large shaggy head, cocked at an angle,
peers warily up at the workmen hanging decorations from hooks
fastened into the twenty-foot ceilings. It really is too early for this
Christmas junk. It's not even Thanksgiving yet, for God's sake. She
never liked the idea, but she was overruled by Present at the last meeting. She wishes she had found the energy to fight back.

Present wears you down with his dogmatic insistence on useless detail
— "This is how MI6 ran the Rostow case in Ankara back in . . ." To
Fletcher this setup seems ludicrous, the staging too transparent. If the
ambassador is only half as intelligent as the files report, he will immediately suspect that the ladder farce has been staged for his benefit. There is
no hope he will dismiss it as more evidence of what Present called "over-
eager commercialism in celebration of the birth of our Lord Jesus Christ."

IN HIS OFFICIAL ROLE as head of the KGB desk in the Counter-
Intelligence Unit, Present spoke with an ambiguous tone of invitation to
conspiracy. He always left his listener wondering whether he was being
sincere or mocking. He pretended an old-world courtesy. He never
cursed, at least not in front of Fletcher, and he reprimanded officers who
did. Everybody knew Present was a deeply religious Catholic. He took
his whole family, wife and five children, to Mass every Sunday. Did that
make him a devout Catholic of the left, right, or centre?

While Present talked, Fletcher could not take her eyes off the photograph of his family on the wall behind the desk. They all had the same vague, round, anonymous faces, fair straight hair, almost invisible eyebrows. They all wore glasses and seemed to be blinking behind their lenses. A dowdy group of little owls seated around a slightly bigger daddy owl: *Portrait of a Bureaucrat with Family*. She stared over his shoulder at the portrait as he lectured her with insistence. "The ambassador has spent the greater part of the last fifteen years out of the country, most of it in Moscow postings. He won't even notice the decorations, and if he does, he'll just shrug them off as more evidence of Western excess. But we must have a reason for those men standing around there, and they can't be doing the usual newspaper-reading act. Come, now! We don't need to waste any more time on this detail of the operation." She held her tongue.

Fletcher sensed another agenda unfolding. What was this American, Merleau, doing here? With Present, nothing was ever up front; you had to find the truth buried deep in the details. He was a difficult man to like. He was notorious for his minutely scribbled notes and his nit-picking procedure memos. And then there was something wrong with that mid-Atlantic accent; affected, she always thought. She sometimes caught a working-class intonation creeping into his attempts at precision. Fletcher recognized the slips — the *eh?* after a sentence. Her own father . . . No, she mustn't let herself think of him, especially in this meeting. She had to keep focused. Why was Present so insecure? Why did he work so hard to cover up his origins? Restlessly she stood and watched the season's first light snow flurries swirling outside. The flakes immediately melted as they hit the streets, making the dark asphalt wet and luminous. A large black crow pursued by half a dozen darting sparrows flapped past the window. Before the Mounties took over this building it had been a nunnery. How many women before her had sat in this space? They at least didn't have to listen to the ravings of men who formed the secret governments of the intelligence world. Present's voice broke through her musings: "Let's just get on with the arrangements, shall we, Fletcher? Or would you rather pass the assignment to Miller?"

He had made a mistake. Present had allowed an extra peevish tone of rudeness to creep into his already querulous voice. Fletcher glanced at

Merleau, sitting there quietly watching them both. Damn these CIA liaison types, always supercilious in their know-it-all silences. She wasn't going to let Present get away with this shit, not in front of an outsider. He should be more careful. Present had seniority because he ran the KGB desk at B Operations here in headquarters, but in the end he was still only a civilian. Every once in a while he needed to be reminded that nobody on the Force would ever address him as anything more than "Mister." Fletcher was an officer, and, while she scorned the Force's paramilitary clap-trap, she didn't hesitate to use it when it suited her. She could pull rank on Present any time she wanted, and in ways Present could never fight.

When Fletcher didn't immediately get up from her chair to leave, Present, the wily old owl, knew he had gone too far. He immediately became more circumspect when she retorted: "None of this makes any sense to me, David." She put special emphasis and icy coldness on his first name, a not-so-subtle way of reminding him of his civilian status.

"I'm listening, *Inspector* Fletcher," the owlish face with the faded blue eyes behind the thick lenses and the narrow, almost lipless mouth replied with reciprocal intent to insult, but careful this time to control the irritation in his voice. How, she wondered, could any woman kiss a mouth like that? You would cut yourself.

"Why would the KGB risk making any contact at all, let alone an exchange, with the ambassador in Montreal, when he is about to return to Europe? They know their movements are constantly under surveillance here. There are just too many things that can go wrong for them in this country and —"

"Think it through, Inspector," Present, with a glance at Merleau, interrupted her. "Think of all the implications and possibilities."

"I have, but from an operational point of view I can't see any implications that make any sense to me. Why can't the KGB wait another couple of weeks until the ambassador gets back to Moscow?"

"I hope this doesn't mean we're going to have another Scharansky foul-up. We can't afford another . . ."

Fletcher was disgusted with that comeback. What a back-stabbing little worm! Still, she maintained her calm and continued in her lucid, icy tone: "Don't patronize me, David. That's precisely why I don't want to be put through the same pain all over again. In the Scharansky operation you made some fundamental errors in judgment. It's true there were mitigating circumstances — you were misled by the expectations of our friends." She gave an imperceptible nod in the direction of Merleau. "But in the end it was me and the other members of the B Operations team who took all the heat for your decisions. Before we get back to the question you're avoiding, there's something else I want to know: Does the Prime Minister's Office know what we're up to? After all, we are dealing with a personal appointment made by the prime minister himself."

In the tense silence that followed, Present scribbled busily. Fletcher waited. But Present held out, making notes on the long yellow pad in front of him. Finally he looked up.

"You know the ambassador is vulnerable because of his . . . ah . . . personal weakness."

"Are you talking about his homosexuality?"

"Yes. That's it exactly, his —"

"Good God! You mean you're putting us all through this very expensive exercise just because he's the last homosexual in the public service who has managed to slip through your fingers? If that's the case, why don't you let the security and intelligence section in External Affairs deal with it?"

She actually forced a blush out of Present. That was a first. Was it because she used the Lord's name in his presence, or because she used the word "homosexual"?

"You should know why not, Inspector Fletcher. External is always too busy protecting its own." This was a not-so-veiled shot at her brother, Murray, who laboured anonymously and silently over in External's unofficial and super-secret security and intelligence unit. But before Fletcher had a chance to reply, the quiet Merleau, a slim man with a knife-like face, finally decided Present needed help. He coughed politely, and they both turned to him.

"The main reason for this joint operation is that we have information gathered from various sources that the ambassador might just be dealing with rogue elements in their intelligence system."

Ah, yes. There it was. Under different circumstances she would have laughed out loud. The old "rogue elements" cover story. Now there's a term, she thought, that's seen a lot of usage in our business since the Kennedy assassination. Did they really think she was so naive? The Americans just didn't get it. Everyone could see how obviously they tripped over themselves. There must be no great talent to playing the "ugly American." Now she understood very well what was happening. But she kept a cool exterior, nodded, and smiled with interest into Merleau's dark eyes. He had olive skin and a black mole on his right cheekbone. On a woman it would have been a beauty mark; on Merleau it looked a bit comic, more like a clown's errant makeup. She decided she would play the game, but she wasn't going to let Merleau off the hook too easily.

"Even if that is so, it still doesn't explain why they would want to make the contact here instead of in Europe."

He answered confidently in a warm and reassuring voice. Present's owl head moved from her to the CIA officer and back again. Merleau was one of those unruffled men with a personality you immediately wanted to like and trust. But he also had a hard edge below the surface — she liked that. He had just been reassigned from CIA operations in Buenos Aires — or so she had heard. He was obviously a man with a lot of experience and skill in persuasion. But, she decided, he's too good, too smooth. His weakness is that he can't resist showing it. And here he is "making do" with what he's been given, trying to talk sense into these hick Canadians and finding a willing ally in this English-trained expert from MI6. Even so, she had to admit Merleau was engaging, and obviously wanted to win her over. He went so far as to take her into his confidence, giving much more information than was necessary for her to know. He zipped open a black folder and took out a couple of red CIA file folders with the usual TOP SECRET stamps on the covers and a designated FOR YOUR EYES ONLY list. "You already have a picture of Poliotov," he said; "here are some others." He spread the photos of Poliotov in front of her on Present's desk. They had been taken at various stages in his career: cadet, university student, Red Army officer. She studied the handsome blond Russian in his mid-thirties, with the classic strong Slavic cheekbones and powerful jaw — a striking figure in his uniform.

"That is hero material," Fletcher observed, "not the usual invisible agent."

Merleau agreed. "Yes, you can see that Poliotov is military intelligence — GRU — not KGB. And you're right. With his distinctive face and presence, the last place he should be is on the ground, trying to make an operational contact. If anything, a guy like that should be lurking back in the weeds, doing the planning and back-channel stuff. Normally speaking, Inspector Fletcher, the KGB would orchestrate any activity first for military intelligence, but we have . . . uh . . . discovered that Poliotov is in some kind of trouble with the KGB. Possibly something to do with competition over turf for recruiting foreign agents. Given the constant KGB surveillance in the Soviet Union on someone like Watkins, it would be even more dangerous for them to try to connect back there in Europe. So, all things considered, the fact that Poliotov's group is willing to take this enormous risk in contacting the ambassador here can only mean that they are trying to do something of an end-run around the KGB."

Fletcher was impressed. The story was plausible. She couldn't help liking Merleau for the air of professionalism that she found sadly lacking in her own colleagues. He stood out in comparison to Present, who was a small-minded bureaucrat promoted way beyond his capabilities, with no wider view of intelligence warfare than the little colonial empire he had created for himself within the RCMP. At the same time, Fletcher wasn't completely sold. Behind Merleau's explanation she caught a glimmer of the first part of the hidden agenda Present and Merleau had put in motion. It was more likely Merleau, she concluded. This scheme was too complex for Present to figure out by himself. She suspected that whatever they had or were about to get on Watkins they would simply use as bait to hook Poliotov, who was their real target. If they could find a way to manipulate the Russian and turn him around, they would have a double agent on their payroll — the dream of every ambitious intelligence officer and an accomplishment that quickly skyrocketed a career. Okay, she would keep her guard up, her eyes open, and her thoughts to herself. "Of course, these are still early days," Merleau had summarized, "and the truth is we don't really know where all this is going and where it will take us. But, nothing ventured, nothing gained, as they say. So, you see, Jane, there is potentially a lot riding on this operation." She noted how smoothly he had moved from "Inspector" to "Jane," and for her it was another little tipoff.

She wanted one last part of the plan to be clarified: "So, after the exchange takes place in the lobby of the Windsor, I am to let Poliotov walk — nobody's to touch him?"

"That's right," Present chimed in. "After he leaves the hotel, the second Watcher squad will pick him up and keep him under surveillance until, presumably, he returns to the Soviet consulate."

"And after Poliotov's cleared the lobby of the hotel, I am to detain the ambassador and hold him for interrogation?"

"That's all we want —"

"By the way, why the safe house?" Fletcher asked.

Merleau and Present exchanged glances. "We're concerned," Present ventured carefully, "or, rather, it's just a precaution against possible defection and . . . uh . . . suicide."

"Suicide?"

"Yes," answered Present, "we don't want another Herbert Norman on our hands."

Merleau stared at them quizzically. God, Fletcher thought, this guy doesn't know anything about us, or has he just been badly briefed?

"The Canadian diplomat stationed in Egypt," Present explained. "Jumped —"

"Possibly even pushed," Fletcher interrupted.

"— from a building in Cairo."

"Oh, yes, now I remember," Merleau muttered apologetically. "Prime Minister Pearson refused to allow him to appear before the Committee on Un-American Activities."

"Something like that," said Present, and hurriedly closed the subject by turning to Fletcher. "That's all we want, Inspector. A few precautions."

"Well, that's what you'll get, David."

Then Present threw in the carrot to keep her on side. "To answer your earlier question . . ." a thread of spittle caught between his upper and lower lip moved rapidly up and down as he spoke ". . . External and the PMO have agreed to permit the interrogation that will follow, but the PMO insists on the proviso that we also allow a uniformed member of the Force to be on hand." For Fletcher that was another clue that there was a play behind the play. "Of course," he continued, "after a bit of back and forth about who would share in the information, we agreed to their conditions. I went one step further. I have clearance from the superintendent of the division for you to conduct the initial phase of the interrogation."

Present smiled his razor-thin smile. Merleau spread his well-manicured hands in a gesture that implied all kinds of possibilities and chided her gently: "You see, Jane?" There it was again, the caress of her first name. "You're not just on to do the shit work. You're in for the goodies, too."

Fletcher had been careful to make all the right noises, but she could read the cards that Present was dealing her. If everything went the way it was supposed to, she would be able to resurrect her career in intelligence from its post-Scharansky decline. But she didn't think for one moment that Present was trying to give her a break. He was just covering his little bureaucratic owl ass. She also got the other side of the message: if the operation went badly, she'd be carrying all the baggage again, taking the heat for another disaster. But this time she'd probably be transferred back to somewhere like Kamloops and be put in charge of transporting women offenders from court to prison. So Jane, she smiled to herself, you really don't have a choice. Just pick up the cards these two guys have dealt you and play them as they are.

She put her notes away in her briefcase: "What's the code name for this operation?"

"How about Starlift?" Present asked.

"Is the code name for the ambassador still the same?"

"Yes, Rock Bottom."

"Very well, we'll be there."

But Merleau stopped her with a question when she had one hand on the door: "Jane, I'm not familiar with the Scharansky case. What was the outcome?"

He had to be lying! She waited for Present to answer, but the owl wisely remained silent.

"He disappeared."

"You mean just . . . vanished?"

Perhaps Merleau did not know. There was something genuine in his tone.

"He was a Czech, an eight-year defector. Someone, somewhere, made a decision to try to reactivate him. One of those theories people dream up at two in the morning and then should forget in the cold grey light of dawn. Unfortunately, they didn't. The plan was to make Scharansky go back and convince his former KGB control officers he was willing to work as a double agent. Naturally he wasn't too keen about it — he really didn't want anything to do with it. But he had no choice. He was here on a minister's permit that could be revoked at any time." As she spoke she kept her eyes on Present. He shrugged.

"It was a simple plan," he said evenly.

"Well, yes, but then so is suicide."

Present shrugged again, seemingly uninterested, and returned to his notes. She continued: "Well, anyway, a meeting was set up in downtown Montreal where Scharansky was supposed to renew contact with the members of the Soviet Embassy staff who we knew to be intelligence officers and who we had let him contact. I was in charge of the perimeter — four city blocks. The KGB officers walked through it according to plan. Scharansky was brought to the boundary. Then, for reasons no one has ever been able to figure out, the Watchers on duty lost contact with him. Nobody ever saw him again."

When she turned back to Merleau, she could see he hadn't been lying. His astonishment was genuine. "No corpse, nothing?" he asked.

"No. Vanished off the face of the earth."

"You mean he didn't even show up on the other side?"

She shook her head and nodded formally to Present. Just before leaving, she said: "By the way, Merleau, let's leave 'Jane' out of it. 'Fletcher' will do fine. 'Inspector' is even better."

She quietly closed the door on his slightly raised eyebrows. But she had not been able to close the door so easily on the lies she was ordered to tell Scharansky's wife: "Mrs. Scharansky, I don't quite know how to tell you this, but without any warning to us, Alexi seems to have suddenly decided to return to Prague." The woman didn't believe a word of it. She carefully put her baby on the sofa and, without any warning, flung herself on Fletcher and raked her nails across her cheek. "You murdering bitch," she screamed. "He told you they would kill him, but you wouldn't believe him." She cursed Fletcher in Czech and violently shoved her out of the house.

DON'T PLAY THE HAND," was Murray's curt and immediate response as they stood in the noisy lineup of secretaries and research assistants in the parliamentary cafeteria. He handed her a plastic tray. "Stay away from the lasagna. It's the government's only truly reliable secret weapon of the Cold War."

Murray pushed back his thick mop of sandy red hair and petulantly studied the steam table. He ordered a sandwich. He had been this way, by turns flip and aggrieved, since their father had died. Jane was conscious of the women around her checking him out. He was tall, especially in the Calgary cowboy boots he wore with his jeans and sports jacket. His big-boned face was too craggy to be considered cute. People's glances always went from him to her and back to him again, as they caught on. She smiled; for her, looking at him was like looking in the mirror. Murray and Jane Fletcher, the Alberta twins.

She followed him to a table that he purposely chose to be in the centre of all the office gossip buzzing around them. She appreciated his discretion. Neither of them wanted this chat to look like a conspiratorial meeting. Just a brother and sister getting together for lunch.

"Why not?" she asked.

"Because the deck is stacked."

"Tell me more, I —"

"Why do you come to me for advice? You never take it anyway."

She was startled and confused by his attack. She glared at him, but he was defensive and wouldn't meet her eye. She watched him wearily canvass the room, his eyes moving on every time a woman met his moody scowl with interest. Why did she always have to feel like the big sister?

"You're still angry with me."

Murray returned his chicken sandwich to the plate untouched. He tapped his fingers aimlessly on the formica. "How did we get here, Jane? Can you explain how you and I, at thirty-two years of age, got to this place in our lives? Working in this paranoid system that feasts off a Cold War that is nothing but a scam wrapped in a flag."

"A scam?"

"Yes! To make a few fat cats even fatter. Or perhaps you can explain it to me, because I can't figure out how it got so fucked up."

She realized at once how desperately lonely and sad he was, and once again she felt guilty. But she didn't know how to answer him.

"I studied Mandarin for five years so I could become a diplomat and I wind up as a spook, a low-level mandarin. That's the joke, eh, Jane? In an office of External Affairs that officially doesn't exist. You started out to become a doctor, to help people, and suddenly here you are too, running around putting together files on people whose lives you can't even experience. You've become just another Cold War spook piling up wood for the final bonfire. And the really scary thing for me is that I think you've suddenly become a true believer."

NO, THERE WAS NOTHING SUDDEN about any of it. It had been a long journey and she had earned every step through the ranks with sheer determination. She disagreed with Murray's cynicism. For a moment she remembered the expressions of discomfort on the Regina boot camp sergeants' faces when they discovered she could ride a horse better than most of them. What else should they expect from a kid from High Level, Alberta? She was also a crack shot on the shooting range. But that hadn't helped her avoid the constant and malicious harassment. No matter, she had borne it with seeming indifference. In retaliation, they had excluded her from the famous Musical Ride, hoping to crush her spirit. They were not about to set a precedent by making her the first woman to ride in the all-male unit. In truth she had been delighted — it was the last place she wanted to go in the RCMP — but again she had disguised her relief with stoic indifference. The sergeants hated her even more for being a law school graduate. Her first tour of duty at Prince

George in British Columbia had been hard and lonely. Nobody, least of all the locals, wanted a woman officer around. Sergeant Bitsky tried to keep her pushing paper like a glorified secretary in the office. Then one morning he had gotten a call from an Ottawa headquarters superintendent looking for recruits, and in a random moment her life had been changed. Bitsky had lifted his head from the receiver and scanned the room. When his eyes fell on Fletcher, they lit up with relief. He suddenly had a solution for his headache. "Fletcher," he announced triumphantly, "pack your gear. You're going to Ottawa this week. They need some warm bodies in security and intelligence."

SHE TRIED TO JOLLY Murray out of his frustration. "I don't know if there are any great truths to be found in our jobs at this particular moment in this Cold War. But I do know for sure, this is one spook who, if she doesn't survive the next few days, will be shipped out for traffic control on Vancouver Island." But his black mood persisted.

"And if you are, Jane, it won't be because you're no good at your job. It'll be because you and I didn't have the right parents, let's face it. And in this town that means everything. We're not part of the old-boys' network — and never will be."

"You really miss him, don't you?"

Murray's eyes reddened and welled up with tears. He propped his head in his hand as he struggled to regain his composure. Finally he gazed at her steadily. "I should never have let you take him out on that canoe trip."

She saw their father's body spinning past her in the water and felt again the icy cold pain of guilt and loss in her heart. "I know, Murray, I know. But nobody knew he was that sick."

"I did."

"No, you just told me he was tired and out of shape, and not to take him on the Upper Churchill because it would be too tough for him."

"I didn't tell you the whole truth."

She waited, puzzled.

"The last time I visited him I discovered he'd been monitoring his blood pressure. Most of the time it was through the roof, 180 over 110."

"My God! If I'd known I would never have taken him on the Churchill. Why didn't you tell me?"

"I didn't want to admit that I'd been snooping, that I went through his desk while he was out on a call. And . . . well, then I had to return to Ottawa and I thought you had taken my advice not to go, so I never knew, until it was too . . ." His voice trailed off.

Her mind spun back to the day of their impromptu decision and departure — the rush to get the canoe and supplies loaded onto the old station wagon. "But he must have taken medication, been on something. He was a doctor. He knew what to do."

"I don't know. Afterwards, I checked all the pharmacy paperwork. You know how meticulous he was. There was nothing there to indicate he was prescribing medication to himself."

She was bewildered, stunned. "On the trip he never mentioned any-thing, and I never saw him take anything . . . Are you sure? Where did you find these notes?"

Murray looked around the room again and heaved a sigh: "In his per-sonal journal."

"You went through Dad's diaries when he was still alive?"

"I know, I know. It's inexcusable. But this job . . . this work deforms the soul and the mind."

She was shocked. She could think of nothing to say.

"So you see, I'm really not upset with you. It's myself I'm angry and disgusted with. Ah, why is it so hard to tell the truth when it should be so simple? I mean, if I had done at least that — told you the truth — Dad might still be alive today."

She was numb, couldn't think. Did this information change anything right now, except to make her understand more fully why Murray seemed so deeply depressed?

"Murray, I can't talk about this right now. I have to think about it. But . . . I'm glad you finally told me." She reached out across the table to take his hand. "We have to take care of each other. We're the only ones left." Tears once again came to Murray's eyes, and he quickly took his hand away to brush them off. She watched him, sad. Their father had tried hard to meet their demands as children equally. But she had been her father's favourite, and Murray had always struggled for his attention. Invariably she had been caught in the middle. They were twins, but she was way older than Murray and always had been.

They stared down in silence at their untouched food. The other diners started to drift away from the nearby tables. She had to force her mind back to deal with the business at hand, the reason she had come to see Murray.

"Murray, I promise you we'll talk about this next time I come, but today I'm under a lot of pressure. I have to get back to Montreal this afternoon. There are some things I need to know about Watkins."

"It's not that I don't want to help; I just don't know much. Since Kennedy's assassination last year, everybody is in a state of permanent paranoia. The most innocuous information is labelled top secret. But today I sent over at Present's request a copy of every dispatch Watkins filed from Moscow. Ask for them. He was a good writer, better than any I've seen so far in this job."

"What could they possibly have on him? I know his files backward and forward. He has no political affiliations from his student days. In fact, he seems completely apolitical."

"It has to be the gay thing."

"But Murray, he's sixty-two, for God's sake — hardly a stud."

"I dunno. All I can tell you is that since he applied for retirement, he has become a non-person."

"How?"

"People who worked with him in the past are rewriting their résumés. It's even hard to find a photograph of the ambassador with any other member of External's inner club."

"And I thought only Stalin did that. What really is his job status?"

"Officially he is on sick leave, but he is still the ambassador."

"What does he do with his money?"

"Well, for one thing, he bought the family farm back in a place called Norval Station, down near Brampton in southern Ontario. And then he seems to give a lot of it away."

"Who to?"

"Mostly to artists. He buys paintings and gives them away to friends."

"But this non-person business is silly. I mean, even your minister knows him well. So does the prime minister."

"Yeah, but you know what they say about Pearson: if he were the captain of the *Titanic* he would say we were just dropping off to pick up some ice."

"You're not cut out for this work, Murray. I think you should request a transfer, soon!"

"No, it's the measure of the man. There's this well-known story in the ministry. Pearson wanted to take George Ignatieff on his trip to Moscow to meet Khrushchev. Someone suggested that the Soviets might be offended because Ignatieff came from the Czarist aristocracy. "Well," Pearson said, "if we get into trouble, George, I'll just dump you.""

"I still think you should apply for a transfer out of the department."

"Ha! I do too, every month. But you know Pearson is distracted. This is probably the worst year of his life. He has no clue how to deal with what's happening in Quebec. The cabinet is in shambles. He can't cope with the scandals shaking the government. And he's totally fixated on this stupid flag debate."

"Let's go back to Watkins."

"I thought I was."

"Are you saying Pearson will just as easily dump Watkins?"

"I guess Watkins is going to find out what friendship really means. By the way, there is something I stumbled on about Watkins. He has a strange kind of friendship with a doorman at the Windsor in Montreal, where he always stays."

"We already know about that. He arranged a scholarship for the doorman's son, Michel. Apparently he does that good-guy stuff quite a lot. But always for poor kids. I think it's to do with his own background. There's no apparent self-interest. The only odd thing is that Michel is involved with the FLQ — those kids who blow up mailboxes in Westmount. But not even his own father knows that, let alone the ambassador."

Fletcher looked at her watch. She had to catch the two o'clock train to Montreal. They walked out of the cafeteria together and along Wellington Street. She took his arm. He seemed better, she thought. Perhaps his confession had unburdened him.

"Next time let's try for a real visit," said Murray. "Maybe you could come and see my latest pad in Sandy Hill. I'll even take you for a ride through the Gatineau in my sporty new Volvo, a 123GT, assembled by those out-of-work lobster fishermen in New Brunswick."

"I will — and you can cook dinner for me. How's your love life?"

"They come and they go — sometimes they pass each other on the stairs."

"I liked the last one I met, the one who went to Alabama to do voter registration work."

"Oh yeah, Wendy from Rockcliffe. Long gone. Disillusioned. Left with a year's supply of birth control pills for an ashram in the Himalayas."

"Sounds like it ended badly?"

"After Medgar Evers was assassinated she came back angry. In her eyes I became the establishment . . . it was just too crazy. Her father is a provincial court judge, for God's sake, but I, Murray Fletcher, the hick from Alberta, was responsible for everything from Martin Luther King's imprisonment to Pearson's policy switch on American nuclear missiles. We had a huge fight before she left. She challenged me to explain what the Americans mean by 'fighting for peace' in Southeast Asia."

"What did you tell her?"

"I told her to try to think of it as fucking for virginity. She left that night."

"It wasn't about you, Murray. But I'm sure you've already figured that one out. I have to rush. Quick! Give me a hug."

She always hated saying goodbye to him, and this time she held on to him for longer than usual. Again she felt a sense of foreboding, of undefined anxiety. She let go when he gave her a little peck on her cheek, but she held on to his sleeve. "One last favour — find out for me what you can about a Z. Poliotov." She spelled out the name. "He's supposedly a military attaché at the Soviet mission in Washington and apparently about to visit the Montreal consulate."

"Sure, I'll do what I can." As he walked away, he called back over his shoulder: "Good luck with the ambassador. You're in for a surprise when you finally see him."

FLETCHER WATCHES the ambassador turn once again to check the front doors of the lobby. Of course, now she understands. She refused to let herself recognize it before. It was just too painful. There it is again. Incredible! How could their mannerisms be so exactly the same? So this was the surprise Murray meant. The ambassador quizzically watching O'Reilly stare at him from the foot of a ladder. There's his sudden lift of the eyebrows in wry amusement, and the way he pushes his steel-rimmed spectacles further back on his nose with his thick first finger. An overwhelming impression of the way her father looked when he said: "My daughter, the cop." A reminder of the gentle, bemused tone with which he pronounced his repertoire of paradoxical aphorisms, so well polished they had become a running family joke. "We must change . . . so that we can remain the same." She and Murray would chime in to complete the phrase in unison when it was still only halfway out of their father's mouth. Oh, this is all too much! Horribly so. She can't control the flow of memories. The same big lumpy male upper body in baggy clothes. Her father used to say: "If I could practise medicine in my overalls and get away with it, I would do it. But these farmers" — for a moment she pictures him holding a vial up to the windows of the out-patient clinic against the white winter light of the snowbound landscape — "really have to see a man in a suit wearing a white lab coat before they'll even listen to a diagnosis, let alone accept it." The quiet of the frozen outdoors descended for a moment on the sterile hospital room. "I imagine it is rather like that in your line of work, Jane. Are intelligence officers ever really believed by politicians until they come out of the shadows and put on their police uniforms?"

Then his bushy ginger eyebrows knit together, squinting at the syringe, the swab of alcohol against the skin, the prick of the needle. Her father murmuring: "Now if we could only immunize humans against political ideologies it would make your work so much simpler for you — but then, quite possibly all too boring."

Fletcher wonders if the ambassador speaks the same way. She has heard him on the phone taps, but the sound quality was terrible. It is never really the same as when you finally speak face to face with the person you have under observation. The possibility that the ambassador's voice might echo her father's is tantalizing. She looks forward impatiently to the moment when she will approach him. She visualizes exactly how it will happen, right after the exchange with Poliotov: "Mr. Ambassador, you are under arrest, please come with me." He will have to speak. There will be no escape from the confrontation.

THE NIGHT SHE LAST WENT to see her father at the small, almost shut-down community hospital he was exhausted from overwork, his eyes red-rimmed behind his glasses. He had stayed on, the only doctor left in the rural community to which he had given his whole life. And now the farmers resented him for wanting to retire. They knew that after he left, the hospital would certainly close. Perhaps a nurse or two would remain to run an outpatient clinic, but no younger doctors would be willing to endure such isolated winters when there were fortunes to be made in the cities.

At two o'clock that morning a pregnant farmwife was rushed, dying, to the hospital. The woman, despite being near term, had been driving a front-end loader in the barn because there was nobody else to help her husband. The tractor had tipped over, and she lay pinned under it for an hour before she was found. Her father had managed to save the baby, but could not save the mother. Losing her left him saddened, quiet. He was reminded of the loss of his own wife, sacrificed to the birth of the twins. As she drove him home through the cold pre-dawn in the beaten-up Chevy station wagon that smelled of his fat old Labrador, Bacchus, they talked about his coming retirement. Not bitter, just resigned. She hated this resignation in him. At the same time she recognized that it had been his greatest strength, his resilience in a long life of struggle. "Old people are like rocks in the river," he used to say when she commented on his affection for his elderly patients. All the same, she wanted to scream at him.

Fletcher still felt guilty about the moment years ago when she told her father she had decided to leave medical school and switch to law. He was at first unable to hide his surprise and disappointment. "A career in law!" He did not think highly of lawyers. But he had been kind, ulti-mately accepting her decision gracefully. Her father had loved her unconditionally. That's probably why she found most other men so difficult. How she missed him!

HERE IN THE OVERHEATED LOBBY of the Windsor Hotel she feels chilled all over, as she relives the cold water splashing over the bow of the canoe. She hears herself screaming to the stern, "Dig in, Dad! Dig!" Then, bewildered by the sense of abandoned motion behind her, she glances back over her shoulder. Her father's face is contorted with pain. The wide stern paddle he had carved himself is slipping out of his slackened fingers. His big body slumps against the gunwale. She throws her weight in the other direction to balance the craft and paddles furiously. But she knows it is already useless. They hang, slowly tilting, agonizingly frozen for long seconds at the head of the thundering river, her father dying as the canoe loses all impetus and drifts stern-first towards the centre of the whirlpool. The icy Upper Churchill ferociously pulls them, their sleek aluminum canoe, and all their camping gear downward in a vertical dive. As they plunge, she instinctively grabs onto a thwart of the canoe. She knows that if she can only hold on, the flotation tanks in the bow and the stern will inevitably bring the canoe up again. Her father's body spins past her face, a huge grey shadow whirling into the downward vortex. The river is a dark pounding monster that has taken her father and now wants her. The force of the current rips the life-jacket in half down the front of her chest. The intense cold and pressure of the water is forcing the air out of her lungs. Suddenly the downward pull relaxes. There's a brief dreamlike second of weightlessness somewhere near the bottom of the river and then the canoe catapults free of the whirlpool current. As it breaks the surface of the river, almost wrenching her arms out of her shoulders, she gasps for air.

God, she's cold. Fletcher urgently waves her hand at the waitress in the Windsor lobby, in a desperate signal for coffee. She tries to stop the too-fresh memories of the funeral from crowding into her mind. What is happening to her? These images are starting to affect her focus on the job. They told her to take time off. But for what — another camping trip? "Go to Europe," Murray ordered her angrily, the blame heavy in his voice. No, this afternoon will be the most important so far in her career. She methodically folds the *Gazette* closed, wrapping the images of her father and the river away into the headlines, and concentrates on what must be done.

Oh no, look at Morissette, what a klutz! She winces at the sight of this scruffy long-haired young man, totally out of place at the Windsor magazine rack, pretending to read *Playboy*, but peering closely over the ambassador's shoulder, attempting to follow whatever has caught the older man's interest. Morissette! Tailing too closely again. What an impossible creep! Always telling dirty jokes too loudly, attracting attention to himself. If he wasn't so dumb you could swear he was working for the Russians.

MORISSETTE IS STANDING right behind the old geezer, so close he can smell his after-shave lotion, probably some cheap Russian shit. What was the old guy reading in *Time*? Oh yeah, another dumb story on the Warren Commission investigation. They must be warming the readers up for next month's anniversary of the Kennedy assassination. He had read it all in the café across the street while they were waiting to go into position. The same old pictures all over again. Kennedy's head blown apart, Jackie holding on to him. And once more all the bullshit about Kennedy taken out by a single assassin, a sniper with a bolt action rifle — give me a break! And all that crap about the magic bullet. This single bullet, after entering and re-entering two guys, is found loose on Kennedy's stretcher with not even a mark on it. How did those politicians and reporter guys ever get the Americans to buy that shit? Everyone knows the CIA set him up because he fucked over their Bay of Pigs invasion in Cuba.

Oh, oh, we're moving again — "The subject moves from the magazine rack to the literary pocketbook section" — what an exciting goddam report this job is gonna make. He glances over at O'Reilly, fumbling around on the ladder, and grins to himself at the joke his buddy told them before the operation. "O'Reilly gets to the pearly gates and St. Peter asks him, 'Well, tell us about yourself, what have you done with your life?' And O'Reilly tells him, 'I've been a good IRA man all my life.'

St. Peter is shocked. 'Well, you're wasting your time trying to get into heaven.' 'Oh no,' replies O'Reilly, 'I'm not here to get in. I'm here to tell you that you've got five minutes to get out.'" What a guy!

Why the hell are we on this job anyway? This old bastard is one of our guys, a Canadian ambassador, for Chrissakes. We're supposed to be on the ass of all those commie diplomats from wherever. Wonder what they've got on this old bugger. Probably been boning some Moscow slut. Doesn't look the type, though. Looks like the basic mad professor. Wonder if he knows something about the Kennedy hit. Nah. What would an old geezer like him know? Still, you never can tell.

Oh Christ! What's that Inspector Fletcher signalling about? She shouldn't even be here. If a contact is supposed to happen in this lobby, for sure she's going to scare it off. Keeping tabs on us, I guess. Maybe she'll learn something. How the guys in the field get the real job done . . . Wouldn't really help, I suppose, when we all know what she really needs . . . Not that it would do her any good — tall, tough-looking bitch like that . . . Probably a dyke, anyway. Not too many guys gonna be comfortable with a broad over six feet. Jeez, this old guy has to be a heavy smoker, his blue suit reeks of it — but then he buys a carton at a time. Oh, no! Christ! The old bastard just made me!

The ambassador takes a paperback copy of *The Quiet American* off a metal rack and turns to cast an inquiring glance at the shabby young man standing too close behind him. "What's that, sir . . . A light? Sure . . . No, it's fine, keep 'em. Got lots more."

FLETCHER WATCHES as the ambassador nods his thanks and pockets the book of matches. So that's what they call state-of-the-art surveillance in I Ops! This breaks all the rules. The idiot has actually just made contact with the target. Nice going, Morissette. Why don't you go ahead now and invite the ambassador into the bar and give him your card, the real one with the Force's coat of arms, and you can have a beer together while we all wait for Poliotov to show up. Morissette, you are done! Sergeant Forbes is going to hear about this. More training can not help an individual like you . . . a brain transplant, maybe. They couldn't foist this idiot off on even the Rhodesian army . . . Oh no! Here is Poliotov, right on time.

The tall Muscovite, military attaché to the Washington delegation, enters the lobby without hesitation. Even though he's never been in this hotel before, Fletcher can tell he has been perfectly briefed. He walks authoritatively up to the newsstand, a folded *Maclean's* magazine in his hand to identify him to the ambassador, just as Merleau's tapes in the Washington embassy had predicted. But Poliotov also has trade smarts. She has to admire him. She can see he has summed up the situation in the moments it has taken to stride from the door to the newsstand in the lobby. He instinctively realizes something has gone wrong. He knows immediately that the ambassador should not be in casual conversation with this long-haired hippie in the upscale Windsor Hotel. Without a glance at Watkins and the paralyzed Morissette, who is gaping, slack-jawed, at the Russian, Poliotov reaches, stone-faced, past both men to lift a *Newsweek* from the rack, turns his back on them, pays for the magazine at the cash register, and strides out of the lobby by the main doors. Total time: thirty-eight seconds.

As Fletcher watches the ambassador stroll to the revolving doors, she is struck by the puzzled expression on his face. Where has she seen that look before? Thoughts whirl in her head. God! The whole operation has been a total disaster. She has to get to her office right away. What she would give for a quiet conversation with her father right now. Yes, of course! It's the same disconcerted expression that haunts her — those final moments on the Upper Churchill before her father disappeared below the river.

WATKINS STEPS OUTSIDE the Windsor Hotel and surveys Phillips Square. A bleak afternoon in October, the air grey and cold, the buildings forbidding. The traffic roars incessantly through the foul air around the square. He fumbles for another Players. He must try to cut down. His heart isn't going to hold out much longer. But then, not very much is what it used to be. And how much difference is one cigarette going to make in the stinking air of downtown Montreal? He examines the matchbook the hippie left with him. Watkins laughs out loud. On the cover is the RCMP coat of arms.

At the bottom of the stairs, Bruno, the doorman, resplendent in his scarlet frock-coat, helps an elderly woman wrapped in fur into a cab, then hands in her lap-dog. When Bruno catches sight of the ambassador, he smiles warmly and comes up the flight of steps.

"The city smells worse every time I come back, Bruno."

"Yes, sir, it's the pollution. One day it will kill us all. Can I get you a taxi, Ambassador Watkins?

"No thank you, Bruno. How is your son?"

Before answering, Bruno looks over Watkins' shoulder at the revolving doors. "Yes, Miss. A taxi?"

Watkins turns to see the tall, red-haired young woman he'd noticed in the lobby, the one being stared at by the workmen on the ladders, pause for a moment at the top of the stairs. He follows her gaze to the other side of the square. There the angular-jawed man, who a few minutes before had brusquely reached across him for a magazine, hangs up the receiver in a pay phone and strides off in the direction of St. Catherine Street. The woman ignores Bruno's inquiry and hurries to commandeer her own cab.

Bruno shrugs, his long crooked face dark under his peak cap, and returns to Watkins. He spreads his hands in resignation: "You see, no matter how gorgeous they get, you always know there's one guy somewhere in the world who is glad he doesn't have to put up with her shit anymore."

Watkins doesn't respond. He's never been able to deal easily with this misogynist working-class banter. He remembers his mother admonishing him, after scolding two sheepish men in the coalyard she operated in Norval Station: "Don't be like that when you grow up, son. Most men are apes when it comes to talking about women." If he was on the farm it would be different; he could play the country yokel, as it amused him to do when the American tourists came by. But Bruno knows him in a different context. They are locked into this tiresome ambassador-footman role. He watches Bruno now, hesitant, transparently casting about for the right words, paving the way for the anticipated rejection.

"Michel is good, doing well at Université de Montréal. A bit too political for my liking . . . uh, we often talk about you, sir."

"Bruno, you've known me too long to call me *sir*."

"Can't break the habit, Mr. Watkins. Uh, last night Michel said we should . . . that's if it's possible . . . invite you at least for a drink with us this time . . . We never really get a chance . . . He wants to thank you. I want to thank you for everything you've done for him. I told him I'd ask, but I know you're a busy man . . . ."

"Of course, Bruno. We must have a drink. How about that tavern over there, the Rymark, on the other side of the square? Six tomorrow evening — Thursday. Or we could do it another time before I leave at the end of the week."

Bruno is delighted. He can't quite believe it. "You in the Rymark, sir!"

"Why not? It's a damn sight better than most drinking places in Moscow. You should see the Aragvi — usually referred to by the diplomatic corps as the House of Aragviphobia and Ptomaine Poisoning. The food in Moscow is dreadful. The only breaks come when I go to a conference in Paris or Rome. Unfortunately, it's too infrequent."

Bruno is caught, fascinated. A lifetime of opening and closing doors for people from all parts of the world — while he has never been west of Dorval or east of the Gaspé — has left him a dreamer.

"What's it like there, sir?"

"Moscow? A big city, full of people."

"Are they like us?"

"In all the basic ways, yes."

"Then they must tell jokes."

Watkins is stumped. "Jokes?"

"Yeah, if they're like us they must tell each other jokes to keep themselves going. Some days on this job a joke is the only thing that will get me through."

Watkins is touched. The problems of the serving class are the same all over the world.

"Tell me a Russian joke, sir."

BEFORE HE PLONKED down the bottle of vodka in the spacious suite in the Tashkent Hotel, Akhundi, with two long, bony fingers, locked the cuff on the sleeve of his jacket, swept the dust from the top of the baby grand piano, and deposited two rough-cut glass tumblers.

"The jokes," he said, "have been getting better since Stalin croaked."

He gazed around the hotel suite. "Almost as good as my apartment," he acknowledged, gold teeth flashing in a warm grin. He tinkled a few notes on the piano and winced at the out-of-tune keys. He made a few adjustments with a spoon and knife, then sat down to play, breaking out to sing in a light baritone voice a wild Uzbek love song he was writing.

True, Watkins had seen Akhundi's apartment. His place was rather grand for a poet, even one regarded favourably enough by the bureaucrats in the cultural department to get a commission for the Pushkin biography. Akhundi was inordinately proud of his plate of four gold teeth. He took a childish delight in flashing them as often as possible. They were a definite status symbol over the usual stainless-steel teeth that smiled at you from Moscow to Samarkand. Akhundi was a dandy, and his wife looked the other way when he openly admired the Uzbek girls on the Tashkent streets where everybody knew him and called his name, asking for a poem or one of his famous love songs. Perhaps she also pretended to ignore the other part of his sexuality, or maybe she took it as part of the price for her comparatively charmed life. Unlike most cultural workers, who could be moved around ten times a year, they had a remarkably stable life. The City of Tashkent Cultural Committee was reported to hang on his every word.

Akhundi broke off in mid-song, rose from the piano, and brought the bottle over to the table where Watkins sat. He flicked the dust off his sleeve and poured them each a half tumbler of vodka. "The chairman of the committee whispered this one to me this morning. The communist and the capitalist are having a beer together. The communist says, 'We have to change the world.' 'Of course! Of course!' the capitalist agrees. 'But,' the communist says, 'first we have to kill a million people.' The capitalist slaps the communist on the back. 'Of course! You are right! I agree with everything you say. But first let me make a million dollars.'"

BRUNO PUSHES the ridiculous red hat onto the back of his head. He stares blankly at Watkins. He just doesn't get it. "That's a Russian joke?"

"Well," Watkins begins — but is saved when Bruno is called away by a guest looking for a cab. Then out of the hotel comes the hippie who gave him the matchbook. Watkins watches as he stops to exchange a few words with Bruno, then slips off into the early evening shadows.

When the doorman rejoins him, Watkins asks: "Do you know that young man?"

"Ah, yes. From my neighbourhood. Kind of a sad case. He grew up with my son, went to the same schools, but they were never really close friends. He's not a serious boy. I knew his dad. He used to spend all his wages every night in the bar and didn't take care of his family. To feed his kids, his wife had to beg food from the church. And, well, you know how it goes, like father, like son. I think the kid has a problem with drugs — the mary-jane. Once when he was high he came around the house and boasted to us that he had some bullshit job working with the cops. But we didn't really believe him. I think he was just trying to impress us because Michel is going to university and hardly anyone in The Point has done that before. And the truth is, sir, we could not have done it without your help."

Watkins waves off Bruno's gratitude. "The boy was ready. And, don't forget, he won that scholarship. Well, then, six tomorrow, Bruno. Bring Michel. The Rymark, best cornbeef on rye in Montreal!"

Watkins waves and escapes inside the Windsor Hotel. Strange, he notices that the Christmas ornaments the workmen were hanging from the ceiling just half an hour ago seem to have disappeared.

2

THURSDAY EVENING. Murray shifts rhythmically up and down through the gears, making his way among the unpredictable drivers on St. Catherine Street. Just past Guy he begins looking for a parking spot. He is in a good mood. He caresses the dark polished wooden head of the gear shift with its carved insignia. There is something very special about this little sports car. The drive down from Ottawa, usually a bore, has been fun. His friend Leo, who runs the Volvo agency in Ottawa, urged him: "Buy it. The car's a steal. The Swedes are being smart. They want to break into the North American market through Canada and capture the unhappy drivers of American shitboxes, so they are making sure these first imports are the best models for export. Lots of quality control on the production line." Well, considering all the junk that comes out of Detroit these days, the Swedes aren't going to have a hard time. Let's hope these European and Japanese imports and this guy Ralph Nader will smarten up the corporate dinosaurs, get 'em to make better cars.

Ah! The god of parking is smiling on him tonight. He shifts down smoothly, cuts into the space, and stops beside the crowded sidewalk. A large group of men are blocking the sidewalk, all gawking up at the second floor of the Bar Go-Go. He glances up to find Penny dancing in the window, sporting only a silver G-string and two very small pasties wobbling around on her breasts. He double-flashes the car lights. She responds with an exaggerated bump and grind as she sticks up a hand in the outspread give-me-five gesture. Okay, he can wait five minutes. Jane should show up in the meantime. He called her earlier, gave her the coded message to go to the pay phone they use, but even then he would only say, "We need to have dinner."

"It sounds like bad news."

"Only you can figure that out."

He peers out at the early evening crowds. Montreal is definitely his favourite city. He has always loved the tension of the city at night — the crowds, the comings and goings in the busy bars, the stylish women. It seems too bad that Drapeau is screwing it all up with his mayoralty election platform of huge downtown projects.

MURRAY FELL IN LOVE with Montreal the first time he visited, a rangy six-foot-three kid out of rural Alberta playing his first year for the Drumheller Juniors in a Quebec invitational hockey tournament. He slipped away from his team-mates, a bunch of yahoos who talked about "beating the frogs" and still thought farting loudly in public was the funniest thing a guy could do, and made his way downtown. Alone, he wandered along St. Denis. He spotted a crowded bar that caught his attention because of the music coming through the door. He paused to slip off his hockey jacket, fold it inside out, and tuck it under his arm. Taking a deep breath, he ducked into the bar. He found a rickety little table in the shadows behind a pillar that partly blocked his view of the musicians on the stage — mostly black guys playing rhythm and blues. Then he held his breath again. Nothing in High Level had prepared him for the absolutely sexiest woman he had ever seen in his life — tight purple velvet pants and what looked like a black lace bra. She glided towards him through the soft rose lights and asked him what he would like to order. "A Blue," he grinned deferentially, trying not to stare holes through the black lace and stoically awaiting the demand for proof of age. "Right away," she murmured huskily, promptly serving him his beer with a smile and a libidinous wink that gave him an immediate hard-on. But he was only seventeen and it was the first time he had ever been in a bar by himself, let alone in a strange city where almost everyone around him was speaking another language and . . . he had been quietly accepted! He had a new sense of himself, his first real taste of independence. For an hour he sat alone in the dark little *boîte* on St. Denis, listening to the music, nursing his beer, and fantasizing about the waitress, who even struck up a conversation with him and bought him a second beer. "On the house," she whispered, leaning so close that the mingled scents of her perfume and her warm body enveloped him in an experience of intimacy that went to his head more quickly than the beer.

That hour was to be more important to him than the two winning goals he scored on the ice the next day for the Drumheller team. He felt he was truly on the way to being a man — that he had undergone an important rite of passage, crossed over a bridge, and left boyhood behind. After that first evening alone in Montreal he was hooked on the night-life, caught up in exploring the bars and cafés, always able to sense the dangers yet move comfortably through the dark hours of any city he visited.

FROM INSIDE THE VOLVO, Murray can read the headlines on the French and English newspapers at the kiosk on the sidewalk: "Another FLQ Bomb Found!" "Alouettes 2 to 1 over Bombers!" Alongside are sedate photos of Queen Elizabeth, in Quebec, of all places, to celebrate Thanksgiving. Her public relations people are really out to lunch in their complete indifference to the complexities of political life in Quebec. Jane met her once: "There I was," she told him later, "dressed in the regulation scarlet tunic, the symbolic woman on parade for the queen, fast-tracked upward to meet the cosmetic needs of the Force, ten years of silent suffering — no, affliction, because I chose it — in one of the most macho police forces in the world! I think I had this childish idea she would give me a moment of wisdom, something I could take and carry with me. It was terribly disappointing. She only wanted to talk about horses. She even suggested I must be grateful that the Force had taught me to ride!"

Murray figures that the queen's presence must account for the strange edginess in the air. The various mouthpieces for the *indépendantiste* and *séparatiste* organizations have said in different but emphatic ways that they don't appreciate the presence of the British monarch in the province and have hinted that there might be trouble. Once again Murray is grateful Jane isn't working in D Operations — domestic counter-subversion — having to worm her way into political organizations, file reports on her politically active friends, engage in union busting. Of course she would do it if she was ordered to, he knows that about her. As his hockey coach once told him: "If you had half that mean streak your sister has, you'd be one hell of a hockey player." Shortly after that he quit playing. The coach just wanted another Spinner Spencer — a banger and a fighter. And look how things turned out for the Spinner. If that's all they wanted from him, if that's all they came to the arena for, then fuck 'em.

Counter-espionage is complicated and ugly enough without having to get into all the ethical questions that come with spying on your own society . . . Ah, what the hell is he doing in External, anyway? Not that different if you really think about it. The minister is always sending his deputy down with requests to get dirt on his own colleagues inside the party. Well, tonight he's not going to think about what he's doing in the spook section of the diplomatic service. He closes his examination into his future and turns his attention to the small group of Hare Krishnas coming along the sidewalk, swaying and chanting.

GOOD! JANE SAYS to herself. Murray is exactly where he said he would be.

"Where do you want me to pick you up?" he asked.

"Make it somewhere close to the Windsor. We've still got surveillance in place. I have to stick close to the hotel."

"Okay, I'll wait for you on the south side of St. Catherine, just east of

Mountain," he said. "You can't miss my new car, Swedish racing green." She didn't get the joke, even after he explained it to her. Fat lot she knew about cars.

But this is one of the things she has always loved about her brother — right on time. Totally Reliable Murray, their dad always called him. But what's this? The snappy little green Volvo is surrounded by a band of chanting Hare Krishna devotees.

She brusquely elbows her way through the skinny, swaying bodies, saffron robes fluttering over their Bob Stanfields (even monks must need long johns on a chilly October evening), then deftly hip-checks a startled young woman in mid-wail out of her way. The tambourine slides out of the woman's hands and under the car, and while she is stooping to retrieve it, Fletcher opens the door and slips in beside Murray.

"Greetings, brother! Your sister is here to guide you on the road to Mahamudrah. Drive me away from these unenlightened seekers of the painfully obvious . . . C'mon, let's go!"

But Murray doesn't smile or move. The garish lights from St. Catherine Street make his face seem harsh and strained. This is how he will look in a few years' time — heavy dark welts under his eyes, the lines at the corners of his mouth beginning to drag. He's living too hard, she thinks. Why so fast? All these women and nightclubs. What's with him? And yet, as she often wonders, is she looking in the mirror at herself?

"Murray?"

"In a moment. I'm waiting for Penny to get off shift." She watches through the windshield as the motley crew of Hare Krishnas encircles the car. Some of the most aggressive begin to tap their wooden and metal begging bowls rhythmically against the car windows.

"Penny?"

Murray points up at the second-floor windows of the Bar Go-Go where, back-lit and seemingly naked, a dancer gyrates as an enticement to the passing throngs.

"Oh God, no! Murray! You're really scraping the bottom of the barrel."

"Relax, Penny's no slouch. She doing her master's in poli-sci at Queen's, and right now she's probably making more money by the hour than the two of us put together. Why did you have to provoke these people?"

She scrutinizes the blabbering painted faces of the Hare Krishnas, and looks up again at the bar window. What's with these kids? Nobody can do anything with them. There's just too many. They're all over the place. Half of them want to live naked; the other half want to run around in weird costumes, playing at being religious gurus or Che Guevara revolutionaries. "What kind of times are we living in, Murray?" she asks out loud.

Murray slips into his Walter Cronkite impersonation: "The best and worst of times. It's Thanksgiving week of 1964. The Doomsday clock has been set back to twelve minutes before midnight, the Soviets are winning the space race, rock and roll is here to stay, Bob Dylan is the great American folk poet, Latin America is on fire . . ." He breaks off to ask: "Tell me, did you ever think we were born about ten years too early?" as he watches the continuing shuffling and chanting around the car.

"Why? You're not missing out on anything — and I wouldn't change places with any of these kids. Not for all the internal peace in China." She pushes Murray out of the car. "Go get your Penny!" and moves over into the driver's seat, swinging her legs over the gearshift. "Tonight I'll be the wheel guy."

Murray catches Penny flying out of the bar, a motorcycle jacket flapping over her bare shoulders and a gym bag in her hand. They squeeze through the ranks of Hare Krishnas. Penny flops into the back seat, Murray into the front.

The white face of the monk with a painted eye in the middle of his forehead gets on Jane's nerves. He raps his metal bowl against the driver's window. She waves at him to move aside, but he ignores her, repeatedly banging on the window. Abruptly, she opens and closes the car door, and the monk drops out of view.

Murray is aghast: "What the hell did you do that for?" With a hand jammed on the horn, she revs the engine, lets out the clutch, and burns away into the traffic, forcing the Hare Krishnas to scatter as their collection of begging bowls bounce off the roof.

"Jesus! Jane?"

"Relax! It's a technique I learned in Prince George to deal with drunken loggers who wouldn't back off from the cruiser." She glances at Penny, who is removing her pasties and struggling under the motorcycle jacket to get dressed in the clothes she has pulled from the bag. "Hi, I'm Jane, Murray's sister."

"Cool! You're the cop, right? I'm impressed."

"Thanks. Like your pasties. That's a nice touch — Lester Pearson's red maple leaves."

"I like to think of it as one woman's contribution to the national flag debate. What could be wrong with a flag of breasts *and* maple leaves waving from sea to sea to sea?"

"An incredible peacekeeper image for the whole world. Nobody could ever forget it."

"Thank you."

Up close she can see Penny is slender — not the raunchy, naked back-lit figure she seemed in the Bar Go-Go's second-floor window. She wants to reach out and caress her delicate Oriental features. A face like that, she thinks, doesn't belong in a topless bar.

"How's Queen's?"

"Bummer. White and tight. You go there?"

"No, UBC."

"Yeah, I'm from the coast. I went to UBC too for my undergrad stuff."

Murray stares ahead as Jane points the car towards the Mountain. He listens to the two women chatting away without inhibition. What is it about his sister? he wonders. Never any men in her life — he has long ago given up asking — and she always gets on so well with his girl-friends. There was only one guy, way back . . . What the hell was his name? "Tell me, what's happening?" Penny asks him in Mandarin.

Before he can answer, Jane has guessed her question and replies: "Don't worry, I just wanted to get some fresh air. I have to get back to work, so I'm going to take a little walk and talk with my brother — family business — and then I'll let you two get on with your evening." She pulls into the parking lot at the lookout that gives a dramatic view of Montreal by night.

As she and Murray get out of the car, Penny asks with a warm smile: "Why don't you join us for dinner? We can go to Chinatown and I'll order you a meal that will make you want to eat Chinese for the rest of your life."

Murray encourages her. "C'mon Jane. Come with us?"

"Well, maybe. I really do have to get back to work, but let's talk first."

They leave Penny curled up in the back seat, snuggled under her motorcycle jacket, and walk to the stone parapet. They are not alone. Couples with their arms around each other stare sentimentally out over the nightscape below Mount Royal. Montreal by night lies below them, but she turns her back on the view. She has never shared Murray's romantic enthusiasm for the city. She reaches out to stroke a wandering lock of his wild red hair back into place behind his ear.

"You're a lucky man, Murray," she teases. "All the nicest chicks really dig you. Where do you find the time to meet them all?" Murray shrugs, ignores her question, leans forward with both hands on the rail, and speaks to the city.

"Poliotov doesn't exist."

"Get off it, Murray! I saw him with my own eyes."

"Sure. You saw a man, but I checked it all out very carefully. There's no Soviet military attaché by the name of Poliotov with diplomatic status in Washington, Montreal, or in any other city in the world."

She is stunned. Again, she fights off the panicky feelings of being in the river. She is conscious of her brother watching her carefully. "What does this mean, Murray?"

"It means the CIA brought in some guy from Central Casting, ran him through the setup, and stood back to see how certain people would react."

"This has to rule out an entrapment of the ambassador."

"I would say so. And from what you told me, somehow or other they tricked the ambassador into coming down from his hotel room and walking around the Windsor lobby at the right time."

"So the bastards are testing me!"

"No, I don't think so — although they could be setting you up for something, at the very least to take the fall."

"Then who are they testing?"

"Well, after the ambassador and you, there's only two left, right?"

"Merleau and Present —"

"Yes, but don't you think Merleau has to be in on the setup?"

"Likely, but not necessarily. He could have been kept in the dark by his Washington people about Poliotov being a dummy. Which leaves us only with Present."

"Yeah, but why would they want to entrap Present? I've heard rumours of an internal super-secret search for a mole inside the security services. But rumours like that have always floated around. We're very sensitive over what appears to be our total inability to catch Soviet spies."

Murray smiles sarcastically. "But the simple answer is so obvious. Canada must be the only country in the world where Soviet spies are not active."

Jane turns away to stare over the parapet. Murray looks at her carefully. If it weren't for her tailored black leather coat and carefully groomed hair, she could be an image right out of their childhood: Jane leaning against the corral fence, gazing out at the big Alberta evening sky but seeing nothing. Now she is leaning against the rock wall, gazing out over the darkened city of Montreal but not really seeing it or anything else, with her arms crossed over her chest, gnawing thoughtfully on the first knuckle of her right hand. When she was a kid she actually had a permanent callous on her knuckle. And since the accident on the river, there have been times when he truly thought she was on the edge of madness. That flash of panic, which she learned to hide as she grew older but he can still recognize, has come back to her face again — he sees it too often. Maybe it's because they are twins that he is so sensitive to her emotions.

She has always been competitive to the extreme. In the high school yearbook the editors described her as the "child prodigy" of Alberta and "the female doctor who will discover the cure for cancer." Of course it was mostly teenage bullshit, but there was a certain amount of truth to it. For two years Jane led the school debating team to the provincial championships. She always had top marks in school, was a phenomenal athlete, and was president of the student council. She made fundraising speeches — which she wrote herself — for any good cause in the community. She carried the flag in school parades. Dad sat in the background, applauding, glowing with pride for his daughter. But what did all that success do to her, or even for her? Jane never had a close friend in all the years they were growing up. She used to tell him, "You're the only real friend I have, Murray." It scared him, made the future ominous. What has happened to her? He puts his arm around her. "Jane, get out of this operation while you still can."

"It's too late, now. I have to see it through." She gently pushes his arm off and moves away a few paces. "Anyway, why should I?"

"Because I think you only stand to lose. There's something very weird going on. I've found out a little bit more about Merleau. He's not a European operative and appears to have no previous experience with any intelligence organization or with what is happening on the other side of the Atlantic. All his postings have been in Latin America. It just doesn't make sense for them to use a guy with his background to do an investigation of a Canadian ambassador caught up in something with the KGB."

"What else do you know about Merleau?"

"I was lucky — or, rather, we got lucky. Normally I would have to go through special channels and there would be all kinds of awkward questions to answer. But a couple of days ago, a member in the House asked a question about CIA activities in Latin America, and I was given the job of preparing the answer for the minister. That gave me a chance to check through our Latin American desk files. From what I can tell, Merleau has never been in Buenos Aires."

She remembers his hands, his quiet serious manner. She had liked him. No, she had *wanted* very much to like him. "Then where was he?"

"Panama. Seems he was mostly stationed in the School of the Americas there. Have you heard of it?"

Jane shakes her head, not sure if she really wants to know.

"The SOA is covered in blood. It's a counter-terrorist school run and funded by the CIA since 1946 to fight communism in Latin America."

Santiago, a twenty-two-year-old Mayan with high cheekbones, ragged dark hair, and wounded eyes, was seeking political asylum in a country that was known internationally as the world's peacekeeper but which had no policy to harbour political refugees. Murray was sitting in as the immigration officer debriefed him. "Do you know any communists in your own country?" "Yes, sir," Santiago replied, speaking softly through the imperfect English of the interpreter. "I knew many communists. Every time the mayor holds a public meeting, people get up to complain about no jobs, no schools for the kids, or to ask the government to help make clean water for the barrio. Then the mayor denounces them, and the captain of the military barracks calls them communists. They disappear or are found dead by the road. And then we are told by the military they are dead because they are communists. These are the communists I have known, sir."

The immigration officer asked him if anybody in his family was a communist. "Yes, sir. The mayor said my father was one of these communists, and one morning we found him by the road. The military had cut off his head and put it on a stick so we could all see it as we went to work in the fields. It was always the same, sir. The communists talked about poor people and schools for their kids and they were killed. The soldiers talked about democracy and capitalism, but the soldiers never died. It is too confusing for me. This is why, sir, I would like very much, please, to stay in Canada." Murray watched the confusion in the eyes of the immigration officer. There was nothing he could do. His hands were tied by bureaucratic red tape. They both watched the RCMP sergeant lead Santiago away to the plane that would fly him back to Gautemala.

JANE ASKS HIM, "Who goes to the School of the Americas?"

"The students in the school are all selected from the officers and ranks of Latin American armies, from Chile to El Salvador. Literally every country has a military assistance program with the United States. The school is wrapped up with the military aid package — you can't get one without the other. If the generals want the tanks and planes, they have to send their best men for ideological training."

"What would Merleau do in this school?"

"Help train chosen people to fight dirty wars — counter-insurgency, stopping peasants from organizing, political assassination —"

"Are you sure Merleau was there?"

"Off and on for the last four years."

He had gone through the reports that were turned in by Canadian consulates and embassies and mailed to the security section by diplomatic pouch. Bad photocopies of photographs of tortured men and women strung out on metal frame beds. CIA instruction manuals from the School of the Americas on the techniques of electric-shock torture using army field telephones with hand-operated generators. Illustrations of the "parrot perch," a bar from which prisoners were suspended behind their knees, naked, five feet off the floor, with their feet and hands tied together. Pamphlets on how to keep a prisoner alive until information was extracted. Manuals stolen by those who wanted the rest of the world to know were slipped to Canadian diplomatic officials in the hope that somehow these materials would surface in the Western media. The documents, of course, never did — External Affairs officers were too protective of their own relationship with U.S. diplomatic staff.

An old hand who had been a first secretary in several Third World postings once told him: "Whatever you do or don't do in an overseas posting, keep it clean and cozy with the Americans. When the shit really hits the fan, it's the Yanks who are going to get you out of town in a hurry. You can never rely on our own government." His wife gave out similar advice to embassy wives: "If you absolutely insist on having an affair, keep it white and keep it in the family — meaning, preferably someone in the American delegation — but most definitely, absolutely no affairs with local commies."

Jane pictures Merleau with his dark and handsome narrow face. Is he the one being investigated? That seems just too clumsy. It is hard to think about him as an instructor in assassination and torture, but somehow — and she is shocked at herself — everything Murray is telling her makes Merleau even more interesting than she has already found him. Could she ever tell Murray that? No, he'd never understand. "What else?" she asks abruptly.

"He's ambitious. He's graduated to a special CIA operations group in counter-espionage run by James Jesus Angleton himself."

Suddenly Jane feels cold and wants Murray's arm around her again, but already he is walking towards the car where Penny is calling to him. Where is Merleau this evening? she wonders.

"So, are you going to eat with us tonight?" Murray asks wearily.

"No." She kisses him gently on the cheek. "I have to put the ambassador to bed."

WATKINS CROSSES PHILLIPS SQUARE under a patter of rain that drips like dirty water through the grey smog of the Montreal sky. The door to the Rymark tavern opens to the dull roar of men drinking, talking, laughing. He hasn't been here since that conference on Scandinavian writers when Dag flew up from New York. They walked down from McGill, about twenty of them, and took over the place until it closed. Nothing has changed, except that the dark wooden panelling is darker now from all the cigar smoke. He chooses a table near the glass-panelled doors that give a view across the square. He orders a scotch and two packs of Players, for he has forgotten his cigarettes in the hotel.

The waiter, in a white apron that covers him from his ankles to his chin, brings his order, along with a bowl of salted peanuts. Watkins smokes two cigarettes and finishes half his drink; Bruno still has not shown up. He pretends to read the *Montreal Star*, but finds himself eavesdropping on a loud, fragmented conversation among four men sitting at the next table. They sound like most young journalists — full of themselves, trying to outdo each other with tidbits of gossip and cutting or demeaning descriptions of the politicians and celebrities they cover. "My girlfriend's apartment is below the one where the finance minister keeps his mistress. It's one of those creaky old wooden buildings where you can hear everything. Every time he comes around to see her he brings some kind of present, usually something weirdly inappropriate that she rejects. My girlfriend tapes all their fights. They quarrel constantly and usually end up screaming at each other before he leaves. The mistress is trying to get him to leave his wife, but he refuses. One night he brings her a gift — a bowling ball — because he knows she likes to go bowling with her friends. But a romantic gift? C'mon! She screams at him: 'Get out! That's it! A goddam bowling ball! I've had enough! Get the hell out of here, you fat bastard!' She pushes him out and slams the door. Then she opens the door again and yells at the top of her voice, so everyone in the apartment block can hear, 'And take your limp dick with you!' She throws the bowling ball after him. It rolls — Bang! Bang! Bang! — all the way down three flights of stairs." The journalists all burst out laughing. They compete to tell the next joke. "Say, have you heard the one about Russian foreplay?" "No?" "He pounds his companion on the shoulder with his fist, screaming, 'Wake up! Wake up!'" They all roar with raucous laughter.

Watkins tries to turn his attention to the *Star* — pages and pages of entries for the Canadian flag. Like every newspaper in the country, the *Star* is running its own flag competition. Bored, he dips into the salted nuts. Probably the worst possible thing I can have for my diet, he tells himself, and orders another whisky. He will drink this one and then, if they don't show up, he will leave. As it arrives, he spots Bruno and Michel hurrying across the square. The father is in the lead, gesticulating angrily. Michel follows with his head down.

"I'm sorry we kept you waiting, sir," Bruno apologizes, even before they shake hands. Michel — slight, prematurely balding, wire-rimmed glasses on a thoughtful face — is quieter, shyly nodding, murmuring his greetings. Bruno prods his son to speak up. "It's all my fault. I kept Dad waiting —"

"It's all this damn political stuff — waving flags and taking over buildings at the university instead of concentrating on your studies," Bruno breaks in angrily. "You have an obligation to the ambassador —"

"Please, please sit down," Watkins breaks in. He notices out of the corner of his eye that the journalists have fallen silent at the mention of the word "ambassador" and have pricked up their ears. He leans towards Bruno and Michel and whispers, "Call me John, please, as a special favour to me tonight. There are reporters at the next table." Bruno catches on and the three of them speak quietly together until the journalists lose interest and resume their loud gossip.

Michel tries to explain again: "There was a political rally at the university protesting the queen's visit. Things got a little out of hand and the traffic made me late."

"You forget to say," Bruno whispers furiously in French, "that you were one of the shit disturbers making the speeches."

Michel is stung. "You make it sound like I'm part of a conspiracy to overthrow the government."

Watkins laughs and joins in, also in French, "And are you?" But he decides to back off when he sees from Michel's reaction that he has either gone too far or there is a lot more going on. "C'mon, Bruno. Every boy has a bit of the rebel in him. It's healthy. After all, we expect the next generation to upset the status quo, don't we?"

Bruno samples his beer and makes a gesture of annoyance. But he won't let go. "I just don't get it, Mr . . . uh . . ." He looks over his shoulder to see if the reporters are still listening. Watkins gently intercedes, "Remember, call me John."

"Ah, yes," but Bruno just can't bring himself to be so familiar. Nor can he give up railing against his son. "He used to be so correct — always got top marks, even went with his mother to Mass once a week."

Michel struggles harder to contain his rage. But Bruno is blind to his son's anger towards him. Michel turns to Watkins and asks in English, "Were you politically active when you were a student?"

Watkins is caught unaware and tries to make a joke of it. "Well, you know, I've been cleared by the RCMP to the highest level of security because, after all, for most of the last fifteen years I've been wrestling with the representatives of the Evil Empire behind the Iron Curtain." Michel smiles a secret little smile, but he can see that Bruno is out of his depth. Watkins decides to lie, perhaps to make some bridge between father and son. The three of them are by now moving easily back and forth in French and English.

"But, of course, in the thirties, as young students, we all idealized the Bolshevik Revolution . . ." Now, why the hell did he say that? Michel stares at him curiously, and another expression passes fleetingly over Bruno's face. A silence falls on the table. Then Bruno excuses himself to go to the washroom. "The beer, you know," he shrugs.

Left alone, Watkins and Michel seem suddenly uneasy, shy with each other. Michel looks up. "I'm sorry about all this family squabbling.

There are reasons . . ." He looks up to see if his father is coming back yet. "This is hard for me, but I owe you a lot and I can only think of one way to repay you . . . uh . . . this is so difficult . . . but I have to warn you to be careful what you say in front of my father."

"Your father?" Watkins is perplexed.

"Yes. You see, I know he is an informer for the police. For many years now the cops have had informers in all the downtown hotels. It's just the way they work."

"Which police?"

"He takes money from all of them — the Montreal cops, the Mounties . . . When VIPs come to the hotel, he tells them who comes and goes with them — which ones use hookers, or order in dope, and so on."

Watkins is speechless. Michel puts his hand across the table and gently places it on the ambassador's wrist in a gesture of empathy.

"I'm sorry," he murmurs.

Watkins can see Bruno returning to the table. He pats Michel's hand. "Thank you. You are a remarkable young man."

"For what?" murmurs Michel in pain. "For ratting on my father?"

Watkins leans back as Bruno rejoins them.

"So, Michel," Watkins asks, "are you still interested in a writing career?"

"Yes," replies Michel, "but more and more I think I would like to do the kind of thing René Lévesque does so well . . . a mix of journalism, politics, fiction . . ."

"And theatre," adds Watkins, and they all laugh.

"Tell me," Michel asks, "about the journalists in Moscow. What do you think of them?"

Now this is something he can handle a little more comfortably. And, given what Michel has just told him, he decides he needs some space and time. Watkins seizes the moment and turns on all the teaching skills that once, years before, made him so popular with his university students. "The leaders and governments of just about every country are fascinated with the problems of getting decent information about the Kremlin and Moscow. I know Mike Pearson was always asking me questions about the press corps."

"Why don't they get the information they want from their own people, like you?" Bruno asks.

"Because," Michel interjects, "the movements of foreign diplomats are so closely controlled that reporters become the other option."

"That's right," Watkins agrees, "and for journalists Moscow is probably the most difficult city in the world to work in."

Michel is impatient: "How could I get to Moscow as a journalist — learn Russian?"

"Don't bother. Spend about ten years establishing yourself as the most strident critic of everything Soviet, from fashion to nuclear weapons. Then you might just stand a chance. I have to warn you, the competition is ferocious — or at least that's how it seems to me after fifteen years of reading the Western press."

Michel toys with his beer glass, rarely looking Watkins in the eye.

"The problems begin even before the reporter gets to Moscow," Watkins continues. Whenever a reporter is assigned by a newspaper — and believe me the paper is really lucky if it can obtain accreditation from the Soviet government — he is automatically looked upon as a potential intelligence source. In our own country, the Mounties vet every journalist who gets sent over there. More important, whenever the journalist takes a trip home he spends hours being debriefed by intelligence officers."

Michel is amused. "You mean to say that with all that pressure from their own cops, Canadian reporters still get to write what they want to write about?"

"Well, I'm sure a staffer doesn't get picked to go because he starts out with an unbiased point of view. For some reason, the press seems to trust only the most conservative writers for the job."

Michel is beginning to enjoy himself. "Is that because the managing editors think their staff are going to be seduced by communism?"

Watkins orders another round from the waiter. "No, it's a bit more complex than that. The Soviet authorities seem to refuse entry automatically to most left-leaning reporters. My guess is they don't want to deal with true believers."

Michel catches on quickly. "Disillusionment is always politically more embarrassing to deal with than prejudice?"

"Exactly. But it wasn't always that way. During and immediately after the war, Moscow was filled with all kinds of characters —"

But Michel is not interested in a history lesson and he shoots the next question at Watkins. "So who at the embassy spies on the reporters?"

Watkins is caught a little off balance. "What do you mean?"

"You said every journalist is looked upon as a potential intelligence source, so who keeps them in line?"

This kid, thinks Watkins ruefully, is too quick. He sees through all the flannel. Then, for the first time, the thought really occurs to him: God, is that what he did? Had they made him into a cop, too?

MIKE WAS ALWAYS ASKING questions: "Give me a background report on the press corps." Had that request really come from his minister? Because of everything that has happened this year, he can no longer be sure. And what did he send in reply? I suppose Michel is correct in a sense: it really was more than an intelligence report. "I have to tell you," he wrote, "the representatives of the foreign press in Moscow have deteriorated in numbers and, to some extent, in quality since the days of the war . . ." Of course, he gave it his usual stylish touch — he was, after all, a man of letters.

"There are very few outstanding Western writers who have made their way to Moscow after the war. Here is a list of the most important representatives of the foreign press: Eddy Gilmore of the Associated Press. Gilmore has been in Moscow longer than most of the foreign correspondents now here. He has a nose for facts, particularly for out-of-the-way information, and is very interested in Soviet personalities. I do not think he is capable of penetrating assessments of broad Soviet problems. He has a reputation of being a lone wolf and has made enemies among other correspondents and members of the diplomatic corps. He is right wing, loathes the Soviet system, and criticizes it as much as he can in view of his marriage to a Soviet citizen. He mixes with Soviet citizens more than most correspondents and knows many of them because of his long stay here and because of his wife's connections . . ."

3

THERE'S A TORONTO JOURNALIST," says Watkins, toying with his glass of Chilean red, "who has put out a terrible rumour about me that I hear whispered wherever I go."

"Yes," agrees Murray, "we know all about it."

Watkins blanches. "He claims that at Khrushchev's dacha, when the prime minister and his group were all present, Khrushchev made a toast, mocking me, suggesting I was the only one present who wouldn't drink to women."

Murray tries his best to reassure the ambassador. "This journalist is a creature of B Operations, counter-espionage. He flies kites for them; they leak him misinformation stories to put out as hard news."

The ambassador is not so easily mollified. "Why would anyone put out such a hateful and petty lie? Many things happened that night.

Khrushchev behaved like the boorish peasant he is. But this incident never happened. Everyone who was there can verify that."

Murray found the ambassador this Friday morning in the second salon of the Montreal Art Gallery's David Milne show. Standing behind him he murmured, "Do you think Vincent Massey could see all those blues and dark purples in the Canadian landscape?"

Watkins turned to peer from under his glasses with amused curiosity at the lanky, red-headed man dressed in a loose brown leather jacket and cowboy boots.

"Or do you think," Murray went on, "he just saw a good deal at $5 a pop when Milne didn't have a pot to piss in and his wife was deathly ill?"

"You sound like a struggling artist," Watkins murmured.

"No, sir, I'm actually here to give you a message from the minister of external affairs. An unofficial message. We don't have a lot of time. But there's a restaurant and bar at the back that looks out over the garden."

So here they are at the bar, with Murray struggling to move the conversation along, and Watkins, hungry to drag out every minute he can with at least this unofficial contact from his ministry. "How does a rumour like that get started?" he wants to know.

"Well, we have friends in the British Foreign Office who tell us that since Prime Minister Wilson was elected, no end of ugly rumours have been put out by those intelligence people at the top of MI6 and MI5, specifically Sir Roger Hollis, who cannot abide the idea of a socialist government in power. He and his agents are doing their best to undermine Mr. Wilson."

Watkins is baffled. "Undermine their own government? How can they do that?"

"It's also done at a very personal level. MI5 have leaked stories to their contacts in the tabloid press that Wilson's wife, unhappy with all the hours he puts into his work, has taken a lover. They've even named some poor man who is a friend of the family."

Murray eyes the older man. Watkins reminds him so much of his own father. "Tell the truth, Murray. It's hard at first, but in the end it's the easiest thing to do," his father said, dropping him off at the high school principal's office. "And you will always feel the better for it."

He takes a sheet of paper from inside his jacket pocket and slides it across the table to Watkins. "This list has been circulated by MI6 officers as suspected communist sympathizers.

Watkins carefully cleans his bifocals on his tie, slips them on his nose, glances down the column, and whispers in wonderment, "Prime Minister Harold Wilson. John Diamond, chief secretary, Treasury. John Stonehouse, parliamentary secretary, Aviation. Sir Barnet Stross, parliamentary secretary, Health. Judith Hart, undersecretary of state for Scotland . . . My God! There's all of a dozen names here — must be at least half of Wilson's cabinet."

"Oh yes, and, unfortunately, that's not the end of it. There's also a long list of Labour supporters, even people like Lord Berstein, chairman of Granada Television. This is only the first page of a file called Operation Featherbed. There are many other lists in this file, many other names. Sir, your name is on one of them."

Murray moves to take the paper back, but Watkins holds onto it and stares at him, puzzled. "What does all this mean? You say you have a message for me from the minister, but you can't even tell me your name."

Murray looks out the window. The leafless trees and dead plants of early October offer him no inspiration. He isn't handling this well. He has let the old guy get to him. Jane's right. He simply isn't cut out for this work, and the sooner everyone recognizes it the better it will be for him. He hates all the lies this job forces him to weave. Hates the lies to his friends, and even to his sister as he tries to protect her.

THE MINISTER OF EXTERNAL AFFAIRS poured himself a generous shot from a bottle of Oban, then held it up to Murray with an inquiring eye. Murray nodded, even though it was mid-afternoon. They were alone in the minister's huge office, with its polished-wood panelling and hanging chandeliers. His secretary had discreetly left for the almost equally large outer office a few minutes earlier. It made him think about the small mean cubbyhole he worked in and the power of all those secrets in that miserable little office — malicious secrets that could bring down a cabinet minister, probably even a government. The minister poured again, brought the glass over to Murray, then led him by the elbow to the window that gave a sweeping view of the Rideau. "Fletcher, they tell me you are a dedicated, bright young man with an excellent future. That's why I've chosen you for this job. Are you up to it?"

Murray looked over the river and thought about his father dying in a canoe. "Fletcher?" the minister asked sharply.

"Yes, sir. I will do it."

The minister clinked glasses. "We need young men like you in External Affairs."

Yes, Murray thought, young expendable outsiders to take the drop when the bottom falls out of your plans and manipulations.

"Young men like you are the department's future. Now remember, most important, above and beyond everything that happens, the ambassador must be made aware that the whole offer is unofficial and off the record."

MURRAY TURNS AWAY from the bleak still life outside the art gallery window to look at Watkins, who is watching him closely. He takes a deep breath and lets it out slowly. "My name is Murray Fletcher. I work in the intelligence section of External Affairs."

"I didn't know we had one."

"We do, indeed, sir. I also work as a special assistant to the minister. Let me try to simplify the message I have been trying to pass on to you from my boss and yours . . ."

"TELL HIM," the minister said, "he will remain on full pay. He is to go to France, stay in his hotel on the Left Bank, not attempt to speak to anyone in the department, and not allow himself to talk to any official from any government agency of any country, including ours, who tries to interview him. He can claim continuing illness. We will keep him on official sick leave at full pay once he arrives in Paris. When things have died down, we will put his retirement and full pension into effect. He will be comfortable for the rest of his life."

"MR. AMBASSADOR, what is it you really want in this world?"

"You mean what is my dream, the way I want to spend the rest of my life?"

"Exactly."

"I know a village in the south of France. There's a café with a sunny table even in the coldest days of winter. I would like to go there every afternoon, take a glass of good white wine, translate Russian poems . . . perhaps even write some poetry myself." His voice is filled with longing, hankering for some kind of peace.

"Then, sir. Leave this afternoon. Whatever it is that you want awaits you. All you have to do is act."

Watkins taps the sheet of paper on the table in front of him. "But what does this mean, that my name is on the list. What do you call it — Operation Featherbed?"

"It means, sir, that the intelligence community of the Western world has labelled you a communist agent."

Watkins begins to laugh silently and uncontrollably. To Murray it is an eerie, mirthless sight. Then another emotion takes over as, stricken by sudden pain, the ambassador's face tightens in a grimace. He watches the older man search his pockets, fumble for a vial of pills. He takes the tube away from the ambassador, unscrews the cap, and helps guide his hand to his mouth. He waits silently as Watkins recovers, fearing he might die at this table in front of him.

Watkins slowly recovers. Again he taps the paper on the table. "No, I'm not going anywhere. At least not before I clear my name. I want to talk to the RCMP's security services."

"Ambassador, I think that is the last possible option the minister would want you to take. From a personal position, it would probably be the worst course of action for you."

AS THEY STOOD looking out the window at the Rideau flowing by, Murray asked the minister. "What if the ambassador doesn't want to take the offer?"

The minister regarded him coldly: "Then he will be on his own." The minister put down his unfinished drink. Murray took the cue that he was on his way out. He also put down his unfinished glass. The minister abruptly walked him to the door, his voice and eyes cold. "But we don't want that to happen, do we, Fletcher?"

"What if he doesn't take the suggestion," Murray also asked Adair, head of External's Department of Security Liaisons. Adair, shaved head, perfectly trimmed mustache, perpetually attired in his dark-blue military blazer, had spent years in military intelligence, mostly working in NATO. Murray had long since learned that Adair had nothing but contempt for the RCMP and all other civilian intelligence agencies. But before he would answer the question, he drove Murray in his Ford Galaxy over the bridge to Hull. There, in a quiet corner of a Legion Hall full of aging French-Canadian vets, he told Murray:

"The minister has selected you for a crash-and-burn mission. Why you? Well, you've figured that out. That's just the way the system works. But if you're lucky you might walk away from the crash. I like you, Fletcher, God knows why. You always come into the office late, and your idea of a dress code is laughable. But I have to admit your work is excellent, and you are willing to stay all hours of the night. So I figure the least I can do is brief you properly.

"Remember that in this business the interests of External Affairs and the RCMP are not the same. If you serve the RCMP's interests, you won't walk away from the crash. You will be lost in the wreckage. I know you have already seen the Featherbed files. The RCMP security services do not have the mandate or the resources to come up with this information. They get everything they know from what little we choose to give them, and from what the CIA and MI6 think is in their interest to give them. Under normal conditions — God, even under wartime conditions — there would be governmental committees, checks and balances. But since Kennedy's assassination last year there has been a power vacuum. Who has stepped into this void? The intelligence structures. The secret governments of the CIA and MI6. The FBI and MI5 are not far behind. But the CIA is completely fucked up.

"Every Soviet defector the KGB has sent over since the end of the war has convinced James Jesus Angleton that his counter-espionage division of the CIA is deeply infiltrated by Soviet moles. Angleton is a psycho. They say that he even wakes up now at four in the morning thinking he himself is a mole. Result? The CIA's counter-espionage is completely paralyzed. But here's the biggest joke of all on Angleton. He was Kim Philby's best buddy. They were like that! So imagine how Angleton must have felt when he woke up one morning last year to be informed that Philby had turned out to be the KGB's prize double agent and that he had got clean away to Moscow. Flew the coop free as a bird and into the KGB's waiting arms! They say Angleton was destroyed. I know he's been a sick and vicious man ever since — a man with enormous power. And, of course, because Philby was British old school and had all the bona fides of the other top MI6 upper-class twits, they were helping him right up to the end. They got him a job as a journalist in the Middle East. So when he made the final run for Moscow to come in from the cold, he could do it easily from Cairo. Result? British intelligence services are distrusted and benumbed. They are now also completely corrupt. They spend their huge budgets to serve the extreme right of the Conservative Party, doing all the dirty tricks to bring down Prime Minister Wilson. Okay? You get the picture?

"Your only way out of this mess is to convince the ambassador to get the hell out of the country as fast as he can. I'm not a political person, but I want you to remember this twenty-five years down the line when you are my age. The intelligence services of the Western world have forgotten their mission. They are all now working for the extreme right, and when the right comes to power, all these opportunists will be going into business for themselves as consultants to corporations. The Cold War, if you haven't already noticed, is hugely profitable. When it's all over, it will have made the rich even richer. Briefing over. We never had this conversation. Finish your beer. It's time for you to head for Montreal."

Adair stood up, saluted the Red Ensign as he marched out of the Legion, and drove Murray back to his apartment in Sandy Hill. "By the way," he asked in the car, "you're not queer, are you?"

"You mean you haven't noticed?"

"Don't jerk me around. I don't think you are, unless all these women are a cover for something. This is important."

"No. But what has being gay got to do with anything?"

"Right, gay, that's the term they're starting to use these days. Just in case you don't know, Present, who runs the KGB desk in B Operations, has been the guy in charge of purging all homosexuals from the civil service. He's also the stalking horse for Watkins."

MURRAY LOOKS UP to realize that Watkins has been watching him.

"What's up, Murray?"

"My father, you remind me of him in some ways."

"He's no longer alive?"

"No, he died six months ago. He had a heart attack . . . he was on a canoe trip."

"I'm sorry. Were you close?"

"Very." Murray nods nervously. He really doesn't want this conversation to get any more intimate.

Watkins senses the reserve and instead opens up himself. "All the same, you're a lucky man. Perhaps if my father had lived long enough I would know what to do in this ignominious situation I find myself in at the end of a career I never really wanted . . ."

Murray knows. He has, of course, studied the ambassador's file. When Watkins was three, his father was injured on the farm in Norval Station when a heavily loaded horse-drawn cart crushed his foot. The wound became infected and he died a few days later from gangrene.

"But I understand you had a close relationship with your mother."

"Yes, a strong and compassionate woman."

"Well, I guess we're even," smiles Murray gently. "My mother died in the hospital when we were being born — twins."

"If your mother had lived, what do you think she would tell me to do now?"

"Well, she used to love poetry. According to my father, she could recite whole poems. Mostly the romantics — Byron and Blake."

"I like her already."

"So I think she would tell you to go and write those poems you want to translate at that sunny café table in the south of France."

Watkins smiles. "If the RCMP has me under surveillance as you say, and the minister is urging me to leave the country immediately, then the RCMP and External must have conflicting interests in my future. Can you tell me what they could be, or do I have to guess?"

"I'm not really qualified to answer that question, Mr. Ambassador."

"Oh, take a shot, and this time we'll keep your mother out of it."

"I think the minister of External and Mr. Pearson are moving pieces around on the chessboard. They don't want to be vulnerable to black-mail."

"You mean, I'm sort of a pawn to be played by the RCMP and the CIA? That sounds a little far-fetched to me, Murray."

"Think of yourself as at least a knight, sir. But you must know that the prime minister is vulnerable. He is barely surviving with a minority government. Any really serious security scandal, like another Herbert Norman affair, would probably bring down his house of cards and totally destroy any chance of getting the Liberals re-elected."

Watkins is embarrassed. "No, I haven't been paying attention to things the way I should . . ."

"Lyndon Johnson wants to internationalize the Vietnam War. He has bullied Australia and New Zealand, and now they are committed to sending troops to Vietnam as part of his new buildup in the war."

"So the president sent Cabot Lodge, his fiercest war hawk, to lean on Mike — to get him to send a division or two of Canadian soldiers to die in this most stupid of all wars."

"Yes, sir, the whole idea is anathema to the prime minister."

"Of course, of course!" Watkins bursts out in real laughter this time. "Only a former governor of Texas would not know that Mike got his Nobel Prize as a peacemaker at the UN over the Suez crisis."

"Yes, seems they're off to a bad start. President Johnson publicly introduced Mr. Pearson to his cabinet as Prime Minister Wilson and his Canadian colleagues."

Watkins chuckles. "It never ends. The Americans are so good at that sort of thing. But, you know, the dark irony is that Mike owes his Nobel Prize to those mischief makers over in Britain's MI6 foreign intelligence service. They were trying to bring down Nasser, the Egyptian president, just the way they brought down Mossadegh in Iran and paved the way for the return of the Shah. A bit of meddling the world will have to pay for in the years to come. But with Nasser, things got out of hand, especially after Eden made his phony invasion of the Suez. The Americans were critical, the Europeans were offended, and the Israelis backed off. Mike and the United Nations had to clean up the mess started by a bunch of English overreachers in MI6, directing death and destruction to rain down on thousands of wretched Arabs. Their safe little enclave at Porton Downs is a lovely place, I must say. I was there a few weeks ago, you know."

Murray is amazed. "You, sir, at the MI6 headquarters in Britain?"

"Yes. You see, Murray, they may have briefed you, but, as always, they leave out the most important parts. I've been this way before. So, as the minister's messenger, you should think about this carefully."

He remembers his father: "There are two ways to lie, Murray. One is you make up the evidence. The second is to leave out essential information. Most people use both techniques of lying as it suits them. And the truth, my son, is something most men stumble over in their lives, but go right on pretending never happened."

"YOU DON'T NEED TO KNOW, Inspector Fletcher." As always, Williams, the director general of intelligence, speaks just above a whisper. Lighting himself another cigarette, he apologizes and casually tosses the package of du Mauriers across the completely bare desk to her. How to read such a gesture? Is it ill-concealed contempt, she wonders, or an effort to be super laid-back?

"No, thank you, sir. Still haven't taken up the habit."

Williams grunts, but leaves the package where it is. In her gut she believes the DGI can't stand the sight of a woman on his force. Still, she wouldn't be where she is today without his support. She remembers him in the first interview when she was bumped up the ladder. "Don't misunderstand me, Fletcher. I don't believe the possession of a vagina necessarily gives you more insight than any man in this department into the human soul. These times are rotten and getting worse, but we have to move with them. So far, you have a good record, Fletcher. Just do your job, don't screw up, and we'll get along fine."

But things hadn't turned out so simply. In most people's eyes she had screwed up in the Scharansky affair. Here she is, going over everybody's head to talk to the DGI, and he is very correctly taking her to task. To her, he also appears pissed off.

Williams stares at her silently from behind a heavy veil of cigarette smoke. A Buddha-shaped man slumped back in his chair, his face pitted and scarred from what must have been terrible acne in his youth. Heavy-hooded eyelids, red-veined from the constant irritation of cigarette smoke, remain half closed. He waits.

"With all due respect, sir, I do have to know. I'm taking orders from the head of the counter-intelligence desk which make me deeply concerned."

Williams curls his lip. "For your own welfare, Fletcher?"

"No, sir, for the counter-intelligence department."

Williams, a man with a chronic bad back, groans as he struggles to his feet and lumbers across the room to close the door. This is not his office. Fletcher had happened upon Williams, down from headquarters, in the corridor and jumped at the chance to talk to him.

"Say your piece, Fletcher."

"Information —"

"You're sure you're not going to repeat rumours now?"

"— information that Present is under internal investigation."

Williams is visibly angered. He growls as he paces up and down the narrow office, kneading the small of his back with clenched fists.

"Where did you get this from."

Fletcher's heart pounds, but she gets the words out evenly: "American sources, sir."

Williams explodes: "Goddam those CIA assholes!"

He gingerly lowers his aching body into the chair and, in a bored voice, lectures her: "Present is undergoing a regular performance assessment, just like you and everyone else undergoes in this department."

Is he lying? She doesn't know what to think.

"Okay, Fletcher? Now get back on the job."

She decides to push it further: "I foresee this case with the ambassador going wrong because of Present's interventions. If it does, for these reasons, I don't wish to be held responsible in the same way as I was reprimanded in the Scharansky case."

Williams sighs deeply and, heavy head bowed and wagging from side to side, casts angrily about for an answer. For the first time Fletcher understands that they need her every bit as much as she needs them — perhaps, she thinks with a thrill of delight, even more. Someone will have to take the fall, if it's needed. She is happy she provoked this confrontation.

"I know all about the Scharansky case. I also know what went wrong and why. But that's behind us."

"Yes, sir. Thank you, sir." Fletcher gets up to leave.

Williams accompanies her down the empty hallway. He puts his arm out to shake hands in a formal goodbye. The hand is huge and softly padded. This is a man, she realizes, who doesn't even have a hobby that is remotely physical. No wonder he suffers so much from back pain. But, strangely, for the first time she feels something like genuine respect coming from him. Still holding her hand, Williams leans in to whisper in her ear: "The only thing I will hold you responsible for is if you let the ambassador slip back to Europe before we are ready to turn him loose."

"You have my promise that won't happen, sir." When Williams doesn't pull his hand away, she sees a glitter of sexual surprise, an expectation of something in the hooded blue eyes. "One last thing," she persists. "Merleau, was his last station Buenos Aires?"

Williams' lip curls in a cynical and disappointed grimace. "No, Fletcher, it was Brazil. But I wouldn't check it out if I were you. It might turn you right off." And the DGI lumbers away down the hall, a bear in an ugly brown suit.

FRIDAY AFTERNOON. Watkins is dressed, except for the jacket of his pin-striped suit, when the phone rings. It is the woman at the front desk.

"Your suitcases have been placed in the limo, sir."

"Thank you, I'll be right down." He packs the last few items into a shoulder bag that is open on the bureau.

He picks up the Swedish copy of Dag Hammarskjöld's *Markings* and puts the book inside the bag. He sorts through the scattered sheaf of papers on the desk, the ones typed in the Cyrillic alphabet and covered in red-inked English translations, and stuffs them into his suit pocket. The last item is the small container of pills, prescription renewed. He opens the tube, shakes a nitroglycerin pill into the palm of his hand, and places it under his tongue. While the pill dissolves, he gazes one last time through the open window. The storm that has been threatening the city for the last two days finally appears to be approaching. He packs the container in a side pocket of his shoulder bag and, with a last glance around, leaves the room. Watkins exits the elevator, quickly crosses the lobby without a glance to either side, moves through the swinging door, and, damn — the sight of Bruno fills him with foreboding. In the Rymark, Bruno had said this would be his day off.

But Bruno smiles warmly, holding the rear passenger door open. "A sudden change in plans, sir?"

"Yes, I'm afraid it's goodbye, Bruno." Watkins pauses to hand him a tip.

"Thank you, sir, but I can't take it. You've already done so much for Michel."

There is more thunder, and heavy drops of rain begin to fall. They both glance up at the sky to acknowledge the coming storm.

"It's the season," shrugs Bruno.

Watkins shakes the doorman's hand.

"When will we have the pleasure of seeing you again, sir?"

"Not for quite a while, Bruno. When this little bit of business is out of the way, I plan to take early retirement."

"And where will you go, sir?"

Watkins recalls Michel's warning. Keep it light and brief, he tells himself. "Oh, I'm dreaming about a café table in a sunny corner of France."

Bruno is delighted. "Couldn't happen to a better person, sir. Who knows? Maybe one of these days I'll get over there to visit you. Don't worry, sir, only joking. I wouldn't disturb your peace."

"No, no, Bruno. By all means. When I get settled I'll send you a post-card with the address. Say goodbye to Michel for me and wish him all the best."

They shake hands one last time.

Watkins enters the limousine, but doesn't recognize the chauffeur. Yes, the driver assures him, his usual man is sick, and his bags have already been taken to Dorval. He feels a bit unsettled, but says nothing.

FROM THE BACK SEAT of the limo, Watkins watches the road ahead with increasing concern. The storm has broken in full force. The afternoon has turned black. The driver has to slow down to pass an accident, surrounded by police officers and emergency road crews flashing yellow lights. The windshield wipers cannot keep up with the heavy rain. Still, Watkins is thankful that the man is expert and continues to drive fast through the downpour. The airport signs point ahead to Dorval, but the driver suddenly pulls off the autoroute and takes an exit ramp. Watkins raps on the window panel that divides them, but the driver ignores him and pulls up under the overpass, where the passenger door is abruptly opened by a woman with a shock of red hair who looks vaguely familiar. Behind her are two men in suits. One of them holds a large umbrella against the rain.

"Mr. Ambassador, I am Inspector Fletcher." She shows her ID. "RCMP Security Services, B Operations. For security reasons I must ask you to come with me."

Watkins is puzzled — and hesitant. "I can't afford to miss my plane. I must be in Paris tomorrow — an important meeting. Then I must make the connecting flight the day after to Moscow."

Fletcher is courteous and reassuring. "Yes, sir, I understand. This is just a momentary delay. Everything has been taken care of and you will soon be on your way again."

Watkins has no choice. He reluctantly follows her through the rain to the other car. But he stumbles and falls to his knees in the flooded gutter. Garbage and debris quickly swill up around him as his legs block off the grating to the sewer. Fletcher pulls him to his feet and the men hurry him to the car. Fletcher stoops to pick up the package of Players cigarettes that has fallen from Watkins' pocket. She stuffs it in her own coat pocket without saying anything.

IN THE CAR, Watkins is silent and apprehensive. After a half-hour's drive he realizes they have returned to downtown Montreal. The car pulls off Sherbrooke Street into the service entrance of a hotel he recognizes as the Ritz.

Fletcher, dressed in a dark business suit, steers Watkins out of an elevator and along the corridor to a large, dimly lit, corner apartment. They enter a spacious room with high ceilings and faux turn-of-the-century decor mixed with contemporary furnishings. There is even a piano in one corner. Huge windows along the walls give a magnificent view of the city as a crack of lightening turns the sky white and illuminates the apartment. Fletcher tries to shut the wooden slat blinds, but they will only half close. A uniformed officer brings Watkins' two suitcases into the room and asks where they should be placed. With a nod of her head, Fletcher indicates the bedroom.

Watkins explodes with anger: "I demand an explanation. I will not tolerate being treated this way!" He goes towards the phone: "I am going to call the Prime Minister's Office —"

"Sit down and shut up," Fletcher screams as she grabs the phone away from him.

Watkins stares at her in shocked silence. He has never encountered this treatment before. "I'm the ambassador —"

"No, not any more!"

Watkins sinks silently into a high-backed chair. The lightning outside continues to back-light the blinds and play bar-like patterns across the walls and ceiling of the apartment. The uniformed officer takes a seat near the door.

A thin-faced deferential man in his early thirties carries a tray with tea and coffee into the room. Fletcher waves his offering aside. He places the tray on the table and pours a cup of tea for the ambassador. They exchange glances.

"Who are you?" Watkins asks.

"Merleau. George Merleau," the man replies.

Watkins merely nods, and Merleau retires like a waiter. After a few moments of silence, Fletcher, in a cold but more normal voice, tells

Watkins: "Everything will be explained to you once the director of B Operations arrives."

Watkins watches through the half-open bedroom door as Merleau searches through his suitcase. Merleau looks up and catches Watkins' eye, smiles reassuringly, and closes the door. Dazed, Watkins does not resist when Fletcher takes his shoulder bag and begins to empty out the contents onto the coffee table. She finds a vial of pills. He anxiously reaches out for them: "I must have them. If I don't maintain my regular medication I will quickly become ill."

Fletcher reassures Watkins: "We will see that you get your pills when you need them, but regulations require that we hold on to the container."

She calls Merleau out of the bedroom and hands him the pills. He slips them into his pocket and begins to make notes on the other items Fletcher finds in the shoulder bag.

She asks for the sheaf of papers in Watkins' suit pocket. He tosses them to her, asking in fluent Russian if she has an interest in Russian poetry. When she doesn't respond, he asks again, and she admits that she neither speaks nor reads Russian. She examines the pages carefully as Merleau makes meticulous notes on his pad. Watkins finds this bizarre. She takes out the Hammarskjöld book of poetry.

"Please be careful," Watkins implores.

"He was your friend?" Fletcher asks coldly.

"Yes."

"How did you meet him?"

"This is silly, I'm a diplomat —"

"Yes, but there must have been a first time. Who introduced you?"

"Mike Pearson, when he received the Nobel Peace Prize. There was a reception at the United Nations, and Hammarskjöld had just been re-elected secretary general."

"So, you were all friends?"

"Friends and colleagues."

"More friends than colleagues?" Fletcher persists.

Watkins doesn't bother to answer. What is the evil that has brought me to this humiliation so late in my life? he wonders. He finds himself muttering out loud: "Is this not that final meeting in the twilight kingdom?"

Fletcher stares at him, her extraordinary green eyes flat in cold incomprehension.

"This is the dead land . . . here the stone images are raised . . ." He must pull himself together. What is he thinking of? This is no time to be rambling on about Eliot. These meddlers will believe he's trying to get off as a loony old man.

He finds himself staring at Merleau. The quiet man smiles back sympathetically and glances at the ambassador's wet trousers and the spreading damp ring on the dark red rug. Watkins begins to shiver uncontrollably.

Merleau stands up. "I'm sorry. You look miserable."

"I must say I have enjoyed the Ritz under better circumstances."

"Come! Let's do something to make you more comfortable."

Merleau helps Watkins to his feet. The older man gratefully lets himself be guided like a patient rather than a prisoner across the suite to the bathroom. Great flashes of lightning momentarily dim the electricity.

Merleau opens the door to the bathroom and switches on the light: "While you dry off, I'll fetch you some trousers from your suitcase."

Fletcher watches them both from across the room, seemingly impassive but secretly amazed at the solicitous valet role Merleau has so easily slipped into. How many other characters can he play?

Watkins immediately latches the door behind him. It's an old-world bathroom, as large as most living rooms, with a sparkling marble terrazzo floor and a gigantic bathtub balanced on lion-claw feet. As he unbuttons his wet pants, a wash of sheet lightning illuminates the lace-curtained French doors beside the toilet. He quickly shuffles over to the doors, pants around his knees, and pushes the curtain aside to peer through the rain pouring down the window panes. He can see the vague outlines of a fire escape outside. He tries to open the glass doors. Perhaps he can get through and find his way down the fire escape to the street. He has no idea what floor the apartment is on — he forgot to look in the elevator. He tries once again to push the doors open, but they are locked tight. He flushes the toilet and, under the noise of the rushing water, pounds with his fists along the centre door jamb to try to force the lock. He is disturbed by a light tap on the bathroom door. "Just a minute!" he calls out over his shoulder.

Watkins repeatedly flushes the toilet as he struggles again with the doors. Perhaps he can at least escape to another suite and raise the alarm. The knock on the door is louder, more impatient. He calls out in an irritated tone, "Yes, yes, one moment, please!" Holding on to his pants with one hand, he puts his shoulder to the doors. Finally they spring open. Rain pours in and soaks the rest of his clothes. He turns his head to find Merleau, the perfect valet, coming through the bathroom door holding a pair of dry trousers over his arm. Fletcher appears behind him. They stare at him curiously. Watkins freezes, peering over his shoulder at them. He feels absurd. In his vigorous attack on the doors his soaked pants have fallen to his ankles, and he still has one hand on the half-open French door. His valiant attempt to escape appears pathetic.

"I . . . I was looking . . . I needed some fresh air," he mutters lamely.

Fletcher snatches the clothing from Merleau's arm, then disappears. Merleau quickly crosses the bathroom and closes the French doors. Fletcher returns with a blanket, which she wordlessly tosses to Watkins. She slams the bathroom door behind her contemptuously, leaving Merleau and Watkins alone. While Merleau holds the blanket, Watkins sheepishly gets out of his wet clothing. Merleau politely averts his gaze from the older man's nakedness.

"Mr. Ambassador," he murmurs, and Watkins wonders why this man continues to address him by his diplomatic rank when the woman officer has indicated he has been stripped of all official status. "I understand you're not a well man. I suggest you try to relax a bit. Trust me, you have nothing to worry about."

Watkins nods, shivering as he towels himself dry.

"By the way, I'm sorry, but the fire escape leads nowhere. It's just part of the balcony that runs around the outside of the apartment."

Merleau hands Watkins the blanket. But Watkins is distracted, anxiously searching through his damp jacket on the floor.

"Have you lost something, sir?"

"You don't have a smoke on you by any chance, do you?"

Merleau shakes his head. "I don't smoke."

Again he hands Watkins the blanket. The old man fumbles, trying to wrap it around himself. He looks at himself in the mirror. He appears ridiculous, and once again he feels humiliated. Who in External would ever believe this?

"So the idea is, if I'm a good boy, I'll get my pants and cigarettes back?"

"I think she believes it's harder for you to run away without your clothes." Again Merleau tries to comfort him. "If you don't mind my saying so, sir, you're overreacting to the situation. I know this must be quite a shock to you and also unpleasant. But please try to stay calm. Everything is going to be okay. Are you ready to go out now?"

Watkins nods, trying to muster some semblance of dignity. The two men return to the living room. Awkwardly clasping the blanket wrapped around him, Watkins sits down on the couch opposite Fletcher. She regards him with cold amusement. Merleau perches off to one side. Watkins is curious about the dynamic between his keepers. Although Fletcher is very much in charge, she also seems to seek Merleau's approval. He watches now as Merleau whispers in Fletcher's ear. All the articles she removed from his shoulder bag now sit in tidy order on the coffee table. She picks up the sheaf of papers Watkins had handed over before the bathroom episode. After watching her examine them, he again asks in Russian: "I see you still have an interest in Russian poetry?"

She doesn't respond, but continues to look at the pages with great care. He remembers the stories Akhundi's parents told him. This is what it must have been like in the early days of the Bolshevik Revolution, when any citizens could be stopped to have their documents examined by illiterate but armed soldiers.

"Perhaps," Watkins asks, "you would be so kind as to comment on my interpretation of Yevtushenko's line, "the shadows of ghosts"?

Merleau silently continues with his note-taking.

"As I said before," Fletcher finally replies, "I neither speak nor read Russian. Tell me, Mr. Watkins, what do these notes in handwritten English refer to? What is the content of these typewritten pages?"

"Poetry."

"Poetry?"

"Just that. I translate Russian poetry."

"Why?"

"Why? . . . Why? Because it's my . . . it's one of my intellectual passions. But I suppose your police mind couldn't understand."

Fletcher, flinty-eyed, once again picks out the poetry book and casually flips through the pages. Watkins watches her apprehensively. He wonders where all the anger in this woman comes from. Perhaps it's the conditioning of being a police officer. He can't shake the sense that he's met her before. As he watches her thumb through the book, it occurs to him that this is a person who has never read anything that has changed her life, her way of thinking. He can't stop himself from saying once again, "Please be careful."

"Yes, yes, I know. You've already told me he was your friend. And the book is important to you?"

Watkins nods. "I'm sentimental about books, especially ones that come as gifts." He attempts a smile, but it only makes him feel even more like a supplicant. Mike, he thinks, how could you have let this happen to me? How could you have delivered me into the hands of the Philistines?

She finds the inscription on the flyleaf and reads it out loud: "'John, Dag's book is finally in print. I must say it brings back many wonderful memories. No wonder you two got along so well. He shared your mystical approach.' It's signed LBP. Who is LBP?"

Watkins stares back at her. "Why are you being so blatantly disingenuous?"

"Please answer the question."

"Violent souls, but only as the hollow men, the stuffed men," Watkins thinks to himself, but he replies patiently: "The prime minister, Lester Bowles Pearson. Perhaps you've been informed?"

Fletcher persists: "And how did you first meet the prime minister?"

"When he hired me for the job."

Fletcher, in a quick underhand movement, flings the open book across the table into Watkins' face. He tries to catch it, but his arm tangles in the folds of the blanket. He clasps the book by a page, which tears out in his hand as the book falls to the carpet. Incredulous, he glares at Fletcher, retrieves the book from the floor, replaces the crumpled page inside, and smoothes out the wrinkles with his palm. Fletcher looks on, unperturbed.

In an indication of apology to Watkins, Merleau raises his eyebrows and ever so faintly shrugs.

Watkins asks wearily: "Isn't this all a bit unnecessary?"

His controlled response seems to provoke Fletcher even more. She flips through the files on the sofa, then returns to her notepad. He notices an odd book in the pile and cheekily leans forward to extract it. "*One-Dimensional Man: Studies in the Ideology of the Advanced Industrial Society* by Herbert Marcuse, just published this year," he says. "Are you reading it, Inspector? Work or pleasure?"

She doesn't answer his question. "I suppose you've already read the book?" she asks.

It's his turn to have fun. "To tell the truth, I tried, but I found it inaccessible. How a book, burdened with all that ideological claptrap — by which I mean pure Marxist jargon that clearly reveals the academic arrogance of the writer — ever gets to be an international bestseller is really a stroke of capitalist marketing."

Fletcher considers him for a long moment. "What does 'sharing the same mystical approach' with Dag Hammarskjöld mean?"

Watkins throws up his hands in an exaggerated gesture of despair. "You know, I've never really been sure. Could be a non-ideological code. But I think just to be sure you should ask the prime minister."

Fletcher smiles to herself. She seems to like it better when he fights back. "Well, what's it been now, two years?" she asks. "I'm sure there are many Americans who were glad to see your mystical and intellectual friend go."

Watkins is openly disgusted by her callousness: "Dag Hammarskjöld didn't *go* — he was murdered." I'm doing everything wrong, he thinks to himself. I'm letting her play me like a hooked river bass.

"Really? I thought he died accidentally in that plane crash over the Congolese jungle . . . When was that exactly, two, three years ago?"

"September 18, 1961." He would never forget that date.

HE WAS AT THE FARMHOUSE in Norval Station on sick leave — the heart again, more tests. He woke up out of a horrible nightmare, bathed in sweat. In the yard, the dogs were howling. He turned on the table lamp and saw it was after five in the morning. He wrapped himself in the Chinese red-silk dressing gown with the embroidered dragons on the back — the one Akhundi had given him as a birthday present — and went out to smoke on the front porch. A waning harvest moon lit up the yard and made it seem like dawn. His presence quieted the dogs. He tried to remember the nightmare: he was lost in the labyrinth of shabby streets behind the Canadian Embassy in Moscow. He tried to ask directions from the shadowy passersby in the street, but instead of his fluent Russian only gibberish came out of his mouth. To his horror, he discovered that his tongue had been cut out. Recollecting the dream, his hand went involuntarily to his mouth. A strange irony for a linguist to suffer! What did it mean? After a few minutes he gave up trying to figure it out — it was too ominous, too impenetrable. He lit another cigarette.

It was already the middle of September, the air was cool, and all around were messages of the coming winter. He didn't want to be here for the cold months. Better to find a way to get back to his hotel room in Paris. As he savoured the cigarette, he heard a large formation of Canada geese flying south through the grey sky, the leader imperiously honking his commands. The geese passed low over the farmhouse, and the dogs moaned and craned their heads upward at the whooshing sound of so many powerful wings beating the air at once. As was his habit, he turned on the six o'clock BBC international news. Then came the awful lead item on the newscast: Dag Hammarskjöld had been killed in a mysterious plane crash over the jungle while on a United Nations peace mission in the Congo. The news was followed by a lengthy obituary:

"Dag Hjalmar Agne Carl Hammarskjöld, born on July 29, 1905, secretary general of the United Nations and fourth son of Hjalmar Hammarskjöld, prime minister of Sweden during the First World War. After a brilliant political career in his own country, in which he was the youngest man ever to hold many critical government posts, Mr. Hammarskjöld, in April 1953, was unanimously appointed secretary general of the United Nations. He was re-elected unanimously for another term of five years in September 1957 . . ." Was it the sense of being a "servant" that sustained him through all those years of pressure?

Watkins wondered. "During his terms as secretary general, Mr. Hammarskjöld carried out many responsibilities for the United Nations . . . one of his most heralded efforts, and one that earned him the gratitude of many Americans, followed his visit to Peking in December 1954 when fifteen detained American fliers, captured while serving under the United Nations Command in Korea, were released by the Chinese People's Republic after Mr. Hammarskjöld's negotiations . . ."

How quickly the Americans had forgotten. All that rubbish about the United Nations being a communist agency, and Dag being attacked in the press as a pro-communist at best and a secret agent at worst. And no mention, Watkins mourned, that he was a distinguished man of literature and an accomplished mystical poet. Sorrowfully he went into the living room and, in requiem, put on a new and prized recording of Shostakovich's 8th symphony that he had recently bought in Paris. He turned up the volume and went back to the porch to listen to the music pouring out of the house. Akhundi had pronounced: "Shostakovich is a Russian who understands and says in his music, 'We are a people living in a cage, but to hell with it. I'm still going to make my music, so hear us, world!'"

WE NORTH AMERICANS do indeed live in a hick society, he reflected, starting past Fletcher's shoulder at the rain and lightning outside.

"Do you have proof it was an accident?" Watkins mildly asks the impatient Fletcher.

"Do you have proof that it was otherwise?" she mocks him.

"At the time, only one of the superpowers had the resources to knock down his plane with a surface-to-air missile."

"But they were all there, weren't they? The French, the Russians, the British mercenaries . . . Even a brigade of Cubans showed up —"

"Why do you leave out the Americans?" Watkins interrupts, and immediately regrets that he let himself be baited by this tiresome and one-dimensional police officer.

"Are you suggesting the Americans wanted to kill the most powerful diplomat in the world?" Fletcher instantly demands.

Well, he thinks, let's not waste time, let's go to the heart of her ridiculous implication. "I have yet to hear a convincing argument that it was in Moscow's interest to kill the secretary general of the United Nations."

"Why? Because he was such a good friend to the Kremlin?"

"Dag Hammarskjöld's death was a great loss to the civilized world."

"Does your civilized world include the United States?"

"Can any culture that produces Disneyland be described as civilized?"

Merleau tries hard not to smile. Watkins sees Fletcher's cheeks redden in anger. It's a waste of time trying to find a way to talk to this woman, he decides in exasperation. Better to stay silent. She is a true believer, a fundamentalist, and her faculty of self-criticism isn't developed enough for her to see her position as a weakness rather than a strength.

HE REMEMBERS one of his last conversations with Dag. They talked for an hour in New York. Watkins was tired and fed up with the politics of External Affairs. "I want out," he told Dag. "I'm not like you. I don't have the same commitment. These national leaders with their transparent lies — I'm getting old and I don't have the fortitude to put up with it any more. When I was a kid working with the harvest workers around Norval Station, they used to say: "Relax, son, we all have to swallow shit, but it's very hard to keep it down.""

Dag laughed and wearily agreed. "The only way to be a diplomat in the Cold War is to be someone who exists for the future of others without being suffocated by the present." That was Dag's mystical Christianity again. Just being around him for a while made you want to try harder to do better.

After Dag became secretary general for the second time, he seemed to age twenty years overnight. To Watkins he seemed to take on the qualities of a Buddhist priest, accepting leaders' ambitions, however cynical and criminal they may have been. In that last conversation, Dag told him he was completely disillusioned with Jack Kennedy. "Diem wants to make a deal for peace in Vietnam, so he and Ho Chi Minh have been meeting for secret talks in New Delhi. Diem and Ho hate each other, but they believe that a buildup of an American war machine in their country will be disaster for Vietnam. So, to keep the Americans out, they're willing to make peace. When Kennedy heard about the peace talks he was furious with Diem."

"Why?" Watkins asked. "He can't believe in the war?"

"No," sighed Dag, "that's what makes it worse. He just wants to keep the war going until he gets re-elected."

"CAN YOU REMEMBER when President Ngo Dinh Diem and his brother Ngo Dinh Nhu were assassinated?" Watkins asks Merleau.

Surprised, Merleau pauses briefly before he replies: "Yes, just last year, November 1, 1963."

"And Kennedy was killed three weeks later," Watkins muses.

Merleau's eyes narrow with curiosity, and for a moment Watkins sees the genial mask drop as a larger interest clearly rises in the man's mind. "What's the connection?" he asks.

"The sword . . . the sword is the connection," murmurs Watkins. "You know, he who lives . . ."

MERLEAU HEARD the whirring of the chopper blades . . . felt the heavy thudding of the .30-calibre machine gun as the port gunner beside him, shaven head and dark glasses, hammered death into the tree line below . . . saw the shiny spent shell casings vibrate on the chopper's metal floor around the blond warrior head of the dying kid from Kansas, Medic scrawled in magic marker across his flak jacket, camouflage pants man-gled . . . The kid's blood a deeper red than the bright red clay tracked in from the hills around Danang. Kansas moved his lips, and Merleau knelt close and put his face against the mouth to hear what he was saying, but the kid was already dead. The chopper pitched wildly from the shock wave of an explosion right beside them . . . Merleau grabbed the dead boy, embraced the corpse to prevent it from falling through the open bay door, and covered his own combat fatigues in blood. He saw, yawn-ing below him, the lush green paddy fields on fire as the helicopter filled with acrid smoke from the napalm strike below.

MERLEAU LOOKS UP to find Watkins observing him closely. "Were you ever in Vietnam, Mr. Merleau?" Watkins asks. Merleau smiles back enigmatically.

"Let's get back to John Watkins," Fletcher snaps.

She is a control addict, Watkins realizes. He notices Fletcher flash Merleau another of her approval-seeking glances, but Merleau, who has regained his neutral expression, registers no response. Watkins leans forward to paw through the objects on the coffee table, looking for cigarettes. They both watch him with clinical interest. "What have you done with my carton of Players?" he asks.

Fletcher ignores his question. "Did Dag Hammarskjöld also share your love for Russian art?"

"This is insane!" Watkins explodes. "Are you keeping me here as part of an investigation into the death of Dag Hammarskjöld? What's the rational explanation for this lunacy? Please! I must make phone calls. People are expecting me in Paris. Allow me at least to contact them."

"Calm yourself, Mr. Watkins." Fletcher is now more placatory. "Don't worry, the embassy people in Paris have been contacted. Everything is under control. But surely you know why you are here?"

"No! Absolutely no idea, none whatsoever! Tell me."

"To prove who you really are."

Watkins is incredulous. "But you know who I am!"

"If you keep on refusing to cooperate, we'll have to wait for the director of B Operations."

"Why?"

"He will make everything clear."

"What on earth is B Operations?"

Fletcher regards him with disbelief: "Now, who is being disingenuous?"

"No! I really don't know. And, essentially, I don't care. But why can't this director get here so we can clear up this 'security matter' and let me be on my way?"

Fletcher pauses to rearrange in neat order all the objects on the coffee table which Watkins has jumbled in his search for cigarettes. "You've been briefed many times, especially by the first secretary of mission."

"I was really too busy with the job to pay much attention to what we diplomats call the spook end of the business."

Fletcher smiles. It's the first time she has relaxed and reacted to Watkins like a normal human being. He can see that, in another place and time, she would be an engaging young woman.

"The spook business," she chuckles. "Strange, that's what my brother calls it also."

All of a sudden, Watkins feels deeply afraid. "What did you say your name was?" he asks.

"Fletcher, Inspector Jane Fletcher."

He remembers, Murray . . . the red hair, the same angular face, the sensitive voice: "What is in your heart, Mr. Ambassador? How would you like to spend the last years of your life?" Yes, of course! This must be the brother she is talking about . . . the twin . . . "My mother died giving birth to us." Is the solicitous Murray, bearing an unofficial message from the minister — "Leave as soon as you can this afternoon" — also part of this elaborate trap he has fallen into? Was he urged to run so they would have the excuse to arrest him? The satisfaction in Fletcher's voice is unmistakable.

"Well, Mr. Watkins, that may just turn out to be a serious oversight for which you have to pay dearly — B Operations is the security service directorate responsible for counter-espionage in what you refer to as the spook business."

Watkins' chest tightens. "Then the director we are waiting for is the head of counter-intelligence, or, in your jargon, counter-espionage?"

Fletcher observes his apprehension with an amused smile. "Yes, you've got that right."

Watkins perceives her disdain and once again feels angry and humiliated. They are interrupted by the phone ringing. Fletcher goes over to the table by the windows to answer it and converses inaudibly in the background. Merleau smiles sympathetically at Watkins and offers him more tea.

Watkins nods absently and scans the room. Fletcher's back is turned while she talks on the phone. A door beside her leads to the balcony. But the apartment is high enough to overlook the city and the surrounding buildings. Besides Merleau, there's also that uniformed officer at the door. No chance to escape.

Merleau has been watching Watkins' examination of the suite. In a quiet undertone he tells Watkins, "We're on the twelfth floor of the hotel and B Operations has control of the entire floor. It would be unwise for you to try and . . . uh . . . leave."

"So this is what they call a 'safe house'?"

"Then you *were* paying attention to those security service briefings."

"Some things stick in your mind. But why a hotel?"

"Oh, logistics. And no nosy neighbours to ask why so many people are coming and going."

"Is she always like this?" Watkins asks, tilting his head towards Fletcher, still on the phone at the other side of the suite.

"Try to stay calm. When the director arrives, everything will be straightened out."

"Is that a trace of an American accent?"

Merleau realizes he has slipped his guard and tries casually to recover. "Oh, probably comes from when I went to school down there."

Watkins smiles in his most diplomatic manner. "So did I . . . Cornell. Of course that was a hundred years ago, but you know, that accent of yours sounds a little bit like Vermont to me."

"Actually, it was Wayne State —"

"No, no, a Wayne State grad would never say 'actually.' I think he would have said 'Really — really, it was Wayne State.' And then, too, a Canadian would never say 'down there' in reference to the United States. It's always 'there' or 'in the U.S.' Do you understand what I'm getting at? I'm very sensitive to these nuances because, you see, my field is linguistics." He smiles benignly.

Fletcher hangs up the phone and quickly crosses the room to pick up on the exchange between the two men.

"You see, to my ears," Watkins rushes on, "you sound like a Notre Dame man. Notre Dame, isn't that where they recruit —"

"The director has been delayed because of the storm," Fletcher brusquely interrupts. "He has asked me to begin the interview for him."

Watkins bursts out in derisive laughter. "Interview! This is an interrogation. I've been arrested by the secret police —"

"No! You were not arrested," she argues. "You were asked to accompany us. You consented freely."

Watkins claps his hands in mockery: "Bravo! Inspector Fletcher, Bravo! You really have a talent for twisting reality."

He senses an uncertainty in her voice and body language. The phone call seems to have knocked her off balance. Her stiffened jaw betrays some anxiety. Has she been informed that she has overstepped her authority? Things may be about to go his way.

"The reality is that the sooner we get these formalities out of the way, the sooner you'll be free to go. Now —"

"What is it, cold feet?" Watkins gambles. "The director isn't going to show up because you're being left out on a limb? A junior officer was urged on by others and by her ambition to take all the risks, and now things are looking a bit shaky? Is that it?"

Fletcher does look rattled. When Merleau turns to look at her, the older man can detect in his eyes a flicker of something else, of misgiving perhaps? Watkins can see Fletcher's fingers trembling as she takes out a file from her briefcase. Surely he would have noticed if she had been so nervous before. What was the context of that phone conversation?

Fletcher takes out a pen and a legal form with a field of printed sections. "Full name and date of birth, please?"

Watkins is astounded. He looks to Merleau, who stares back impassively. "You two are completely mad!"

"We know —"

"Of course you know who I am! The Canadian ambassador to the Soviet Union, impatient to continue on his flight to Europe and hoping to return to duty in Moscow in the near future!"

This time Fletcher feigns patience. She laces her fingers together in her lap to control them. He can see that she is searching for the right words to launch the interrogation. This is the kind of moment Anatoly had told him about.

WATKINS DISLIKED HIM the moment they met. They were introduced by
Nina Krymova, the expert in Scandinavian writing at the Moscow
Academy of Literature, on the snowy steps of the Music Conservatory
after a performance by the precocious young pianist Bella Davidovich.
Nina, not yet forty, but already a stout Russian matron, was still exhila-
rated by the magic of the performance and was humming strains from
Prokofiev's Piano Concerto No. 2 as they descended the steps. A short
rotund man in a fur hat forced his way through the crowd to them.
Nina's humming suddenly stopped. She hesitated, and then, as if on cue,
said in a rehearsed voice, "Please, Mr. Watkins, I would like you to meet
my brother, Anatoly Nikitin." The bespectacled man with the bland
moustached face stuck out a plump, gloved hand. In the late December
cold, Muscovites rarely struggled to remove their gloves for salutations
on the street. "He is a historian at the Moscow Academy of History,"
Nina continued, as if repeating phrases learned by rote. "You two will
have a lot in common. Anatoly is a specialist in American history."
Watkins didn't believe for a minute that Anatoly was her brother; he
knew right away it was a setup. But like every other diplomat in Moscow,
the ambassador was starved for contacts. Indeed, the minister of external
affairs had often urged him to be more aggressive in the quest for connections with people in power at the Kremlin. It was much later, long
after Anatoly had introduced him to Alyosha, that out of the blue one
evening, after several vodkas, Anatoly offered him some oblique advice:

"My uncle works for the state security apparatus. He is a specialist in
interviewing criminals — that is, political criminals. The other day he
told me this odd thing: the first officials sent in to interview a suspect
are trained to disassociate the suspect from his own identity. It creates
confusion and disorientation, you can imagine. But, you know, they've
found that the people who are best at that part of the process usually have
little sense of identity themselves. After a couple of years being employed
in this kind of work, they often suffer serious nervous breakdowns."

"Why are you telling me all this?" Watkins asked. "And besides, I
thought you told me the other day that your uncle was a psychiatrist?"

"He is, he is. That's what makes him so good at his job."

Anatoly downed another vodka, nervously wiped his unkept moustache with the back of his pudgy little hand, and smiled. "Come now, Ambassador. We're men of the world. You know by now that life often takes many sudden and surprising turns. Men like us can never know too much about such things."

"PLEASE, MR. WATKINS . . ." Fletcher's tone is equivocal. "I know you find this tiresome, but —"

He wants to make her work harder and decides to affect even more outrage. "A career diplomat in External Affairs for fifteen years!"

"I'm just following orders. Please cooperate with —"

"Why should I? You've lied to me and manipulated me all evening."

Fletcher holds on to her temper tightly, bites her lip, and perseveres. "I have to hear it from you, sir. Now, please, name and date of birth."

"Does this official form mean that sooner or later you'll want me to sign some kind of statement — a confession, perhaps?"

Fletcher looks to Merleau for help, but his head is bent over his own notes. "Yes," she slowly admits, "it might possibly work out to something like that."

"Inspector, don't expect me to sign anything today, tomorrow, or ever without having a legal adviser present."

Inspector Fletcher stares back at him bleakly. "I'm simply obeying orders, Mr. Watkins, doing my job."

Watkins gives up and, in exasperation, falls back in his chair. "Then I simply refuse to answer any more questions until you let me put my clothes on."

Without waiting for a signal from Fletcher, Merleau motions to Watkins that the two men should go to the bedroom.

FLETCHER IS LEFT to ponder her phone conversation with Present. The chief of the KGB desk was furious: "Nobody, Inspector Fletcher, nobody gave you the authority to detain the ambassador in such a manner."

"He was making a run for it. As soon as we picked up the tip from our informant at the Windsor, I tried to reach you. I left you three different messages. But you weren't available. We were running out of time, so I had to make a decision." She was about to tell him that Williams was on her side, but that information might make life even more difficult for her. Instead, she retaliated: "You almost sound as if you wanted the ambassador to get away." After a long, tense silence from Present, she decided to push it further: "Why didn't you get back to me?" Present still did not answer. "You know I'll have to follow standard procedures and make a report tonight in writing to DGI Williams regarding all the events that led up to my detaining the ambassador. I will also have to include my notes on this conversation."

With deep exasperation in his voice, Present replied: "I've ordered a car. I'll be there in two hours. It may take longer because of the bad weather. Proceed with the preliminary questions we talked about before." And he slammed down the receiver.

WATKINS TAKES HIS TIME dressing. He chooses a more comfortable pair of slacks. He needs to start thinking about Anatoly and Alyosha. They are inevitably going to come up. He finds his carton of Players, breaks open a pack, lights a cigarette, sighs deeply, and lies back on the bed for a moment. Merleau watches him silently from an armchair.

"George — May I call you George?" asks Watkins. Merleau nods. "It seems to me that when I mentioned Vietnam it had a powerful effect on you. You seemed to go there in your head, or am I mistaken?"

"You're a perceptive man, Mr. Watkins. I was in Danang briefly, as an observer."

Watkins nods, hoping that Merleau will be more forthcoming, but he remains unruffled and leaves the room with an enigmatic look. As he disappears, he says: "The windows are sealed for the air conditioning. But by regulation, we have to leave the door open a little."

Watkins smiles agreeably, "As soon as I finish my cigarette, I'll join the party."

Watkins knows there's much more to come from Merleau. He hears

Fletcher and Merleau in conversation, but even though he sneaks off the bed to listen at the door, he cannot make out any words. They have moved to the far end of the suite. He lies down on the bed again and lights himself another cigarette.

WHEN WATKINS RETURNS to the living room, he sees that Fletcher is again determined and icy in her manner. He wonders what she and Merleau talked about.

She starts in immediately: "Name, date of —"

"Yes, yes, yes — John Watkins, born Norval Station, Ontario, 1902."

"Month, day of birth?"

Watkins gets up from the couch. He's determined to assert his presence more firmly. "Excuse me, I need my cigarettes." And, without asking permission, he goes into the bedroom.

"You have to re-establish control," Merleau whispers to Fletcher.

Fletcher glares back. "I will. Give me a moment."

Watkins returns to the sofa, settles himself comfortably, and announces, "I was an only child surrounded by women —"

"This is not a psychotherapy session, Mr. Watkins."

"Afraid of the psychiatric dimension, Inspector Fletcher? Why? Isn't your whole game built around the dark psychosis of betrayal? The story is the same wherever you go — Moscow, Washington, Ottawa — if the security services betray you, you're justified in betraying your country. Isn't that how it works? Of course, I'm speaking hypothetically."

"I don't believe that you're so naive as to view this as a game. Besides, what you've just told us is not true."

Watkins chuckles good-naturedly. "Come now, betrayal, or rather your perception of it, is the juice that drives you people to do what you do."

She smiles triumphantly. "No, you just made a bad slip."

Merleau puts a file in front of Fletcher and points out a line on the page for her. She reads for a moment, then looks up to study Watkins carefully. "John Watkins was not an only child. He had two sisters, Elizabeth and Isabel."

Watkins' mood changes.

Fletcher continues: "Isabel died of TB when she was twenty-seven years old. And Elizabeth died at the age of . . . ?

But Watkins refuses to fill in the blanks.

" . . . fifty-one, after many years spent in mental institutions."

Watkins tries to recover: "I said I was an 'only boy surrounded by women.'"

Fletcher marches over to a cabinet by the wall and opens the cupboard to reveal an audio control panel. She pushes a rewind button. When she activates the tape, they hear again Watkins' deep, heavy voice booming through the suite: "I grew up as an only child surrounded by women."

"Then I simply meant to say *boy* — a psychological slip, perhaps."

"Or a slip in the legend? We've spent a lot of time reconstructing your life from day one —"

"Legend?" Watkins exclaims. "Are you trying to suggest that I'm not who I say I am?"

"No, it's not as simple as that. We have experts who believe you may have been planted, many years back. Besides, I thought you didn't know anything about the spook business? How did you immediately know that 'legend' meant 'cover story'?"

"Some things stick —"

"— in your mind!" Fletcher catches herself and shakes her head. For a moment he has been her father sitting there on the couch, and she has been mocking him good-naturedly. She becomes aware that Merleau is looking at her. She stares down into her notes to recapture her thoughts.

Watkins tries again. "There is a literary allusion in the word 'legend' that —"

"— things or people are not always what they seem." Damn, she has done it again! In the same jesting way she and Murray used to finish off their father's more pompous aphorisms.

"This is ludicrous! Why am I suddenly defending myself? I am John Watkins." But he realizes how hollow it sounds.

Fletcher cannot hide a smirk of satisfaction. This is a turning point in the interrogation. She takes the file from Merleau without looking at him, keeping her eyes fixed on Watkins. "John Watkins, with no living relatives to confirm his story."

He reaches for another cigarette. "For a sick man," she says, "you smoke too much, Mr. Watkins."

He lights up with relish and, ignoring Fletcher, turns to Merleau: "I find Canadian cigarettes a bit mild, don't you? You know, when I spent ten years in the States, I always preferred Camels. When you studied in the States, what did you smoke? Lucky Strikes, I bet."

Merleau keeps his distance: "Remember? I don't smoke."

"Yes, of course, of course, excuse me. As you get older you forget the details. But listen, can I take advantage of all the remarkable research you've done into my personal habits. I mean, would you just happen to have on hand a tumbler of my favourite whisky?"

Without missing a beat, Merleau gets up, pours a drink from a decanter on the sideboard, and brings it over to Watkins.

Watkins samples it. "Bushmill's! I'm even more impressed. My, you people really have done an exhaustive job into my likes and dislikes." A tone of artificiality creeps into his voice. He knows why it's there. He's afraid and he's trying to mask it. How can he stay on top in this cat-and-mouse game? He's aware that he is losing position and credibility in the eyes of his audience.

Fletcher produces the packet of Players that Watkins dropped in the rain when he was taken from the limousine. He reaches out for it. "Ah, my cigarettes. Thank you. You found them."

But Fletcher doesn't hand over the pack. She flips open the lid to reveal the name *Khamal* followed by a telephone number scribbled on the inside. His heart sinks.

"This is your writing, isn't it, Mr. Watkins?"

"Yes, yes, I suppose it is."

"Suppose, yes or no?"

"Yes, yes, of course it is."

"And who is Khamal?"

Watkins doesn't answer. "Where did you find it?"

"You dropped it when you got out of the limo and agreed to accompany us here."

"Yes, I suppose I must have." He knocks back the rest of his whisky and holds out the glass. "Perhaps another, George. Care to join me this time?"

But Fletcher grabs the glass from his hand and puts it on the table between them. "Or perhaps you were trying to get rid of it?"

Watkins shrugs. "Have it your own way, Inspector."

"Who is Khamal?"

He fights for time to think. How stupid of him! How careless! But then, how could he know? How could he have anticipated the events of this evening? He thought Murray had given him the green light to get out. He hears himself say: "I can't quite remember. Does it really say 'Khamal'? Such a strange word . . . sometimes I can't even read my own handwriting. You know how it is — you scribble a name, a phone number on a cigarette package, then you can't quite recall who it was or what the context was, and you remind yourself once again to be more methodical . . ."

Fletcher knows she has him on the run. "What city is this phone number for?"

Again Watkins shrugs. "I wish I could remember, as I say —"

"Then let me help you try to remember," Fletcher interrupts. "You were on your way to Paris, correct? Perhaps it's a phone number in Paris? A friend, a contact — someone you were going to meet there?"

Watkins is blandly polite. Does she already know the answers to these questions? "Again, I wish I could help you . . . but I really can't remember."

Fletcher rises, paces around the room for a few moments, then returns. "Do you realize that when you lie, you're unfailingly polite?"

Watkins is at a loss for words. Khamal, he thinks, my dear Khamal. What have I done to you? Fletcher turns to Merleau: "Perhaps, Mr. Merleau, you would be kind enough to check this phone number in Paris?" Merleau makes a note of the name and phone number and, before leaving the room, passes another file to Fletcher. On his way past, he gives her an approving tap on the shoulder. She's obviously pleased, and follows him with her eyes as he leaves the room. Then she takes up the attack on the ambassador from another angle.

"Before you allegedly studied Russian, you spoke several Slavic languages?"

"That was my job at the university."

"Before you joined the diplomatic corps?"

"Yes. I always thought it was a mistake."

"Becoming a diplomat? Or learning foreign languages?"

"No, External Affairs." And tonight I regret it more than ever, he reflects morosely. "How about that drink?"

Fletcher ignores his question and gets up once again. "So, why did you go against your better judgment, or was it instinct?"

"Neither. I went against what was in my heart."

Fletcher is amused. "Your heart?"

"Yes, Inspector. My heart. You know, there are times when I think that my heart disease literally comes from going against what was in there all these years. When you do that, Inspector Fletcher, your heart becomes a prison — a labyrinth. You spend years trying to find your way out, but you can do that only if you kill the monster."

"The monster?" she asks, begrudgingly curious.

"Yes, the monster you have created in your mind which waits for you in what is left of your heart, somewhere deep in that labyrinth you have made out of your life."

Fletcher tries to maintain her amused mask, but she looks a little off balance. Watkins perceives her reaction. He remembers Murray: "My father died six months ago . . . a heart attack on a canoe trip."

"Tell me, Inspector, did your father ever talk to you about things before he had his heart attack?"

Fletcher stops in her tracks. Her face pales. Her hand rises to her throat. For a moment she looks to Watkins like a child caught out. "How did you know about my father?"

Watkins waves a hand dismissively. "One hears things. But be careful, Inspector. Do you know what's in your heart?"

Merleau re-enters the room. Where did he come back from so soon, Watkins wonders, and what did he find out? Merleau takes a look at Fletcher and sees that she is rattled. "Are you all right, Inspector?" he asks.

Fletcher, upset and mystified, but not knowing what else to do, returns even more malevolently to the attack. "Why did you betray your heart, Mr. Watkins? You still haven't answered my question."

"Ah, yes. Why did I go against my instincts and go to work for External Affairs? Simple answer: Mr. Pearson convinced me the country needed my talents. You must have been all of twelve years old."

Fletcher dismisses his thrust with a wave of her hand and continues: "So it was the prime minister himself who put you in place?"

"You use a strange appropriation of the language, but I suppose in your lingo that's right. If it hadn't been for the prime minister, I would be an obscure but happy academic today."

Fletcher leans back and, despite her shock at the ambassador's knowledge of her father's death, is able to transcend that moment and regard Watkins with pleased speculation. Again she glances at Merleau, who for the first time allows himself a flicker of a smile — a "you're doing well" smile — then hands her another file. Watkins studies them both. What is this moment of triumph they're secretly sharing? What is this business about Pearson that makes them look so smug? But there's no time to think it through because Fletcher shifts gears and takes aim again.

"Before you allegedly studied Russian, I understand you were already fluent in Danish. Where did you learn that language?"

"As a boy — growing up in Ontario."

"How old were you?"

"Nine . . . ten."

"Who taught you?"

"Nobody taught me."

"So, you're a fatherless nine-year-old boy, growing up in rural southern Ontario, and you teach yourself Danish — from a book, perhaps?"

"In the summers I worked with a Danish farmhand. He had two sons. I learned, just by being around them. They didn't speak much English."

He remembers those summers in what now seems like another country, another land . . . lying on his back in the warm moist earth, looking up at the green leaves of the corn stalks against the vivid-blue sky . . . The knowing hands of the others . . . his first experimenting with youthful flesh . . . understanding who he was and knowing that it would be like that for the rest of his life — and being at peace with it all . . .

Fletcher stops pacing and comes around behind Watkins. Leaning her hands on the back of the sofa, she speaks softly above his head: "Your father was dead. What was it your mother operated — a coal yard? But she did own a farm."

"That's right, we rented the farm out. Some summers I worked for a neighbouring farmer — we weren't poor, but we weren't comfortable either. I went to university on scholarships."

For the first time Merleau asks a direct question: "Scholastic?"

Fletcher winces. She senses that Watkins has also twigged. He must know for certain now that Merleau is a CIA man. Sports scholarships didn't exist in Canadian universities in the forties. They were strictly a facet of the American education system and were frowned upon in Canada. But Merleau is unaware that he has given himself away. Before Watkins can say a thing, Fletcher leans forward and whispers venomously in his ear so softly that Merleau can't hear: "You son of a bitch! I'm going to find out how you know about my father."

Out loud she continues: "But you didn't do so badly for a poor farm boy from Norval, Ontario. Here you are, some forty years later, rubbing shoulders with prime ministers and world leaders — really one of the old boys."

"That's true. I have come a long way. But if I was really part of the old boys' network, I wouldn't be in this room tonight having this conversation with you two troublemakers."

"Dear, dear! You sound bitter, Mr. Watkins."

Watkins can only stare at her. He has underestimated the relentlessness of this policewoman. "But you have powerful friends," she continues.

Watkins desperately needs to know. "Does the prime minister know I am here?"

Fletcher ignores his question and returns to her seat in front of him to refer once again to her notes. She has obviously spent a great deal of time preparing for this interrogation.

"What was this farm worker's name? The man you learned Danish from just by being around him?"

"Luc."

"Luc . . . or Luke what?"

"I don't remember his last name."

"Let me help you . . . Matter? Luc Matter?"

"Yes, that's right."

"The man or the name? You're sure?"

"Yes, yes! Luc Matter."

"But we know that Luc Matter was Dutch, not Danish." She gleefully scores a point.

"How do you know that?"

"Mr. Watkins, we know everything there is to know about you. Are you still insisting that you learned Danish from a Dutch farmhand who didn't speak English?"

"Why don't you ask him, for God's sake?"

"He's dead, drowned in a boating accident when you were fourteen. But you knew that, didn't you?"

"I had forgotten — it was a long time ago," he stammers.

"Why, Mr. Watkins? Why such a clumsy lie about Luc Matter?"

"It wasn't a lie, really. I was just trying to protect him."

"From what? He's dead!"

"Loyalty to old friends. Force of habit, I suppose. As I remember it, they had to flee Denmark after a dispute with the rural landlord became a violent eviction from their farm — his wife was killed. Luc and his sons fled to Holland and illegally, I suppose, assumed Dutch citizenship. They swore me to secrecy. I was just a boy, and I thought it all thrilling and mysterious. So you see, Inspector, there's a very simple explanation for my momentary lapse of —"

"And no close living relatives to support your story . . . How very convenient for you. Or, maybe, Mr. Watkins, just maybe, your handlers forgot to brief you properly on that part of your legend?"

Watkins shakes his head in annoyance. "My handlers! What is this nonsense?"

Fletcher takes her time. She carries his glass to the sideboard and pours him another shot of Bushmill's. Despite the situation, his diplomatic courtesy remains intact. "Thank you," he murmurs.

Fletcher continues to walk around the room. Outside, the storm begins to abate. It's like this woman, he thinks. Her moods are just as mercurial, and at this moment she seems serenely confident. "Mr. Watkins, you've heard of the Lonsdale case?"

Watkins shakes his head. He's not going to make anything easy for her, he decides, unless it suits him. "I'm tired. What time is it?"

Merleau looks at his watch. "Almost midnight."

"I would like to rest for a while."

Merleau looks at Fletcher, who nods her head from across the room. "We'll take a break in a minute. But surely you read about the Lonsdale case. It broke in mid-1961. A sensational story about Soviet intelligence work."

"I don't read the sensational press," Watkins mutters.

"No? Then let me tell you about it. Gordon Lonsdale was the assumed name of a Soviet illegal who was sent to the United States as a potential spy at the age of eleven. Now, that shows incredible planning, don't you think? The true Gordon Lonsdale was a boy born in Canada who was taken by his mother to live in Finland at about the age of five. They were both killed in 1939 during the war between the Soviets and Finland. Somehow the Soviet intelligence machinery obtained the Canadian documents of both mother and child. At the same time, a boy of the same age, named Conon Molody, was growing up in Moscow. His father was a well-known science writer, his mother a teacher of languages. They separated, and his mother, at the KGB and GRU's instigation, sent Conon, then aged eleven, to live with her sister in California. The sister pretended to be Conon's mother. After spending six or seven years in the United States, where he learned to speak perfect and unaccented English, Conon returned quietly to the Soviet Union. There he was taken into the navy and given anything he wanted. He became an officer and was trained in military and industrial espionage techniques. Finally, in his mid-twenties, he came to Canada on a grain ship. He used the original Gordon Lonsdale documents to obtain an updated passport for himself. You must remember the rest?"

Watkins is weary. All he wants to do is lie down. "Yes, I do remember now. I believe he was arrested in 1961 in England, posing as a Canadian businessman supplying services to military bases. But he was actually spying on British military underwater research programs for the Soviets."

"That's right. I knew you would remember if I helped you out. And, just to finish the story, you know, of course, that he was traded this year for the English spy, Grenville Wynn."

"I take it there's a reason for your telling me this story?"

"Oh yes. The moral in this adventure of Conon Molody, a.k.a.

Gordon Lonsdale, is that it helps to have a wife, Mr. Watkins."

"Now I am totally baffled."

"Because Mrs. Wynn and Mrs. Molody got together for a couple of days and came up with a plan. They suggested to the two enemy governments they should do a swap. Surprise! The wives got their husbands back. But you, Mr. Watkins, never married, did you? So who will be there on the other side to bargain for you? Will it be Akhundi or Khamal?"

Watkins slowly takes off his spectacles and cleans them on his shirt with exaggerated care. He holds them up to the light to inspect the lenses and returns them to his face. "You are a malicious and cruel young woman. I think your father would be ashamed of you if he was here today."

"Oh, I don't think so," Fletcher answers airily. "I think he would be proud of all the groundwork I've done. Because, you see, Mr. Watkins, there is now a lot of information on the table to suggest that it is quite possible that perhaps the ambassador is a "sleeper" — put in place years ago by the KGB. If it was possible to do it for Lonsdale, it would be possible to do it for you. When they arrested Londsdale, they also arrested four other Soviet spies, each with similarly manufactured identities."

Watkins decides to call her bluff. He slams down his empty glass. "These are serious and criminal charges. I want you to call the prime minister right now. You have the means to reach him wherever he is and inform him of what you've just told me."

"How long have you known Prime Minister Pearson, Mr. Watkins?"

"Since 1948 — that's sixteen years. Something like half your lifetime."

Fletcher is unperturbed. She throws a questioning glance at the taciturn Merleau. He nods in agreement.

"I must inform you, Mr. Watkins, the Prime Minister's Office knows full well you are here. People there have been briefed every step of the way. Likewise the minister of external affairs."

Watkins is shaken for a moment. No, he can't let them get away with that. She's lying.

WHEN HE WAS ON a brief leave home from his posting in Norway, he had a meeting late one evening in Mike's office on the Hill. As more and more external-affairs aides crowded into their minister's office, the meeting turned into a spontaneous brain-storming session. He marvelled at Mike's charm and popularity, the magnetism that attracted so many loyal followers. It was 1953, and the American media were frothing over Mike's refusal to allow Igor Gouzenko to testify in the U.S. Congress before Joseph McCarthy's crew of inquisitors in the State Department's hunt for communists. That week Mike himself had been denounced by the *Chicago Tribune* in an editorial written by its publisher, Colonel McCormick. It had reported a "communist infestation in Canada," and described Mike as "the most dangerous man in the English-speaking world." Mike wasn't at all shaken. When someone brought up Dean Acheson's name, Mike dismissed him as "that empty glass of water" and vowed he would never let the best people in Canada be destroyed the way the best Americans were being ruined in the United States.

MURRAY ROLLS AWAY from Penny's sleepy, warm flesh and remembers the events of the previous afternoon. Cold stone hallways, heavy pillared archways, echoing footsteps. What a repulsive place to spend your life. The corridors of power? More likely the corridors of the supplicants and the inept. The West Block, the whole damn Hill for that matter, has always given him the creeps. Unimaginative architecture, built with the naive idea that a building could project the idea of permanence. The place reminds him of those god-awful Scottish Presbyterian churches his forebears constructed in their march across the country. Great bloody stone monstrosities, built at enormous expense, clinging to the reluctant Canadian landscape and now mostly empty on Sundays — not much balm for the soul to be found in those places, despite the angst of living in the age of instant nuclear warfare.

He remembers those American propaganda shorts they ran before the main feature in movie houses: huge red arrows representing Soviet bombers as they zipped over the North Pole and dumped nuclear pay-loads first on northern Alberta. When he was a teenager he had developed a fearful certainty that they were all going to vaporize in their beds in one of those huge golden-red mushrooms. Some nights, after their father had gone to his bedroom, he and Jane would get to talking about "the bomb"; too afraid even to sleep, they would stay up all night in the big living room, whispering to keep each other awake until the first grey light of dawn showed in the windows and they knew they were safe for another day. Dad was great — didn't try to tell them they were being silly. Just acknowledged it all with a shrug: "Scariest damn time the human race has ever known." Somehow that took the edge of their obsession, made it more manageable. It was about then Murray swore he was never going to get married and have kids. Why bring them into this nightmare?

Come to think of it, what could the conventional religious beliefs do for anybody in this world where the two superpowers are posed for "Mutually Assured Destruction"? Kubrick had the answer. What a director! Now there's a guy who speaks to the times: starts out to make a serious movie about the end of the world by nuclear warfare and, halfway into the production, realizes the overwhelming absurdity of the official Pentagon strategy of MAD — those generals just loved the acronym — and makes this black, bitter, goddam comedy. Stanley, you are one fucking genius! You are the one guy who knows what's going on in the hearts and minds of my generation.

Who are all these people? Where do they come from? He examines the intense young men and women in suits scurrying past him, loaded down with files and briefcases. The smell of Friday and the long Thanksgiving weekend is in the air. All those MPs the aides will be slugging their guts out for over the holiday are flooding the corridors, leaving the political dung behind. No, politicians aren't even that useful.

Ah, but now he's getting closer to the PM's office. He hums "We'll meet again." What a great scene that was, Vera Lynn singing in the background, dark little mushroom clouds of nuclear explosions popping up all over the world. Slim Pickens going out the bomb hatch astride the A-bomb like it was a rodeo bronco. What did the *Time* movie critic say? "A moment of pure dark cynicism unequaled in the history of the cinema."

Whoa, what a babe! Look at those legs going by. Wonder what she's doing tonight? No, no. Get a grip, brother, you are a man on a mission. No time to be distracted now.

Officially, *Time* didn't like the movie — "over the top," the critic said.

What the hell did *Time* know about anything? In its editorial eyes, any-body with an independent thought — a world view that didn't coincide with Washington's and Henry Luce's — was a commie fag.

What is this? Long Legs is slowing down! She's looking over her shoulder, smiling! Talk about a smooth pickup. "Hi!"

"Hi, I saw the movie too, last night."

He doesn't click to what she's talking about. "What movie?"

"You were just singing to yourself as I went by — the song Vera what's-her-name sings in *Dr. Strangelove*."

"No kidding! Was I? Out loud?"

She smiles and begins a fairly good Vera Lynn imitation. Strong, throaty Joan Baez kind of voice — similar face too, long black hair. He joins in, "Don't know where, don't know when, but we will meet again —" They break off laughing, as a couple of passing suits turn to stare at them.

"Hey, maybe we should quit our day jobs," he suggests. "I just know everything will be all right — soon as we get the band together."

She has a nice laugh. "You don't look like a Vera Lynn fan."

"These days Otis Redding is my guy."

"Far out! It's not every day you find a guy in cowboy boots who digs soul."

"So what's a talented singer like you doing trucking a load of files around?"

She sings lightly, "Heading for the PMO," giving it a little "Dock of the Bay" riff.

He decides she's irresistible. "I'm going there too. Here, let me help." He lightens the load in her arms by taking a handful of manuals. He reads the title on the top one, almost as thick as a phone book, "Regional Effect of Grain Subsidies on Crowsnest Pass Freight Rates." "Fascinating! I like your writing style. You got a movie contract yet?"

She can't stop smiling. "What's your name?"

"Murray. And yours?"

"Gabrielle."

"You got time for a drink later?"

"Such a fast worker!"

They have reached the outer offices of the PMO and the first layer of security. The guard eyes his long hair with suspicion, but as soon as he sees his special security clearance ID, waves him on in. But Gabrielle can't proceed any further. The guard tells her a clerk has to come out and take delivery of the files. "Could take about ten minutes."

Murray feels obliged to keep Gabrielle company while she waits. They chat about working life on the Hill. He feels uneasy. He shouldn't be standing around like this if he wants to catch the PM.

"How can you possibly work here? Jeans, all that hair, cowboy boots."

"You know the new Dylan song 'Things Are a-Changing'? All these old farts," his gesture takes in the Parliament Buildings, "are going to have to move over."

"Don't talk like that about my uncle. He's one of the real old farts — a senator."

"I promise you, give it a year and even the parliamentary under-secretaries will be running to Cabinet meetings in Beatle haircuts. And besides, in that blouse you look like a flower child yourself."

"Thank you."

He looks at his watch. "Listen, I gotta run."

"No! You can't leave me alone like this, with all these dirty old men staring at me."

He smiles, but sighs inwardly. "Murray, Murray," he hears his father, "when are you going to let the big head do the thinking for you, boy?" Unasked, Gabrielle writes down her phone number. He thanks her for it and prays for the PMO clerk to show up quickly. He's got to get going. If my mother had lived, he wonders, would I be spending all this energy on women? No, that's just *Reader's Digest* psychology crap. Look at your sister, Jane, she doesn't run around chasing men. Yeah, well, face it, Murray, your sister's gay. Strange. That's the first time he's ever allowed himself to think that, to really confront something he's known intuitively for a long time. Jesus! What a creep he has been. His own twin sister, and she's probably too scared to confide in him because he's never appeared open enough to her. Frightened at this new and clear perception of Jane, he tunes back into Gabrielle, who is chatting up a storm. Turns out she got to work on the Hill because of the uncle. She prattles on — too quickly. She's only twenty-five and she feels it's already all over for her. Why? he asks. Because she missed out on the "summer of love" in Haight Ashbury. She'd give everything to live in San Francisco and be singing with a rock band.

Suddenly Murray feels very old, from another generation. He thinks about John Watkins, sixty-two, and wonders how he sees young men like himself. How will he himself feel connected to the world, if he ever gets to that age? "It's got nothing to do with age," his father told him once, discussing a bitter old rancher who was one of his patients. "He's the same miserable, selfish bastard I knew forty years ago. I don't think we change much in this life. We're the same boneheads going in as coming out."

"I'm sorry, Gabrielle, I really must go."

"Oh, is it something I said? I don't usually talk this much. I'm just . . . uh . . . a little nervous, meeting you and everything . . ."

Oh sweet Gabrielle, you're breaking my heart. "No, no. Everything is cool. You see . . . I have this appointment with the PM."

She laughs uneasily, not certain if he's putting her on. "I'm already impressed. You don't have to lay it on any thicker," she protests.

"I'll phone," he lies, and backs away intoning "We'll meet again" and almost tramples the PMO clerk, who has finally shown up and appears to be a permanently exasperated little man in a shiny suit that's too tight for him. Gabrielle giggles at his clumsiness. Damn! She looks even better than Joan Baez.

The PMO appointments secretary wearily hears him out with a sceptical glint in her eyes, then turns him over to a self-important executive assistant who looks about twenty-eight going on fourteen. One of those super-bright creeps right out of McGill, probably president of the Young Liberals. The EA peers at him suspiciously while he examines his ID and listens to Murray's pitch.

"What's happening over there in External?"

"What do you mean?"

"The Ministry turning out hippie cops for foreign postings?"

He lets the cold sarcasm go by. "Look, I just want the PM's ear for two minutes."

Mr. Young Liberal hands him back his ID. "That's what they all say.

But even if I could, which I wouldn't under the circumstances, you're wasting your time."

"Why?"

"He's just left for the weekend — five minutes ago. See?" The EA points out the window at the doors closing on the PM's limo below, then walks away from Murray without so much as a goodbye. With a sinking heart Murray watches the PM's car slowly sweep around the driveway and out onto Wellington Street. He feels deeply ashamed. Old Man Watkins now has to spend the whole weekend detained in the Ritz just because he got a hard-on for a strange babe called Gabrielle. Damn! When are you going to grow up, Murray? He thinks about the ambassador and his sister at the Ritz. And then the irony suddenly strikes him: his gay sister is investigating John Watkins because of the RCMP's suspicions of his homosexual liaisons with Russian spies. God, what a bind she must be in!

WATKINS TURNS TO FLETCHER. "I don't believe you. You're bluffing. I know the prime minister too well. Mike Pearson would never condone this kind of a witch hunt. He stands by his people."

Fletcher doesn't miss a beat. "Oh, you think he stood up for your colleague Herbert Norman? Or do you think Norman jumped from that building in Cairo to save the prime minister's career?"

Watkins is exasperated. He slowly lumbers to his feet. "This is dirty work, isn't it?" he asks. Before she can respond, he holds up his hand. "Yes, yes, I know you're doing your job." Now it is Watkins who moves around the room to assert his physical presence. Fletcher and Merleau watch apprehensively. The ambassador knows how to hold attention. He goes to the sideboard, pours himself another drink, and gives them a mock "Cheers!" He pulls up the blind and gazes out the window. The uniformed officer makes a move to bring Watkins back to his chair, but Merleau signals him back. Watkins broods at the view below him. The adjacent buildings are no higher than this twelfth floor, and most of what look to be apartments and offices are in darkness. "Tell me, Fletcher," he asks, using her name without a prefix as one would address a junior in the diplomatic service, "what postgraduate degree do you have?"

"Law, from Queen's."

"Hmm . . . so that explains why you are here. I mean, it accounts for your getting to ask the questions."

"Perhaps —"

"No *perhaps*, Fletcher. The Mounties are not renowned for seeking out people with a decent education. I'll wager you're in the ten percent of the Force who even have undergraduate degrees."

Fletcher remembers her father objecting: "Why are you going to waste all that education on a bunch of cops who will only resent you?" But she stays silent, letting Watkins push this line wherever it is going. Merleau passes her a scribbled note — "Don't let him take over." But she crumples it up in her hand and tosses it back to him. Watkins seems deep in thought, and she's confident now that she will be able to stay on top no matter what happens.

"But have you ever thought about it from another angle: Why are they letting you do this softening up work on me? That's what it's all about, isn't it?"

"I have a director. I follow orders. Just as you have a minister. When you were in Moscow, whose orders did you follow? Mr. Pearson's?"

"Ultimately, yes. The difference is that there was a policy — an entire strategy on how we should approach and deal with the Soviet government. We had a series of long-term positions with goals that were worked out by the minister, advisers, and policy analysts, with considerable input from me."

"Did this policy take into consideration the interests of our allies?"

Watkins laughs. "There's not ever a consistent American foreign policy, Fletcher. I mean, you can't call the Cold War a policy. It's just too one-sided — Gary Cooper as the sheriff in *High Noon*. I always wondered what would happen if that movie continued for another ten minutes. The very day after Gary Cooper and Grace Kelly drove their horse and buggy off into the sunset to enjoy their mythical American romantic Puritanism, a whole other bunch of bad guys would ride into town to set up business, and the film would have come full circle. It's the same with American foreign policy. It's a day-to-day thing. I suppose that's why they play poker in Washington, and in the Kremlin they play chess."

Fletcher forces a grin to cover her returning uneasiness. That is just how her father would have argued — except that she can never remember her father going to the movies. Movies and TV bored him. Watkins, she decides, is a man who prides himself on his avant-garde role. "What movies do you go to?" she asks.

"I see everything I can, but I have favourites. For example, movies by Fellini. Now there's an artist who understands our world profoundly. Have you seen his *Dolce Vita*? That was the last one he made, all of four years ago. But I understand he is working on a new film, *Juliette of the Spirits*."

"I saw *La Dolce Vita*," Fletcher says, "but I didn't really understand it."

"The Catholic Church put it on its register of banned films," Merleau interjects.

Bravo, thinks Watkins, I haven't lost my touch. Whenever a lecturer can push the most silent student in the class to speak, he knows he's getting through. "Well, that's true, but I understand many long-awaited reforms are about to take place in the Catholic Church. The *au courant* critics say *La Dolce Vita* is the most insightful film of the last two decades. It will be the first of a phalanx of pictures that will help to smash public confidence in the social order."

Merleau is right, Fletcher acknowledges. She has let Watkins take over. The interrogation has suddenly spun out of control. She realizes that, when the pressure is off, Watkins quickly reverts to his enduring role as raconteur and teacher, forever lecturing a class on social history. She must find a way to shut him down, push him back into the corner she had him in a few minutes ago. "To me, Mr. Watkins, that all sounds like the usual whiny left, with its condemnation of Western values."

"Well, Fletcher, I have a totally different analysis. But first let me ask what you didn't understand about the movie?"

"I couldn't understand why that intellectual friend of the reporter murdered his two children and then killed himself. It seemed gratuitously evil. In fact, at that point I walked out of the movie."

"My, my, Fletcher. For a police officer, you are a delicate child."

"Just why are we talking about this movie?"

"Fletcher, it was you who asked me what movies I go to. I'm trying to respond to the best of my ability. But there is a relevant point in all of this. My own interpretation is that the suicide of the intellectual is symbolic for Fellini of the death of Marxism, the collapse of communist ideals during the Stalinist era. Of course, hardly anyone agrees with me, but . . ."

"THIS, MY FRIEND, is what your American friends call bullshit," Khamal contends. "Fellini does not have a political bone in his body. There is absolutely nothing in Fellini's life that would give him any experience with the problems of the masses . . ." They were both good-naturedly drunk in the darkened hotel room in Oslo. He revelled in the sight of Khamal, naked, smoking by the window, his muscular back highlighted by the city lights as he leaned casually against the window sill. How had Khamal been able to get travel passes for this trip? When Watkins had heard his voice on the phone and rushed delightedly down to the hotel to greet him, Khamal had mumbled something about the international poets' conference in Copenhagen. But Watkins knew it was a transparent lie. Khamal, unlike Akhundi, was an unknown young poet. The authorities would only have given him permission to travel abroad after extracting exorbitant conditions. Watkins knew what they must be, but he didn't want to think about it then. He only wanted Khamal's hard young body beside him. He followed Khamal's movements as he limped around the room looking for his shirt.

"Not true. Fellini was a conscientious objector. He served his military time in a labour camp —"

"No, no, my friend," interrupted Khamal, strapping the brace on his shrivelled leg, "you are confusing him with Mastroianni. It is Marcello Mastroianni who did his military service in a labour camp."

"My God! You're right. I'd forgotten. How did you know that?"

"We study contemporary film in the institute. What do you think? That we're all little robot scientists working on the atomic bomb? We see and read many things — everything — and work like crazy. Since Khrushchev came to power, we have to catch up on . . . what do you say in English . . . 'the whole shebang'? What a word! Explain to me please what is a 'shebang.'" It's true, Watkins thought, there is probably not a better-educated population in the world than this generation of the Soviet Union. What an incredible irony!

"ARE YOU STILL WITH US, Ambassador?" Merleau asks.

"Yes, yes." Watkins suddenly spins to attack Fletcher. "You're nothing but a careerist, Inspector Fletcher, willing to do the dirty work that other officers in security services would refuse to do. Why? Because you are a woman wanting to get ahead any way you can. And for what — to destroy people's lives? Is that what you're using your ludicrous law degree for? I see you as part of the vanguard of a new management ideology that will be as disastrous for the world as communist collectivization has been."

When Fletcher opens her mouth to reply, Watkins again cuts her off: "I know, I know, you're just doing your job." He walks to the bedroom door and, before he closes it behind him, calls out: "Inspector Fletcher, you're a part of the future I don't much care for. I'm glad that I probably won't have to live in this country while people like you are running things."

The ambassador closes the door, collapses fully dressed on the bed, and falls immediately into a feverish sleep.

LESS THAN THIRTY MINUTES out of Moscow they turned right onto a dusty country road and drove towards Volodya's dacha on the other side of a community called Bolyshevo. "All the quaint airs of a small Russian village," Nina called out from the back seat, "but no doubt the city will soon engulf this lovely place." They passed two or three charming dachas where men and women were loafing about. "They're rest homes for artists and actors," explained Anatoly, who seemed to become more mellow the further they drove from Moscow.

Volodya's dacha was not the usual log cabin but a large stuccoed house in the centre of an estate: a couple of acres of land with many large trees, lilac bushes, dwarf cherry trees in blossom, flower gardens, and a vegetable garden. The property was surrounded by a high wooden fence, and there was a small wooden cottage beside the gates in which the gardener lived with his family.

Maxim asked if he could leave the embassy car there overnight and walk on to his own dacha, which was not far away. "Of course," Anatoly replied, forgoing the hemming and hawing he applied to every little decision he made in the city. Watkins thought the arrangements all seemed a bit too convenient, a bit prearranged. He wondered where Volodya kept his own car, and Anatoly replied that Volodya had the use of an official car and chauffeur. Ah, thought Watkins, a lowly paid agricultural professor with both an estate and an official car?

Volodya and his wife shook his hand warmly and insisted on carrying his bags into a large airy bedroom with several windows. It was a plainly furnished room with two narrow beds, a large old desk, a rug, and a couple of chairs. The house had been spring-cleaned especially for his visit, they explained. Everything was certainly fresh and clean. He never wanted to go back to Moscow again. The ceilings were high, and the light-coloured walls were papered in small patterns. Quite a contrast to the flamboyant wallpapers in most new apartments in Moscow.

Anatoly and Watkins shared this room, and Nina and Volodya's wife were in the other large bedroom. Volodya had a cot in a wide hall off the bedrooms, bathroom, and kitchen. Watkins apologized for putting them out, but they shrugged and told him Russians were used to crowding in together. "It makes for a more interesting visit," they laughed. "Besides, Alexei will be with us soon and he is always lots of fun." Alexei would sleep on a couch in the glassed-in porch, where they would also have their meals.

The living-room was furnished simply, but contained a large dining table for use in the colder months. The house had no upstairs, but there was an attic for storage over part of it. Watkins fantasized briefly about living there — a quiet expatriate life, a Canadian defector to the Soviet Union for non-political reasons — except that the Crimean countryside was the perfect place for a poet translator living out his dreams . . .

When he asked if the house could be lived in all year round, Volodya told him that, in winter, Russians traditionally closed off most of their houses and lived only in the part that could be heated. One side of a

Russian tiled stove in the kitchen protruded into the living-room, and the other side went into the bedroom in which he slept. "For the long Russian winter, it's alright for one man and a very good friend," said Nina flirtatiously.

The plumbing was old-fashioned but it worked, except for the wood stove that was used for heating the bath water. When he asked if he could take a hot bath after the long journey, everyone looked askance and explained that it was a lot of work. The water had to be heated on the kitchen range and carried to the bathtub.

"There is an alternative," Anatoly pointed out. "The back of the property goes down to the Klyasma River. There's a locked gate in the wooden fence along the riverbank, but anyone who wants to take a dip is welcome to the key."

Watkins took them up on the offer, but only Anatoly was keen to join him. Had the Russian been ordered to keep an eye on him? They couldn't have an ambassador drowning in a river. The Western tabloids would call it a communist assassination. But Anatoly wasn't cheerful about his duties, and he whined that the water was too cold. So much for the myth of hardy Russian comrades, Watkins smiled to himself. Strolling back along the riverbank, Watkins stopped to talk to a fisherman who had been there since five o'clock that morning and in six hours had caught only one small fish. A few cows and goats graced the bright green banks of the river. Groups of young people were lying lazily in the sun, reading, chatting, or singing folksongs accompanied by guitars.

The whole village was rustic and unspoiled. Most of the inhabitants got their water from the well in the centre of the village green. As soon as they discovered where he was staying, their manner changed, and Watkins realized he must be with a group of highly paid bureaucrats who had gone to some sacrifice to spend this weekend with him in the country.

As if to confirm his suspicions, Alexei Gorbunov, Anatoly's colleague from the Institute of History, arrived in a huge shiny Zim driven by a chauffeur. Alexei apologized to Watkins for being late and for appearing in a formal dark suit, but he had just come from the office. "Call me Alyosha," he insisted. "All my friends use this nickname." Watkins realized he was serious, and promised he would. Half an hour later they sat down to supper. Watkins had brought along some Canadian rye and French red wine. They had vodka, beer, and a dry white Georgian wine. The table was well laden with *zakuskis*, or hors-d'oeuvres — cold ham, sausages of different kinds, sliced cucumbers in sour cream — a whole meal in themselves, but not to Russians. The cold collation was followed by an excellent soup, beef stroganoff, cake, and coffee.

Later, they played Russian dances, tangos, and waltzes on an ancient Victrola. Watkins was invited to join in the dancing, but he begged off, protesting that he felt too stuffed from the huge meal. "Huge?" they exclaimed. "But we are all on diets out here in the country."

The Victrola was enormous and was paired with a radio that barely worked. Alyosha insisted on fiddling, and it responded in fits and starts. Nina disliked the loud squawks, but at last Alyosha, an avid Torpedo fan, got what he wanted: the final result of the Czech-Torpedo football game that day (2–1 in favour of the Torpedos). He turned off the set with laughing apologies.

Watkins was charmed. The moon was full, and they sat in the garden for hours, singing song after song. Alyosha in particular had a good tenor voice, though untrained. Watkins sang with them and they applauded his deep baritone.

"Where did you learn to sing like that?" they wanted to know.

"In the church of my small home town," Watkins explained. "I also played the organ on Sundays."

"Are you a believer?" asked Anatoly.

"I'm keeping all the options open," Watkins smiled, and caught Alyosha and Volodya exchanging a quick glance.

Nina, who as usual had been working too hard on her Scandinavian translations, went to bed about midnight. The rest of them stayed out in the garden, singing and passing around the Canadian rye for another hour. Not once did they raise any topic of conversation that was remotely political.

On Sunday at two o'clock they had chicken with rice and tea, and at three they all left for Moscow. Alyosha had a lecture to prepare for the next day. Watkins invited them for dinner at the embassy the next Saturday evening, and they accepted with alacrity.

Alyosha said he hoped Watkins would visit him again at his dacha near Yalta over the summer. Anatoly went down every year, and was planning to fly out around July 1. Watkins said he had been thinking about a trip to the Crimea and could probably get away for ten days after July 5. What about driving? Volodya said it would be much more interesting to drive than to fly, and it would be useful to have the car there. Watkins asked Anatoly if he would like to drive with him instead of flying? Anatoly thought this might be managed. Nina had taken her vacation in May, when her husband was ill, so would not be able to get away again. Besides, she had to go to Helsinki as translator for the Soviet peace delegation around the end of June. Vera, Volodya's wife, was anxious to go, but Volodya, who expected to be too busy with his *kukuruza* (maize) at that time to take a holiday, was not sure he would trust Vera in such company. After the way Anatoly had acted the previous evening, he would have to think it over. Everyone roared with laughter and further discussion was postponed until Saturday evening, when they would all meet at Watkins' place.

4

THE ROLLING STONES vibrate through the apartment. Murray inhales deeply and passes the fat hand-rolled joint in the brown Brazilian paper on to Penny, who is stretched out on the llama rug, her small, lithe body moving with the beat, singing along with the Stones: "I just want to make love to you, baby."

"Penny!" He calls out through the spaces in the music, but she waves the joint off. She's had enough and sings back, "When you gonna take me home, baby?"

"Soon, soon." Murray returns the joint to Steve, who yells, mystified: "What the hell do you want to go to Brazil for?" The music suddenly ends, but Steve, chubby and bespectacled, is still shouting in his high-pitched voice: "The Brazilians don't speak Chinese worth a damn." A neighbour pounds sharply against the wall. "Jesus!" mutters Steve,

"Welcome back to Ottawa! At two on a Saturday morning things are just starting to liven up in Brazil." He turns down the amplifier before the next LP drops to the turntable and the Beatles go into the first lines of "A Hard Day's Night." This time Steve joins in with Penny: ". . . But when I get home to you, I find the things that you do will me make me feel all right . . ."

He breaks off and asks Murray, "I mean, why would you blow off a career specialty like Mandarin? I bet all the people in External who actually speak and write Mandarin could fit in that phone booth down there outside my apartment."

"I know," sighs Murray. "But they're never going to let me use the lingo, especially now. I'm on the minister's shit list. I was his golden-haired boy. Yesterday I couldn't get an appointment to see him. And by next week he won't even remember my name."

Murray gazes moodily around Steve's meticulous apartment. The walls are adorned with framed photographs, Brazilian masks and dolls, and all kinds of necklaces and accessories that Steve has picked up through his involvement in one of the Umbanda sects in Brazil. He can picture Steve eagerly dressing up in the robes and beads — any chance to get up in drag. Steve is just back from Latin America, where he has spent three years as third secretary in the embassy in Rio de Janeiro. Murray focuses on a blownup colour photo on the mantelpiece of Steve taken with a Mountie. The policeman stands at attention in full dress — scarlet tunic and broad-brimmed hat. In the background are the Parliament Buildings and the Peace Tower. Beside the Mountie is Steve, his choir-boy's face grinning widely. They each have one foot resting on a beautiful hand-tooled leather trunk in front of them. The same trunk sits on the floor below the mantelpiece. Steve, who has been watching Murray's gaze move from the photograph to the trunk, gets up from his Italian-designed chair and flips open the lid of the trunk for Murray to see inside. One glance and he realizes this is Steve's stash for his marijuana.

Laughing uncontrollably, Steve explains the connection. "I'm coming home from the airport, happy to be back and totally ripped — it's the only way to put in fourteen hours on a plane. The customs guys are real darlings and wave me through on my diplomatic passport, including my leather trunkload of righteous Brazilian grass." He grandiosely waves the joint around in the air. "Frankie, the little bitch, meets me at the airport with a couple of queens from Hull, all in drag, completely bombed. What a scene, my dears. Thank God no one in the department was at the airport! We're smoking up in the cab. 'Go by Parliament Hill,' I tell the driver, 'I've missed the old whore house.' It warms my heart to see the Mounties standing guard for the tourists. Then I suddenly have this lovely idea. I get the cabbie to wait, haul the trunk full of mary-jane out of the back, and lug it over to the Mountie. I tell him this is the trunk my grandmother brought over from the old country, and she always wanted me to join the Mounted Police. Instead, I broke her heart and joined the Jesuits. 'But,' I explain, 'she would die happy to have a picture of her grandson priest alongside a Mountie and behind the trunk with which she started her life in this country.' The beautiful young lad takes one look at Frankie and his two queens, and sheer terror passes over his innocent face, his cheeks turning as red as his uniform. You can see he thinks we are all crazier than a bag of hammers, and he's obviously grateful I never made it into *his* Force — I mean, with friends like that. But in that truly great Canadian way that separates us from all other nations, that ineffable inability to assert ourselves, he goes along with it! Frankie, bless her little balls, takes the picture. We whip the incriminating trunk literally from under the Mountie's feet and scurry back to the taxi before the poor boy can blurt out any questions. And *voilà* — there it sits on my floor, a testament to the liberal values of our great nation's police force."

Penny, who has rolled on her stomach to listen, bursts into a fit of giggles. Murray shakes his head. "Only someone with an angel face like yours could have gotten away with it," he marvels.

"Yes, if they only knew how this dope-smoking little gay fox had once again pulled a fast one on them!" Steve roars with joy, but is met by the pounding on the wall from his neighbour. "This brute next door is getting on my nerves! That's it! Tomorrow I start looking for a house to buy."

"How did you get away with it, Steve?"

"What exactly?"

"You know, escape the investigation of —"

"You mean the Great Fag Purge of the civil service by the guys who 'always get their man'?"

"Yeah . . . Hundreds went down, and, well . . . you never made too big a secret of it. How did you beat them?"

"Well, you know how they went about it?"

"Not exactly, no."

"The Mounties started with each personnel department and then went to the heads of each section and asked them to supply names of anyone in the department they thought might not be 'one hundred percent straight.' If your name showed up on the list, the Mounties invited you into a meeting." Steve's soft face hardened. Murray could see that under the easy-going and bantering exterior Steve presented to the world, there was a strong-willed man.

"My head of section at the time was queer with bells on and the creep turned me in. Wanted to save his own limp dick, I guess. The interview was very intimidating. You were all alone, no lawyer. You sat facing a panel of three or four cops behind a desk, and a tape recorder running. That prick Present in security services was in charge of the show. He asked me if I had anything to say. 'About what?' I asked." Steve mimicked Present's mid-Atlantic accent perfectly: "'We have information you are a homosexual and therefore a possible threat to national security,' he said in that phony accent. 'The Cabinet has passed a special order in council which rules that if you are a homosexual, you must immediately have your security clearance revoked.' What crap! All the time I was in Brazil, the RCMP visa control guy attached to Immigration down there was bonking himself blind every night with a different Brazilian babe. Did anyone think for a moment that might make him want to betray his country and become a risk to the security of the state? My God! What a dark age we live in."

Steve lapses into silent disgust. Penny rolls over on her side and immediately falls asleep on a cushion that Steve has tucked under her head.

"She has a high-energy job," Murray explains. "She sleeps whenever she can." Steve puts on a Bob Dylan record, turns down the volume even more, and softly sings harmony, "There once was a woman, a child I am

– 116 –

told." He breaks off to look down and admire Penny. "What an incredible face! Who was it who said, 'Eroticism doesn't work without a winning face'? Had to be a Frenchman. It would be genetically impossible for an Anglo to say something like that. You have an eye for the beautiful ones, don't you, Murray? That's too bad because then you're in for a hard life — the beautiful ones are always trouble. I know, my boy, I suffer from the same self-destructive affliction."

"So how did the meeting with the RCMP end?" Murray wants to know.

" 'Prove it!' I challenged them. 'Let's go back to the basics of English common law, the Magna Carta, the legal principles that are the foundation and the building blocks of our great nation. Show me my accusers. Let them speak to my face.' That really pissed them off because, of course, they didn't have any evidence. They had to let me go without any further questions, except the threat that they would be keeping an eye on me. I pulled my job performance gradings for the last five years out of my briefcase and shoved them under their noses. 'Take a look at that,' I said. 'Exemplary! Steve Tagliatti performs at all times above and beyond his duties.' God, they were furious! A fag who does his job really well! I went straight from there to my section head's office. I told the little Judas if he didn't get me out on the Brazil posting that was up for grabs that week, I would turn him in. Luckily he believed my bluff. I mean, even if he deserved it, I would never have turned him over to the inquisition. That's exactly how it was. The guys who were trapped into being honest and admitted to being gay were fired or shuffled off into oblivion. I hoped that, by the time I got back, the witch hunt would have blown over. But it seems not."

"Why, are they still trying to nail you?"

"No, but from what you've told me that's probably why they've got that poor darling Watkins trapped in some hotel room in Montreal. Who else is in there with him besides Present and your lovely sister?"

"A CIA type by the name of Merleau."

"Merleau! Not George Merleau!"

WATKINS WAKES UP. How long has he slept? It seems like a few minutes. There is no bedside clock in this room and his wrist-watch seems to have stopped. He holds it to his ear. Nothing. Is everything winding down? Get a grip on yourself, man. Not the time for self-pity. Perhaps the watch got wet in the rain, or when he stumbled in the overflowing gutter. He feels exhausted. He pats his pockets, looking for his pills, but remembers that Merleau has them. He must try to contain his anxiety, stay calm, and think things through. When he considers it now he can see it is a long, slow chess game. The opening moves and the shuffling of the pawns began on the snowy steps of the Moscow Music Conservatory when Nina Krymova introduced him to her "brother," Anatoly Nikitin.

Dispatch S367 to the Minister of External Affairs
Copies to the Internal Security Branch

A month after my last reported meeting with Anatoly Nikitin, he has gotten into the habit of dropping by the chancellery every four or five days. He behaves casually, giving the impression that it is quite normal for a Soviet citizen to have the freedom to visit informally the ambassador of a foreign country, when everyone in the diplomatic corp knows only those with special clearance with the KGB can get past the Soviet policemen on guard outside the gates of the embassy.

Following your orders to pursue this relationship to see where it will give us an opportunity to make political contacts at a higher level, I usually drop the task I am busy with and at least take the time to have a cup of tea or refreshments with him. He is quite keen to borrow whatever Western newspapers or magazines we might have on hand. He invariably returns them, and one can judge from the condition in which they are returned that they are read from cover to cover and certainly not just by one person. If he truly is a historian at the academy, then they must have no budget for Western periodicals.

He also likes to talk about the current political situation. He seems especially to want to get from me a feel for the American public support for Taiwan. I have the curious feeling that he is following some kind of line of instructions on how to deal with me. And, more important, that his advice may not be from another Russian, but perhaps a Western adviser. At any rate, he is obviously trying to feel me out. Unfortunately, his questions are ponderous and clumsy.

I replied that I wasn't really well informed on the subject of Taiwan/Formosa, but following the security branch's suggestions, I tried to keep the conversation open. He said he could not understand the American attitude on the question of Taiwan and assured me that the average Soviet citizen found it quite inexplicable. Nobody in the street could understand why there should be any doubt that Formosa belonged to China, he said. It seemed to Russians that the Americans were taking the same unrealistic attitude towards the Chinese Revolution that some of the Western countries had taken towards the Russian Revolution. I smiled politely, but, following your suggestions, did not enter into any debate.

Mr. Nikitin then went on to ask me if there had been anything recently in the Western press on the question of a Soviet-Japanese peace treaty.

I told him the last I had seen was that the Soviet and Japanese governments had agreed on New York for the negotiations. That has already been announced in the Soviet press, he replied quite huffily. He supposed, in a sarcastic tone, that the Japanese would probably have some kind of observer status in the United Nations and that the head of their delegation would be in charge. Yes, I replied, and then, to provoke him, I suggested that the Japanese would probably like to have the southern part of Sakhalin back. Yes, Mr. Nikitin shot back, and probably the Kurile Islands, too. And why stop there? Maybe they should even have Okinawa returned!

I'm sure he was hoping to get me to choose an anti-American position. But when I said nothing and stared back at him without expression, he seemed to become a bit unnerved, looked around for his fur hat, and abruptly took his leave. I await any further orders you may have.

MURRAY KNEELS, picks up the sleeping Penny in his arms, and gently places her on the sofa. He returns to his chair and declines the wine bottle Steve is waving around to refill his glass. "Tell me what you know about Merleau," he asks.

"Just stumbled into it. As you know, most of the security stuff for the embassy — cables, codes, and so on — is handled by the first secretary. But we were so overwhelmed with work down there, and the first being sick a lot, many things got passed down the line to yours truly, who had established a reputation of getting all the bore-you-shitless jobs done! So I got to do the contact work with the spooks over at the American Embassy and others. Mostly a lot of incoherent for-your-eyes-only documents and several bore-your-ass-numb meetings. Best part was my liaison work with the Brazilian cops, especially a couple of guys who were loyal to President Goulart and detested the CIA. We would hit the bars regularly and so, after three months, I bet I had better contacts than anyone else in the embassy as to what was really going on, the *réal politique*. So what happened next didn't come as a surprise to me.

"In August '61 Quadros, who had been elected president by a record majority, was forced to resign by the military and Goulart, the vice-president, took over. It was really the old American squeeze play behind it all. The U.S. State Department got upset with Quadros because he wanted to buy guns and helicopters from Hungary and Czechoslovakia — where they were a lot cheaper than in the States. So the State Department began calling him a potential left-wing dictator. What a joke! Quadros was a conservative. He jailed students who demonstrated at the university. He sent the army in to beat up starving peasants in the Norde Este when they staged sit-ins in the towns. But for the last twenty years the Americans have pumped millions of dollars into establishing 'client' armies in Latin America. They own all the military generals from the Mexican border to Tierra del Fuego, and Quadros was just too independent for Washington's liking — the guy wanted to choose his own cabinet, for God's sake."

"But what's all this got to do with Merleau?" Murray interrupts, impatiently rising from his chair.

"Everything, dear heart. But if you're going to pace around, at least take those sexy cowboy boots off or I'll have that moron downstairs banging on *his* ceiling." Murray reluctantly sits down again.

"Merleau was supposed to be some kind of military attaché to the U.S. mission. But everyone knew he was CIA. You could see he had enormous power, although he never said very much. The U.S. resident staff were terrified of him. Behind his back they called him 'Doctor Destabilizado.'"

"How did you know that?"

"I used to have drinks with a darling boy in the U.S. press section. We had a little thing going, a sweet boy in charge of what you spook guys call 'press assets.' Basically his job was to meet Brazilian reporters in bars, hand them brown envelopes full of U.S. bills, and, over a beer, tell them what kind of anti-government stories the embassy would like to see in the press. Nothing very subtle, but very effective. He also warned me not to get on Merleau's bad side. The story was that Merleau was the CIA guy who drove around for hours with former president Lumumba's body stuffed in the trunk of his car, trying to find a place to dump the corpse."

"Those are just rumours."

"Perhaps. But everywhere he pops up for the CIA, whether it's Africa or Latin America, a few weeks later an elected president resigns, or a military coup ousts the constitutional leader, or, like Lumumba, he ends up dead."

"Are you suggesting that's what he's here for?"

"I'm not suggesting anything. All I can tell you is that I was at two meetings in Rio at which Merleau was present. At the first he said only one thing: 'Quadros wants to normalize diplomatic relationships with the Soviet and Eastern Bloc countries.' Nobody responded — just a dead silence, like a judge passing sentence. Two weeks later Quadros was out. Later he named the U.S. ambassador to Brazil and other top-ranking Americans as the key men responsible for forcing him out of office. He said he would lead a personal crusade in Brazil against corruption and the communists. Some left-wing dictator!"

"And what happened in the second meeting?"

"It was early this year, after the Goulart government passed a law limiting the amount of profits foreign multinationals could ship out of the country, and then went on to nationalize a subsidiary of ITT. Goulart promised to pay compensation, but couldn't do so immediately because of a cash-flow problem. All the diplomatic secretaries responsible for security of mission were at this meeting — the Australians, the Brits, the French, and so on. Again Merleau said only one thing: 'This is Fidel Castro and Cuba all over again. It's an inevitable drift to the left and must be stopped!' Two weeks later Goulart was arrested in a military coup led by General Castello Branco, one of the 'Yankee Generals,' who immediately installed himself as a military dictator. He swears it is necessary for the military to be in power for the next three generations to save Brazil from the communist threat. That's American foreign policy for you. Goulart was about as much of a communist as Eisenhower. He was a multimillionaire land holder who wore a medal of the Madonna around his neck. So you see, my sweet, idealistic Murray, I'm not suggesting anything. I'm just telling you what happens around that guy Merleau."

Murray is silent, staring down at his boots, thinking about Watkins. "Poor old guy. He reminded me of my father. There's got to be some way to get him out of there. Who could do it?"

Steve chuckles. "Murray! Murray! I do worry about you. Listen, there's only one man who can do it — all he has to do is pick up the phone."

"You mean the prime minister?"

"And the big question is, Does he know?"

"Christ, Steve, I can't even get to see my own minister, let alone bend Pearson's ear."

Steve reaches for a pad, writes down a name and phone number, and hands it to Murray. "Here's your best hope — Ken Banks. Pearson, Banks, and Watkins all know one another from way back, just after the war. Shit! What am I talking about? The three of them created the Department of External Affairs as we know it today."

"So what happened to Banks?"

"You don't know? What kind of a spook are you? He's like me, another arse bandit. No, he's not like me. He's a gentle, civilized, remarkably intelligent, well-educated, especially capable civil servant from another generation. But! . . . still a homosexual! And so, in the eyes of the spooks, he had to go. Have you ever seen the Cabinet directive that talks about us — here, hold on a second." Steve gets up and opens a drawer of his desk to reveal alphabetically arranged files. "Ah, here it is — not the whole thing, just an extract." He stands reading in a flat mechanical voice: "It's titled 'Security Cases Involving Character Weaknesses, with Special Reference to the Problem of Homosexuality,' prepared for the Cabinet's special security panel in May 1959, blah, blah, let me see . . . Oh yes, here we go. 'Characteristics of homosexuals: instability, willing self-deceit, defiance towards society, a tendency to surround oneself with persons of similar propensities, regardless of other considerations — none of which inspire the confidence one would hope to have in persons required to fill positions of trust and responsibility.' Blah, blah, blah, it goes on and on. Dear sweet weeping Jesus!" In disgust he tosses the paper over for Murray to read.

"How on earth did you get hold of this?"

Steve ignores his question. "Anyway, Present and his mob of Neanderthals made sure Ken Banks got shoved out sideways. True, they found a mattress for him to fall on and he's okay. But . . . ah, to hell with them. Anyway, if anyone can get to Pearson, I think Banks just might."

Steve's angelic features look suddenly drained, and Murray has a sense of the deep anger and resentment the man carries inside him. He stands up, finds Penny's motorcycle jacket, and wraps it around her softly protesting body. "C'mon babe, let's go home." But Penny mumbles unintelligibly and turns over on the sofa to sleep more comfortably. Murray scoops her up in his arms and carries her to the door, where the watching Steve opens the latch, smiles wearily, and pats him softly on the cheek.

"That's good, Murray. Let Stevie the Wonder Boy get his beauty sleep. Take your woman-child away to bed and, if you wake up in a few hours from now and throw away that paper with Banks' number on it, nobody except me is going to know. And Stevie is not going to think badly about you for one moment because he knows it's not your fight — and even if it were, you don't stand a chance of winning."

WATKINS KNOWS he is dozing off again. Flashes of dreams interweave with the reality of his imprisonment in the Ritz. He senses he has fallen back into that slippery place in the mind where the will cannot overcome the weariness of the brain and body to stay in control. For a few moments he struggles to engage with the voices he hears outside the suite. It is Fletcher, arguing with a new voice, a man's voice that somehow is familiar, but then he is drifting . . .

WATKINS WAS EXCITED. His chauffeur, Maxim Constantinovich, was driving the embassy Oldsmobile and they were both looking forward to getting out of Moscow for a few days. The only disappointment was that they had to pick up that bore, Anatoly, at his apartment before they could set out on the long drive to the Crimea. Watkins was finally about to meet the mysterious Alexei Mikailovich Gorbunov — the man Anatoly has been talking about for six months, the "historian" the security types have been urging him to contact. They have all been invited to spend a few days as guests at the Gorbunovs' summer dacha near Alushta, about 45 kilometres from Yalta. It was a three-day drive from Moscow and already Anatoly was gushing: "You will love them, especially Anya. She will want to practise her English on you, you'll see. This will be the trip of your life."

Watkins was looking forward to getting away from the oven-like heat of Moscow in July, especially to the unknown countryside — a closed territory, usually, for foreigners. No Canadian ambassador had ever before been invited for a holiday at a dacha, and, after some discreet inquiries, he learned that the visit would be like a journey into outer space for the Americans. He carefully planned the 1,500-kilometre trip many days in advance. Anatoly suggested they take it easy on the way down and spend the first night at Oryol, the second at Kharkov, the third at Zelyonny Gai (Green Hill) — the name itself aroused idyllic expectations — and arrive at the dacha on Friday.

On the first day the road was excellent all the way, with the exception of some detours between Moscow and Tula, and it was possible to drive at a steady speed for long stretches. The traffic was not heavy, although many Russian families were taking the same sort of holiday.

"You see," said Anatoly, the master of the obvious, "the hotels at Yalta and Alushta and all the other coastal towns are full to overflowing.

So it's good that you booked rooms so far in advance."

Watkins realized that the regime had not even begun to understand how much Soviet life and society would change as more of the people acquired automobiles. The drivers were frighteningly casual about the rules of the road, and they would not survive long on a North American expressway. Food was always a problem in the Soviet Union, so Watkins and Anatoly had packed lunches, and they picnicked for the first two days. Watkins had wired ahead for reservations, and three comfortable rooms were waiting for them in the old-fashioned hotel at Oryol. Two of the rooms had baths, but, unfortunately, it was Tuesday — not a hot-water day. They had to make do with a cold bath that evening, but got a warm one the next morning.

There was also a shortage of electric power in Oryol. When they went for a walk around the town in the evening, they found the street lighting very dim. But the true comedy began just before they reached Oryol, when they drove into a gaudy new *zapravoochnaya stanzia* (gas station) elaborately fitted up with red gasoline pumps, garages for storing cars, and workshops for repairing them. The architecture for these wayside stations was too eclectic for precise definition. It certainly was not Russian. Anatoly thought that the high square ornamental towers and their steep tile roofs suggested South Germany. Perhaps the man does have a sense of humour after all, thought Watkins.

When Maxim reported some difficulty in getting gas the next morning, Anatoly took over. He got the secretary of the City Soviet on the phone and explained he was speaking for the Canadian ambassador. Immediately Watkins knew he was not travelling with a lowly academic. Anatoly quickly extracted a promise of personal delivery of gasoline for the ambassador's needs. This was the only time in the entire trip that there was any difficulty in getting gasoline or service for the Oldsmobile. From Oryol on, they were always able to fill up with the best-quality gas in fifteen minutes at any gas station, despite reports from the British that when travelling through the country, simple gas fillups frequently became two-hour bureaucratic nightmares.

After a couple of hours on the road the next day, the engine began to sputter and Maxim decided that the gas they had got in Oryol had not been of high enough quality. He would have to add some from an emergency can kept in the back. Also, the accelerator pedal had come off and needed to be screwed on again. Watkins viewed these events with suspicion, but said nothing. They decided to have lunch by the roadside sitting under a tree on a rich carpet of grass and clover amid many kinds of wild flowers. Maxim soon discovered that in the rush of getting ready he had forgotten to bring either a screwdriver or a piece of hose to pour the gas through. So he began waving his hand at passing vehicles. As if on cue, a shiny green Pobeda with sheer pale-green window curtains pulled up. An exceptionally tall, slender, smartly dressed young woman got out, and Maxim announced in jubilant tones that he had found a "good soul" to help him.

The woman introduced herself as Natasha, and the young man with her as her cousin Boris. Both of them were travelling to the Crimea for a holiday, they said. But to Watkins' eyes, it all seemed a bit staged. Boris, it turned out, had the necessary tools for Maxim. The repairs were quickly made while Natasha all the while flirted outrageously with Watkins. He was grateful when they were soon able to continue to Kharkov.

Watkins knew Kharkov well. He had spent almost a week at the Intourist Hotel in the fall of the previous year when he first met Khamal. They had both been very comfortable there. He was delighted to find the same old Intourist official on the job as well as his assistant, a young Ukrainian woman who practised a little Finnish with the ambassador. They both extended a warm welcome and asked after Khamal. Anatoly, taken aback by all the fuss they made over Watkins, sulked in a corner. The food in the hotel was excellent — much better than in Moscow — and the service perfect. The waiter remembered Watkins and greeted him cordially. They had caviar with toast and butter, steaks done exactly as ordered, salad, and strawberry ice-cream. All through dinner and their later walk, Anatoly talked about Natasha, their "roadside angel." "I'm sure she likes you," he ventured. "She said as much when you weren't listening."

Watkins was aghast at the man's gaucherie. Anatoly also kept asking at the desk if Natasha had registered, although his inquiries were complicated by the fact that he did not know her surname. He seemed strangely obsessed by her. Watkins wondered if this was all a clumsy attempt to mask the too coincidental rescue of the "breakdown" on the highway.

While Anatoly again began to natter on about Natasha, Watkins escaped into the streets of Kharkov. What a sad sight it was when he first saw it in 1950. It had changed hands several times between the German and Russian armies during the war and had been bombed by both sides. Although many new buildings had been constructed, there were still whole streets of empty shells. However, it looked infinitely more cheerful five years later. There had been a tremendous amount of construction, with many grandiose official buildings. Streets had been widened, squares and gardens laid out, and the banks of the river turned into parks. Anatoly noticed nothing, except to point out proudly a billboard that declared the population well over a million.

When they came out of the hotel the next morning, they found a large group of youngsters collected around the car. It attracted a lot of attention everywhere they stopped, even in Moscow, as it was the only Oldsmobile in the Moscow diplomatic corps. The onlookers were curious and asked many questions. Unfortunately, Maxim was very short with them and objected to their touching the paint-work with their dirty hands.

Just as he was getting into the car, Anatoly remembered that he had left his passport in his hotel room. Watkins insisted on walking back with him to get it. In the lobby the manger introduced Anatoly to a Professor Sidorov. The scholar had received a request from a Kharkov communist youth group for a lecture on current events, and since Anatoly, who he had just learned was a distinguished professor from the Moscow Academy, was in Kharkov, perhaps he would give the lecture and save getting somebody from Moscow? Anatoly was flustered and protested that he was on vacation. He would not give any lectures on anything for a solid month. Sidorov was greatly disappointed.

Watkins thought it all passing strange. Events became even more comic when, stepping by chance into the dining room, he came upon Natasha and Boris tucking into a breakfast steak. They looked up, flustered and embarrassed. Anatoly came in and there was a lot of phony joking about the mysterious ways of Russian destiny. Finally it was agreed that they should all have a picnic lunch together somewhere along the road and that the cousins should join the others for dinner at Zelyonny Gai that evening.

Anatoly and Watkins stopped for a dip in the Oryel River, and Anatoly proudly pointed out the prevalence of bathing suits at the various swimming holes in the region as a sign of advancing culture. A great improvement, he thought, over people swimming naked or in their underwear. Watkins kept quiet, not so sure. He found the bathing suits ugly and poorly designed.

As they finished dressing, the green car with Natasha and Boris pulled up from out of nowhere and they agreed to lunch at the first shade trees they found. Large trees were scarce in this region. There were only steppes for miles, and they had to drive almost a hundred kilometres before they found a small grove on the edge of a little village of small white-washed and thatch-roofed cottages. Anatoly persuaded the housewife in the nearest cottage to boil some water so they could use their Nescafé. Although the cottage was small and had a rather tumble-down look from the outside, Anatoly said it was clean and tidy inside. At first the woman feared it would take some time to get the water to boil because she had just let the fire go out, but Anatoly spotted a primus stove in the corner and they used that. Boris bought a jar of butter-milk from an old man who lived alone in another cottage. His cow was tethered on the roadside in front of the house, and his mongrel dog was keeping watch. As in all these little villages, chicken and geese were wandering along the side of the road. All the men and women were away at work on the Kolkhoz, haying or harvesting.

In a small town called Nuvomoskovsk, they visited a large and beautiful old wooden church, which stood out against the horizon for miles with its cluster of nine onion-shaped cupolas of different spires and heights. It had been built 300 years before by the Zaporozhye Cossacks. The priest, who was just preparing for a service, told them that not one nail had been used in its original construction. It had been struck by a shell during the war, but had not been seriously damaged, as a stone or brick church would have been by a similar blow. The shell had simply come in through one wall and gone out through another. The interior was beautifully finished, entirely in wood, the work of highly skilled craftsmen. The priest showed the visitors the oldest icons, including a fine twelfth-century example from Byzantium, and drew their attention to an enamel cross bordered with large diamonds that he was wearing. He also said that the handsome new automobile standing in the courtyard belonged to him. The congregation was just assembling — mostly old and middle-aged peasant women with a few men and children. One old woman informed them that they should not hold their hands behind their backs in a church, but they had no idea why.

Zelyonny Gai, where they were to spend the night, was nothing but a large gas station, with a hotel and a few restaurants, garages, and workshops. The hotel rooms were spacious, clean, and comfortable, but, strangely, most were without baths or even washbasins. The contractors had forgotten to instal them. When Watkins asked for a bath, the receptionist said there was no hot water. When Anatoly complained, he agreed to light the wood stove at the end of the large communal bath-tub. Although the hotel, with its ornamental square tower and red tile roof, was only a few years old, it was disintegrating quickly. Tiles had fallen off the roof and not been replaced, and there were water stains on the ceilings. The plumbing was of poor quality, the locks were difficult, and some of the doorknobs had disappeared.

They dined in a pleasant open-air restaurant, but the food was not very good. Natasha seized on the opportunity to vamp Watkins when he offered some French wine he had brought from Moscow. The rest had to make do with a harsh Ukrainian Vodka and mineral water. By now Boris and Natasha had given up all pretence of travelling independently and they joined the larger group for every meal. Watkins could not believe he was still supposed to show a romantic interest in Natasha, but from the way Anatoly and Boris behaved, Natasha still thought she had a chance. It all became too absurd. When Natasha coyly asked him in front of the others if he had ever married, he replied starkly: "No — and I don't ever intend to." A stunned silence followed, and Watkins got up from the table and walked away.

The evening turned into a clear, silent, moonlit night. After dinner, Anatoly and Natasha wandered off together in close conversation and it became obvious to Watkins that Boris had been assigned to keep him company. They walked around the garden, though Boris remained guarded and uncommunicative. Watkins soon excused himself and went to his hotel room.

"MR. WATKINS?" There is a tap on the door, and Fletcher's curt voice interrupts his sleep: "Please come out. The director has arrived."

As Watkins emerges from the bedroom, he senses a different tension in the apartment. He pauses in the doorway until his eyes adjust. He's wary. What are they up to now? It's like a scene change on the theatre set. Most of the lights in the suite have been turned off or dimmed. The blinds are open and the ambient lights of the city, barely able to penetrate the curtain of rain that has followed the storm, create an atmosphere of soft blue light in the room. The coffee table has been replaced with a large table, behind which three figures silently sit. On this side an empty chair waits for him. A single tubular table lamp with a heavy green shade illuminates the papers and documents neatly arranged in front of the inquisitors. Disembodied hands and sleeves disappear into indistinct upper bodies, the faces in shadow. Rembrandt would have liked this tableau, he thinks, and painted it on canvas. Watkins can make out the forms of Fletcher and Merleau. The unknown figure in the middle stands up, an arm reaches out, and a hand emerges from the darkness. "Mr. Watkins, we meet again."

Watkins is too surprised to shake hands. He stares at the dimly lit face on the other side of the lamp, ignores the hand, and lets his body sink slowly into the free chair at the table. Unbalanced, he steadies himself by gripping his hands tightly on his thighs. He tries to mask his surprise. "Well, well, Mr. Present, then it must be true."

"What must be true, sir?"

"Beneath every upright presence a murder is taking place."

"Ah, yes," Present says. "I wish I had a dollar for every time I've heard that one. My wife delights in it — daily."

"All those discussions we had in Paris, the places I took you for a good meal, excellent wine — and you never once mentioned that you were the director of counter-espionage."

Present remains silent. Fletcher brings her hand to her mouth and begins, nervously, to chew on the knuckle of her first finger. At no time has Present ever mentioned anything about previous interviews with the ambassador.

"The last meeting," Watkins continues in his heavy, accusing voice, "you thanked me graciously for my time —"

"There's a reason for that," Present interrupts.

"— you said I had cooperated in every way possible, and that all the points we had discussed —"

"If you will listen for a moment —"

"— had cleared everything up."

Present fiddles with the papers in front of him and pretends to be busy making a note on his pad.

"Your premise for those discussions — what you called 'a debriefing' — was that they would allow your intelligence organization to gain as much information as possible about the security and intelligence-gathering functions of the Soviet Union."

"All that is true, Mr. Watkins," sighs Present.

"Then why have you brought me to this place against my will? What more could you possibly want to know about my life and my service in Moscow?"

Present clears his throat. "To help you clear your name —"

"Clear my name! Of what?"

"Because of evidence that has been brought to us by our American allies, I must officially warn you that you are now the subject of an intensive and serious investigation."

Watkins laughs derisively. "Before we go any further, I want a lawyer here. What time is it?"

"Just after four a.m.," Fletcher answers.

"Where can I get a lawyer at four on a Saturday morning of the Thanksgiving weekend?"

"Your question is academic," Present replies. "Under special authority granted by the Cabinet to the security services, I have the power to detain you and question you without legal counsel."

Watkins waves his hand wearily. "I see. So you are effectively above the law."

"No, we operate strictly within the powers that have been granted us."

"Then what is happening here tonight is a corruption of those powers."

Present tries a more conciliatory approach. "We're not off to a good start. I was delayed by the rain, and I can understand the difficult position you now find yourself in —"

"No, you can't — you can't even come close to understanding, so stop all the flannel."

"— and, of course, you can always refuse to answer my questions."

"This is not a court of law, so you can hardly throw me in prison for remaining silent."

"We can't compel you to answer, but . . ." Present purses his tight, narrow mouth into an even finer line and frowns down at the blank yellow pad that lies in front of him. His whole being yearns to fill up that space with notes.

Watkins winces as he gingerly pushes his body forward. His back is beginning to act up again. He can feel the pain spreading from his lower vertebrae down through his hips. He knows that sitting for protracted periods of time will soon become an agony.

"But *what*? Mr. Present. What are the penalties?"

"We can detain you for as long as we wish."

"You're bluffing."

"We can also recommend that you be stripped of your post and that your retirement pension be denied."

"This is blackmail!"

"No, of course not, but I urge you to cooperate, Mr. Watkins. You've had a long and illustrious career in External Affairs. Let us go about this sensibly and help you clear your name —"

"Help me! And clear my name of what, for God's sake? What exactly are the charges that support this investigation?"

"You have been named an agent of influence."

"What on earth does that mean in your secret policeman's jargon?"

"That, as Canadian ambassador to the Soviet Union, you discharged your duties in a way that shaped the foreign policies of Canada and the West to the benefit of the Soviet Union, rather than serving the best interests of Canada and our allies."

"Where is your evidence for that, Mr. Present?"

"We will get to that in great detail later —"

"But what would be my motive?"

"We believe you were a victim of entrapment by the KGB, a plot that made you vulnerable to . . . uh . . . blackmail."

"Well, at least you had the modesty to stumble on the dirty word."

Present shrugs. Watkins rises to relieve the painful tension in his lower back and begins pacing around the room. He can feel his heart racing. He knows he needs his medication, but he's damned if he's going to ask for it at this point and appear even more of a supplicant. He must think his way through this situation. Looking down into the street he can see the headlights of a car reflecting a moving swash of light off the slick pavement, and he remembers a splash of sunlight across the doll-sized café table outside Le Coq d'Or on a new spring day. Yes! That's what awaits him on the other side of this nightmare — gentle mornings in Paris at his favourite haunts on the Left Bank, with an espresso and perhaps a little shot of absinthe to start the day. A pad of paper in front of him, a book of poems to translate. Yes, those are the images he must hold on to. After all, he has earned them. Why shouldn't he live out the rest of his life with peace and dignity? He moves back to the others and leans over the table, taking the weight off his back by balancing on his clenched fists. He towers over Present, looking down into the man's strained, pinched face.

"'A man whose desire is to be something separate from himself invariably succeeds in being what he wants to be. That is his punishment. Those who want a mask have to wear it.' Do you know who said that, Mr. Present?"

"No, and I'm not interested. Could you please —"

"Oscar Wilde. And you wore a mask of betrayal through all those many hours of supposed friendship we shared during a month of conversations in France this summer."

Fletcher feels panicky. *My God! They've been at this for a month already. Why wasn't she briefed?* She can see now that Present never wanted this interview to take place. It was he who tried to sabotage the "exchange" in the Windsor Hotel lobby by substituting the Watcher crew at the last moment. That means he couldn't have known that Poliotov was a fake. She feels completely unsure of herself, out of her depth in the river. Has she really been manipulated by the DGI to put the ambassador through all this turmoil so someone can settle old scores with Present?

Watkins won't let up. "Do you remember when we said goodbye? I took you for a fine meal at the Café DeLuca. We toasted each other, and afterwards you shook my hand, looked me in the eye, and said, 'Everything is now satisfactory, Mr. Ambassador. All the questions have been answered.'"

Watkins reminds Fletcher of a wounded old bear, trapped in an alien environment where he has lost all power and is beginning to lose any sense of himself. She feels only dismay. She's unable to take even clinical satisfaction in the effectiveness of her interrogation tactics that have set him up so well for Present.

"Please sit down, Mr. Watkins," she urges. "You must be very tired."

But Watkins shakes his head and moves away again to stop in front of the cabinet, only to find that all the liquor bottles have been removed.

"You know where I first heard about you, Present, long before you came over to see me in Paris?"

Present remains silent, quizzically glancing at Watkins over the rims of his bifocals.

"In Moscow, no less. Your fame has travelled a long way. Even the Kremlin has heard about the iron-fisted purges over the last fifteen years in External Affairs and other government departments. It was Gromyko who asked me. 'How does this happen, Mr. Ambassador,' he taunted me, 'in a democracy like yours, that such an individual as Mr. Present can have so much power to —?'"

Merleau gets up abruptly and walks out of the darkened room. There is something in the way the man moves, Watkins thinks — like a predatory animal slipping through the shadows of the jungle.

"When did Foreign Minister Gromyko say this to you?" Fletcher asks. Present frowns at her question. Nothing in this interview is going the way he wants it to.

GROMYKO LOOKED LESS SOUR and formidable than the last time Watkins had seen him. To Watkins he seemed shrunken and ill, but the other diplomats sensed weakness. Charles Bohlen, the American ambassador, bent over to whisper in his ear: "Do you think that rapid weight loss is normal? Looks to me like the ancient war horse has cancer, don't you think? Perhaps this will make the old bastard a little easier to deal with." Sir William Hayter, the British ambassador, overheard Bohlen and chuckled: "At public occasions like this he always claims he speaks only Russian. But when I see him alone and without an interpreter, we do our whole business in English. Good thing too, old chap, because I don't speak a word of their lingo. Just can't get my tongue around it."

When Gromyko shook Watkins' hand, he made a special effort to appear friendly. He took Watkins' elbow and steered him out of earshot of the two other Soviet deputies present, Valerian Zorin and Vasily Kurnetzov, and waved off the translator. He spoke in Russian and complimented Watkins. "Soviet president Comrade Kliment Voroshilov tells me you're the first Western diplomat he has talked to so far who speaks fluent Russian. I must congratulate you. Canada has gone up several notches in his personal estimation. We had a long conversation on how we would like to make our relations with Canada a priority, an important part of our new international outlook."

"That's good news, Mr. Minister." Watkins was pleasantly surprised. All the drudgery of developing and maintaining contacts, the hours of putting up with boring clowns like Anatoly, the endless struggle to master the nuances of the language were finally starting to pay off. God knows, none of it had been easy.

"Yes," Gromyko continued. "I don't think we will have any serious problems in working out those trade deals we have been talking about, but this is not the time and place to pursue that business. You can rest assured things will be easier now that Comrade Khrushchev is calling — " slipping out of Russian and into English, "— how do you say, the shots?"

Watkins made no attempt to hide his pleasure, and voiced a few notes of appreciation.

"We want," Gromyko continued, "to have a more friendly and open communication with the West. The Stalin era is over. Our hope is that Canada will have some ameliorating affect on the harsh anti-Soviet U.S. policies."

"Thank you, Mr. Minister. I will await your phone call."

Gromyko became even more outgoing than he could remember. "Comrade Khrushchev knows many things have to change. We have much to learn from the West, and many things have changed since we last talked. Have you noticed how the Moscow Metro is now much more efficient? This rethinking of priorities is at every level in our society. We have to do more to reward our citizens for their past sacrifices. Even the hours of work for the bureaucracy are changed. We are on a strict regime now in the Kremlin. We work from nine to six, and that's it! We think it will be more efficient in the long run. Even the deputies must set an example. But something strange has happened socially and it's difficult for our civil service to adjust to this new rhythm. For years our whole family life has been structured around long hours." He laughed. "It's very difficult for the wives to have their husbands around so much."

Watkins wanted to find out if the old man had a sense of humour. He looked into the still bright blue eyes and took a gamble. He told Gromyko the joke he had carefully rehearsed in Russian only that morning — the one about the husband who comes home from work unexpectedly to find his wife in bed with her lover. The husband draws his revolver. His wife throws herself in front of her lover, crying out to her husband: "Don't shoot the father of your own children!"

Gromyko laughed uproariously, slapped Watkins on the back, and beckoned over a waiter with a tray of drinks. As they clinked their glasses of vodka together, the minister kept chuckling and repeating, "Don't shoot the father of your own children!" He roared again with laughter, so loud that many of the other diplomats cast an inquiring and envious glance over at Watkins. Then it happened, almost it seemed as an after-thought, but still a subtle message meant to convey that the Kremlin knew exactly what was happening around the world. "But I understand you don't share the same problem in your own ministry, Mr. Ambassador. I've heard that so many people have been purged from your civil service at home that those who remain in External Affairs have to work long nights, and weekends too."

PRESENT DOESN'T RESPOND, but his expression becomes glacial. He watches Watkins walking back and forth.

"Please sit down, Mr. Watkins. We must get on with this —"

"No! I don't want to get on with this farce!" His voice rising, Watkins demands: "I insist you release me immediately from this interrogation. I have meetings to attend in Paris. There is a trade pact that must be discussed with the Russians. People are waiting for me at Orly —"

Merleau enters with a dispatch that he wordlessly passes to Present. The owl-eyed man reads, smiles, and with cold delight tells Watkins: "We know who is waiting for you in Paris."

Watkins is shocked. "You know?" He falls silent.

They watch his reaction carefully. Merleau speaks to Present as if Watkins were not in the room. "French intelligence services have detained this individual. He carries Soviet travel documents and goes by the name of Khamal. Ring a bell with you, Mr. Watkins? No?" He addresses Present again: "They are talking with him now and will let us know whatever they get out of him."

Present nods, wincing at Merleau's brutal language.

Watkins, completely deflated, sits down in the chair. Khamal! Where is this going to end?

Present observes Watkins' distress and smiles with satisfaction. He turns once again with persistent but unfailing politeness to the business at hand. "Your case has been reopened and you have come to the attention of the security services because B Operations has developed information —"

"You mean you have had me, your own ambassador, under secret surveillance? What did you do, put microphones and cameras in my apartments?"

"Please don't pretend to be so naive. You must know every Western ambassador or journalist who has contact with the Soviet Union is kept under constant surveillance. In your case, the CIA is most concerned because —"

"So it's the CIA that's at the bottom of all this! What are you — a slave to the paranoia of American anti-communism and the manipulations of their intelligence operations?"

Merleau's face hardens. Watkins feels a certain satisfaction that he has at last gotten under the silent man's skin. For a moment, Present too seems to lose his cold intensity and answers Watkins more heatedly: "We will come to the details of the evidence later —"

"Why can't I hear these accusations directly from the CIA? Better still, why not let me be confronted by my accusers?"

Present impatiently waves his demand aside. "That is impossible. This information, and the means by which we obtained the evidence against you, would, if released, seriously endanger the security of the state."

Watkins appreciates the deep irony of this logic and shouts out in despair: "How can you expect to create democracy by undemocratic means? Not even the security services can be above the law. Otherwise, we behave like just another totalitarian state. Isn't that, gentlemen, what you claim to be fighting — the totalitarian communist state?"

Present takes time to lecture Watkins patiently one more time: "Yes, Mr. Watkins. We are indeed empowered to operate outside the law, whenever it is necessary to protect the state against internal subversion."

"Then at least give me a sense of what all this CIA nonsense is based upon?"

Merleau breaks his silence. Even though Present raises his hand as if to protest, he cannot stop Merleau's angry outburst. "It's very simple. Over the last ten years you have articulated in Moscow and in other European capitals many anti-American positions: on nuclear weapons, on Cuba, on the American two-China policy, and most recently the communist guerilla war in Vietnam — now a threat to peace in the whole of Southeast Asia. The list goes on and on. And the CIA would like to know why you have become such an implacable enemy of American foreign policy?"

Present cannot restrain a small gesture of exasperation over Merleau's blowup. But Watkins reacts with delight. He has finally got to the man he believes might be calling the shots.

"Aha, so now it's out on the table. You are the official CIA man here. And what right, in God's name, do you have to harass an ambassador of a foreign country in such a lawless manner?"

Merleau is silent. Watkins notes that Present leans even farther back in his chair and into the shadows. "These accusations are absurd! Mr. Present, I pointed you to my dispatches from Moscow. I'm sure that, being the methodical man you are, you have gone through them with a fine-tooth comb. Did you find any statement that remotely suggests I became an 'agent of influence'?"

Present squirms in his seat. Watkins is becoming more difficult by the moment.

"All these diplomatic positions," Watkins continues, "have been taken strictly on order from the government of Canada."

"You mean the prime minister?" Present shoots back.

"Yes!" Watkins shouts in reply. "The prime minister!"

The director flashes a satisfied smile, and exchanges glances with Fletcher and Merleau.

In that moment everything clicks into place for Watkins. He has unwittingly walked into the first stage of a trap. He studies them thoughtfully and adds, emphatically: "Yes! The prime minister, the Cabinet, and the legally elected government of Canada."

But Present continues to smile smugly: "Are you trying to push the blame onto the prime minister, when for years you were the most senior policy adviser to the prime minister on all Soviet affairs?"

"I have been and always will be completely loyal to the prime minister."

"Over and above loyalty to your own country?" asks Fletcher, more curious than unsympathetic.

"Once again you have all left out a vital reality: "What could possibly be my motive for acting as an agent of influence for the Soviet Union?"

With another patronizing smile, Present replies: "We'll get to that piece of business — all in good time."

Frustrated, Watkins strides around the room for a few moments. Then, in mid-step, he turns and challenges them: "It's not really me you're after, is it?"

Present looks uncomfortable and hurriedly tries to cover himself.

"Who else could it possibly be, Mr. Watkins?"

Present, Fletcher, and Merleau all wait for him to answer. But Watkins keeps a long silence, staring intently at each in turn. He walks over to lean very close to Present, their faces almost touching, and whispers, mockingly: "Mr. Present, if you don't know who the target is here, tonight, then we're all in trouble, and most especially you."

Merleau can't contain himself any longer and, with a snort of disgust, he stands up. "Cut the crap, Watkins. I guess the next thing you're going to try and sell us is that you didn't know that your two principal contacts in the Soviet Union were top KGB officers. You didn't know that Anatoly Nikitin is really Anatoly Gorsky, the KGB colonel and control officer for Philby and those other English fags Burgess and Maclean." His voice heavy with sarcasm, he asks: "Are you going to try and tell us you didn't know? And that you had no idea that your other buddy — Alexei? — is really Oleg Gribanov, the second-highest ranking officer of the KGB's Second Chief Directorate? No? Shit! Who do you think you're kidding? The man who led you to Gromyko and Khrushchev was in charge of all intelligence operations within the Soviet Union, and you had no idea! Bullshit! You may speak Russian fluently, Mr. Watkins, but in this room we understand American — and in American the evidence shows you're nothing but a commie fag."

He stalks out of the suite. Fletcher looks to Present for some indication that he will reassert his authority. But the director has disappeared inside himself and is staring morosely out the window at the rain. It seems to Fletcher that there is no longer any emotional centre in the room. A vacuum has replaced the previous acrimonious tension.

Suddenly Watkins explodes in rage: "You have no legal right to keep me confined." He leaps to his feet and charges for the door. The police officer jumps up to grapple with him. But Watkins is a big man and he puts up a surprisingly furious fight. The director yells orders ineffectively in a high-pitched voice above the cursing, struggling men. Only Fletcher is calm. She opens the front door of the apartment and waves in two more uniformed officers to come and assist. Watkins suddenly collapses under the pile of men, clutching at his heart.

"Please, my pills!" he gasps.

For a moment, everyone stares at his grey sickly face, twisted in pain and covered with a slick of sweat. He pleads again for his pills. "Please, I must have them!"

The pain in his chest is excruciating. He feels himself slipping into shock. Watkins watches desperately as Fletcher looks to Present for orders. But the director is aloof, silent. He didn't really want this interview to happen, and now the ambassador might die, she thinks. Merleau, drawn by the commotion of the brawl, reappears. Fletcher stretches out an open hand. "The pills," she urges. Slowly and reluctantly Merleau withdraws the medication from his pocket and hands the container to Fletcher. Watkins holds up two fingers, a signal he wants two pills. She gives them to him and he clumsily stuffs them into his drooling mouth. Present and Merleau exchange a long stare, broken only when Present turns away.

The policemen adjust their clothes. One has a bloodied nose, another a torn shirt. Fletcher slips Watkins two more pills. He conceals his surprise and pockets them. They exchange a quick glance. The transaction has not escaped Merleau, however, who silently shakes his head.

Present orders the two guards to return to the hall, closes the door, and signals to Merleau and the other policemen to half carry the humbled Watkins to the sofa.

"That was foolish," lectures Present, as they lower him onto the couch.

"Not as foolish as you will feel once the prime minister finds out what you're doing in this place," Watkins retorts.

Present takes a deep breath: "The prime minister —"

"Perhaps it may be a good idea for Mr. Watkins to take a rest in the bedroom," Fletcher interrupts.

The director looks at her askance for taking control of the situation. She whispers in his ear. Watkins gets the impression that Fletcher has probably saved him from a serious blunder. Of the three, Present looks the most upset by what has happened. He curtly nods to Fletcher and pauses to thrust his face very close to Watkins. "I know what you're hiding," he threatens, "and I promise you I will get you to confess."

Fletcher almost laughs. It is out of character for Present to speak this way, so it can only be for Merleau's benefit.

"You don't fool me with this good-cop-bad-cop act," Watkins shouts after Present in a hoarse whisper as the director stalks from the apartment.

"We resume this interview in two hours," Present commands.

Fletcher is thoughtful, even gracious. She asks Watkins if there is anything he needs. He asks for a pen and paper. Quickly he writes a note and tells Fletcher to deliver it to the Prime Minister's Office immediately.

"Yes, of course," Fletcher agrees. "I will personally make sure it is delivered this morning."

For a fleeting moment Watkins feels like his old self — a man of dignity, with certain powers of authority.

Fletcher motions one of the guards to help Watkins to the bedroom and solicitously inquires about his diet. She will order some food so it will be ready for him after he rests. Watkins lists the fats and sugars that must be avoided. Then she coolly humiliates him once again. She orders the guard to take away his belt, tie, and shoelaces, and to search his suitcase for anything he might use to kill himself. From now on the ambassador must shuffle around holding up his pants.

When Watkins finally closes the bedroom door and lies down on the bed, he sees Fletcher, through his half-closed eyes, open the door and leave it ajar. A police officer is watching him from a chair in the living room.

"DID YOU GET SOME REST? Eat something?" Fletcher asks.

Merleau is once again silent. He seems to have fully recovered his composure. Watkins tries to appear contrite. "I apologize for my behaviour. I'm . . . I'm not myself these days."

The two men regard him without expression. Fletcher turns her eyes away from the rumpled, pale-faced man to look out the window and hears her father: ". . . a canoe trip? I don't know. I haven't exactly been myself these last few weeks." And her cajoling response: "C'mon, Dad! You need to get away from this place for a while."

Present leans forward across the table, "This is very important. When was the last time you saw Oleg Gribanov, alias Alexei Gorbunov?"

Watkins sighs heavily. "We've already been through all this. I'm sure you have a copy of the memo I filed with the ministry after my last meeting with him in Paris.

"Yes, but it's important that we go through it again. You may have missed out some small detail. When was it?"

"Two years ago, just after what's become known as the Cuban Missile Crisis — that was our main topic of conversation."

Fletcher's curiosity is piqued. She's never seen this report that Watkins is talking about. Why hadn't Present shown it to her? "You sound as if you don't think it was such a big deal," she says.

"The Cuban crisis? . . . Oh, it was definitely an extreme emergency, but I don't share the conventional perception that it was a crisis the Soviets created all by themselves. But then, the public didn't have the advantage of having all the information. My meeting with Alexei Gorbunov offered quite a different perspective."

"So, Mr. Watkins, where did you meet him in Paris?"

"In the Coq d'Or, a small bar just around the corner from the Lennox Hotel."

Present, as ever, was curious about the way arrangements were made. "Did you have a special calendar, an agreement to meet on a certain day of the month?"

"Good God, no! He just gave me a ring at the Lennox and we agreed to meet the next day for a drink. Why do you keep trying to turn me into some sort of master spy? I don't even have the basic spy materials."

"What do you mean by that?" Fletcher asks.

"To begin with, procrastination and personal disorganization are my greatest weaknesses. And these days I get bored very quickly with the sheer banality of most of the human activity I see going on around me. Perhaps it's just another sign of age."

FLETCHER AND HER FATHER sat quietly in their canoe on the first day of the Churchill trip. Drinking in the peace and solitude of a lake the river had led them to, they rested, paddles balanced across the gunwales. Her father's deep voice resonated more than usual close to the dark, placid water.

"Why did I become a doctor? Because when I was a young man I knew that I wanted to do something, to make some contribution, that wasn't just measured in money."

"One can make a contribution as a firefighter or a poet or an engineer, so why specifically medicine?" she questioned.

"At that age it was all intuitive. I didn't understand why until I was much older. I had to overcome my major character weakness, my lack of personal discipline, and to do that I had to have people who needed me twenty-four hours a day — people who would impose their life demands on me and create an inescapable structure for my own existence. Patients tend to do that . . ."

"YOU HAVE ANOTHER DEFICIENCY of character?" Fletcher asks. "You did say, 'to begin with.'"

"Yes," he replies. "I'm handicapped by neither a greed for money nor a belief in politics. If I am to understand the historical view of human nature correctly, all your spies and double agents get sucked in by one or the other. Money, you see, never interested me. My mother passed on to me a non-material attitude towards life, so, although I enjoy a good meal and a decent glass of wine, I've always had more money than I could spend. And . . . well, politics bores me. The only thing that really absorbs me is art. Unlike your friend Kim Philby, I'm not ideologically predisposed. Not even vaguely interested.

Present stiffens. Fletcher's interest intensifies. "Whose friend Philby?"

Watkins realizes he's touched a nerve and files the perception to use when the opportunity presents itself. "I was speaking generically about intelligence services. I mean, he was one of yours, wasn't he, before he made the run for Moscow? Or at least you thought so."

"Generically speaking, you're correct," Present agrees.

Then Watkins, seemingly innocent, presses the point. "Surely, Mr. Present, you must have known the man in a professional capacity?"

Present is uneasy. "It appears nobody really knew him."

Watkins keeps on needling: "Not even those who worked closely with him? All the same, an interesting man, don't you think? Surely you must have met him? . . . Wait, it's coming back to me, that chat we had in London. Didn't you tell me —"

"Yes." Present is caught. He can feel Merleau's eyes studying him.

"Right! In person, wasn't it? Not just one of those shake-hands occasions?"

"Yes, I mentioned that I had served with him in Turkey. It was brief . . . a long time ago . . . and —"

"Fascinating," Watkins murmurs sympathetically, and continues in his best professorial tone. "But, of course, that must be a terrible professional burden for you. I mean, here's the most infamous double-crossing agent in the long life of Western intelligence services, and, well, I would have thought anyone who had just shaken his hand even at some distant point in the past would have automatically become suspect, quarantined, and pensioned off. Isn't that how you people do things?"

Watkins finds himself smiling keenly into three taut and serious faces. They each know he is laughing at them, and not one shares his amusement of the moment.

"There is a third entanglement, in addition to the money and ideology," Present whispers hoarsely, "one you have conveniently left out of the equation."

"What could be more powerful than belief in your own righteousness or the greed for gold?" Watkins banters. "It seems to me that the great betrayals of the world have always turned on those two — especially in your occupation."

"Blackmail!" announces Present emphatically. "But we'll return to that in a minute." He smiles thinly as Watkins recoils and a shadow of apprehension crosses his face.

Fletcher steps in again. "Was there anyone else with you when you met with Gribanov, alias Alexei Gorbunov?"

"No. As I explained, he phoned me up at the Lennox and —"

"How did he know where to find you?" Fletcher persists.

"Simple. The last time we met in Moscow I told him where I would be staying in Paris. The Lennox is more or less my home away from home."

But Fletcher is tenacious. "Isn't that rather unusual — that you would leave your address and phone number in Paris with a Soviet government official?"

"Not really. Alexei and I were friends by this time, and . . . I was also encouraged to do so."

"But Mr. Watkins, this is a man you had come to think of as Khrushchev's 'right hand.' Didn't you think it strange that he would suddenly seek you out in Paris."

Watkins is amused at Fletcher's provincialism — the girl from a small western town. But he is not cruel, and replies only, "We held each other in high esteem."

"Who encouraged you to maintain this private and personal level of contact?"

"The minister of external affairs and —"

"And who?"

"Well, your boss, Mr. Present — Williams, the director general of intelligence."

Fletcher collapses in astonishment against the back of her chair. If Merleau is surprised, he doesn't show it. He just continues writing careful notes in the book on his lap. Present carries on with a masklike face, as if he doesn't even notice Fletcher's reaction to Watkins' bombshell. "What did you and Gribanov talk about when you met at the Coq d'Or?" he asks.

"Mostly about the Cuban Missile Crisis. It's all in the report I gave you in London."

"Mr. Present, a moment, please," Fletcher demands.

Present frowns at Fletcher as if her interjections are interrupting the flow of his interrogation, stopping him from gaining any ground in his attempt to corner Watkins. He gets up and gestures to Fletcher that they go to the windows to talk out of earshot.

Watkins watches them. The scene reminds him of the evening in Zelyonny Gai when he toured the garden outside the small hotel with Boris while Anatoly and Natasha whispered in a corner. What were they trying to do? Work out a strategy for making him vulnerable? To whom? He can guess by his captors' body language now what it's all about — Present trying to assert his control; Fletcher insisting she has the authority and the mandate from Williams to participate, but complaining that she hasn't been given the full information. He can see Merleau glancing over his shoulder at the RCMP officials, and for the first time he senses that Merleau is getting fed up. He's beginning to hunch his shoulders — a man of action trapped in a room of talkers. Ah, Watkins understands only too well. What he would give to be sitting right now with a glass of *rouge* in the comfortable, refined ambiance of the Coq d'Or. They used to say that Hemingway wrote there in his Paris days, and Bertrand, behind the bar, claimed that the Coq became the model for the short story "A Clean Well-Lighted Place."

OCTOBER AND NOVEMBER were always magic months in Paris. The tourists were almost all gone. Only the hardiest expatriates, writers, painters, and artists still hung around the bars and cafés to mingle with the tolerant natives of the Left Bank. Many of the artists knew him. He would often drink and talk with them late into the night — marvellous sprawling conversations about music, writing, and film. Visual artists, he had long ago decided, were the best conversationalists. He sometimes bought a painting or a drawing. Not that he had any wall space left to hang his purchases. Most of the time they went into the trunk under his bed in the Lennox. He was happy to give the artists a little something to keep them going. He envied them. He should have investigated that life, given in to that creative side his mother had made him so afraid of exploring. If he had betrayed anyone, he had betrayed himself.

"Greetings, Mr. Ambassador!" Alyosha was suddenly at his side, dressed as usual in one of his dapper dark-blue suits, smiling his pinched smile. It was always so peculiar meeting with Alyosha. No matter how Watkins positioned himself in a bar or on a park bench, he never saw the man coming. The way he sidled up made Watkins think of a garter snake slithering through the long grass behind the barn at the farm in Norval Station. They shook hands, a Canadian diplomat on sick leave and a high-level Russian *apparatchik* in God knows what branch of the Soviet government (certainly one that had nothing to do with the Moscow Academy of History), sitting in a Left Bank bar to share a drink. And just two weeks before, the Western press had painted a terrifying picture of a world unable to pull back from the edge of nuclear self-destruction.

Watkins poured Alyosha a glass of wine. "It's a good thing neither of us believes too strongly in what we read in the papers."

Alyosha lifted his glass. "To Cuba! And a future world without nuclear weapons!"

More partisan to his own profession, Watkins shook his finger at the Russian, clinked his glass against the one extended by Alyosha, and whispered, "To Ambassador Anatoly Dobrynin!"

Alyosha nodded his accord. His grey face showed a little less exhaustion than usual. "And it's my pleasure to tell you our side of the story, seeing that you are such a fan of the diplomatic abilities of our ambassador at a very difficult moment in world history, and knowing that you are really — what do the French say — *un historien manqué*? Yes?"

Alyosha reached into his briefcase for an envelope, broke the seal, and fished out a few pages held together with a large brass paperclip. With a ceremonious flourish he placed them on the worn zinc table top before Watkins. "Voilà! I have brought along a small but special gift for you to read: a copy of Ambassador Dobrynin's cable, written after his final secret meeting with Robert Kennedy, the president's brother." Alyosha couldn't resist teasing him: "Let me know, my dear friend, if you need any help with the Russian."

Watkins was aware of the privilege being extended to him. Almost any historian in the West would probably give his right arm at this particular moment in the Cold War to see this cable. He controlled his excitement by methodically changing to his reading glasses, and then calmly reached across for the document. He skipped the bureaucratic jargon — Cable to the Soviet Foreign Ministry, from Ambassador Dobrynin. 27 October 1962: TOP SECRET. Making Copies Prohibited. Copy No. 4. CIPHERED TELEGRAM — and began to read with astonishment.

Late tonight Robert Kennedy invited me to come to see him. This was the second time. In all, we have met three times in secret. Always we talked alone. Robert Kennedy began: "The Cuban crisis is rapidly becoming more serious. The President has just received a report that an unarmed American plane was shot down while carrying out a reconnaissance flight over Cuba. The U.S. military is demanding that the President arm such planes and respond to fire with fire. The American government will have to do this."

I interrupted Kennedy and asked him, "What right do American planes have to fly over Cuba at all, crudely violating its sovereignty and accepted international norms? How would the United States have reacted if foreign planes had appeared over its territory?"

Kennedy quickly responded: "A resolution of the Organization of American States gives us the right to such overflights."

I told him that the Soviet Union, like all peace-loving countries, resolutely rejects such a "right" or, to be more exact, this kind of true lawlessness, when people who don't like the socio-political situation in a country try to impose their will on it — in this case on Cuba, a small state where the people have established their system themselves through a revolution.

"The OAS resolution is a direct violation of the UN Charter," I added, "and you, as the Attorney General of the United States, the highest American legal authority, should certainly know that." Kennedy said he realized we had different approaches to these problems and it was not likely we could convince each other. But the matter was no longer in these differences, since time was of the essence. "I want," Kennedy stressed, "to lay out the current alarming situation the way the President sees it. He wants Khrushchev to know this. This is the thrust of the situation now."

"Because of the plane that was shot down —"

Watkins breaks off to ask Alyosha, "Dobrynin is here referring again to the U2 spy plane the Cubans shot down over the island?"

"Exactly!" responded Alyosha, refilling their glasses from the carafe. "Please take your time, my friend. You will understand that I cannot let you take this document away with you, but read and ask any questions you like."

"— there is now strong pressure on the President to give an order to respond with fire if fired upon when American reconnaissance planes are flying over Cuba. The United States cannot stop these flights, because they are our only means of getting information about the state of construction of the missile bases in Cuba which we believe pose a very serious threat to our national security. But if we start to fire in response, a chain reaction will be initiated that will be very hard to stop.

"The same holds true in regard to the essence of the issue: the missile bases in Cuba. The American government is determined to get rid of those bases, to the extent, in the extreme case, of bombing them, since, I repeat, they pose a great threat to the security of the United States. But in response to the bombing of these bases, in the course of which Soviet specialists might suffer, the Soviet government will undoubtedly retaliate against us somewhere in Europe. A real war will begin, in which millions of Americans and Russians will die. We want to avoid that outbreak in any way we can; I'm sure that the government of the USSR has the same wish. However, taking time to find an honourable solution is very risky." (Here Robert Kennedy mentioned, as if in passing, that there are many unreasonable U.S. generals and politicians who are "itching for a fight." The situation might get "out of control, with irreversible consequences," were his exact words.)

"Do you believe that Robert Kennedy was really worrying about a coup d'état by the U.S. military against his brother, the president?" Watkins asked Alyosha.

Alyosha spread his hands in front of his small chest. "You mean, was he bluffing? We don't think so. We know that ever since the Bay of Pigs disaster, the president has been very unpopular with his own military."

Watkins put the pages down. "Would it be in the Soviet Union's interest if the U.S. military assassinated John Kennedy?"

"Believe me, Khrushchev would shit his pants if that happened. I know he's a peasant, but he's not stupid. He might even feel a certain sympathy for the president in his struggles with the military. Remember Khrushchev barely escaped an assassination attempt in 1956. The military tried to kill him when the battle cruiser *Red Ukraine* blew up in Sebastopol minutes after Khrushchev had disembarked from what was supposed to be an inspection. No! No! Can you imagine what life would be like with all the Cold War hawks wanting to drop nuclear bombs on the Kremlin and all our cities?"

Watkins had never heard Alyosha speak so openly. Hungry for more, he returned to his reading of the Dobrynin cable.

"In this regard," Robert Kennedy said, "the President considers that a suitable basis for regulating the entire Cuban conflict might be contained in the letter Khrushchev sent on October 26 and the letter in response from the President, which was dispatched today to Khrushchev through the U.S. Embassy in Moscow. The most important thing for us," Kennedy stressed, "is to get as soon as possible the agreement of the Soviet government to halt further work on the construction of the missile bases in Cuba, and adopt measures under international control that would make it impossible to use these weapons. In exchange, the U.S. government is ready, in addition to repealing all conditions of the quarantine, to give the assurances that there will be no invasion of Cuba and that the other countries of the Western Hemisphere are ready to give the same assurances."

"And what about Turkey?" I asked Robert Kennedy.

"What is this business about Turkey?" Watkins interrupted his reading to ask Alyosha.

"This is what really started the whole business — the installation of the missiles in Cuba," Alyosha replied excitedly. "The U.S. military have for the last year been placing nuclear missiles in Turkey and Italy, all pointed at and just minutes away from Moscow. Khrushchev felt the increasing pressure. He complained several times to Kennedy. He was ignored, so he said, 'Okay, if Kennedy doesn't want to take his missiles out of Turkey, I'll put some in his backyard, too.' So he sent them off to Cuba."

Watkins shook his head and went back to the cable.

"If that is the only obstacle to achieving the arms regulation I mentioned earlier, then the President doesn't see any unsurmountable difficulties in resolving this issue," replied Robert Kennedy. "The greatest difficulty for the President is the public discussion of the issue of Turkey. Formally, the deployment of missile bases in Turkey was a unilateral decision by the United Sates. To withdraw missile bases from Turkey would jeopardize the U.S. position as leader of NATO and seriously damage the entire structure of the organization. In short, if such a decision were announced now, it would seriously tear NATO apart.

"However, the President is ready to agree on that question with Khrushchev, too. In order to withdraw these bases from Turkey," Robert Kennedy said, "we need four to five months, taking into account the procedures that exist within the NATO framework. On the whole Turkey issue, if Khrushchev agrees with what I've proposed, we can continue to exchange opinions between him and the President, using me and the Soviet ambassador. However, the President cannot say anything publicly in this regard about Turkey," he repeated. He then warned that his comments about Turkey are extremely confidential; besides him and his brother, only two or three people in Washington are apprised.

"That's all the President asked me to pass on to Khrushchev," Kennedy said in conclusion. "The President also asked Khrushchev to respond (through the Soviet ambassador and me) if possible within twenty-four hours in order to have a businesslike, clear answer in principle. He asked not to get into wordy discussions that might drag things out. The current situation is so serious that, unfortunately, there is very little time to resolve the issue.

Events are developing too quickly. The request for a reply tomorrow is just that — a request, and not an ultimatum. The President hopes that the head of the Soviet government will understand him correctly."

I noted that it went without saying that the Soviet government would not accept any ultimatums and it was good that the American government realized that. I also reminded him of Khrushchev's last letter to the President appealing that he demonstrate state wisdom in resolving this question. Then I told Kennedy that the President's thoughts would be brought to the attention of the head of the Soviet government. I also said that I would contact him as soon as there was a reply. In this regard, Kennedy gave me the number of a direct telephone line to the White House.

I must say that during our meeting, Robert Kennedy was very concerned; in any case, I've never seen him like this before. True, once or twice he tried to return to the topic of "deception" (that he had talked about so persistently during our previous meeting), but he did so only in passing and without any edge. He didn't even try to get into fights on various subjects, as he usually does, and only persistently returned to one topic: time is of the essence and we shouldn't miss the chance. He said that after meeting with me he was immediately going to see the President, with whom he spends almost all his time now.

Watkins put down the pages and drew a deep breath. "Truly staggering."

"Yes," Alyosha agreed, as he carefully returned the pages to a file inside his briefcase. "Dobrynin attached a note saying that previous meetings between him and Kennedy had usually degenerated into shouting matches. During these recent secret meetings the attorney general kept his emotions in check and took the ambassador into his confidence in an attempt to cooperate on the resolution of the crisis."

"If Kennedy hadn't agreed to pull the missiles out of Turkey, would Khrushchev have backed down?"

"Backed down! You're talking like one of these Western tabloid reporters. I sometimes wonder who is brainwashing whom! I mean, the American and European press have never mentioned a word about the removal of missiles from Turkey being part of the U.S. obligation."

Watkins hastily recovered his diplomatic manner. "I mean, when Kennedy agreed not to make the removal of missiles from Cuba an ultimatum, was this the moment of agreement between him and Khrushchev?"

"Yes, of course."

MERLEAU FINALLY BREAKS the silence. "And you reported every word of this meeting in the Coq d'Or to your government?"

"Absolutely," replies Watkins, secretly amused at the effect the information and his account of the meeting have had on these three intelligence officers sitting opposite him.

Merleau turns a questioning face to Present, who nods reluctantly in agreement with what Watkins has said.

"Come now," Watkins smiles, "surely we shouldn't be surprised that governments, especially the most powerful in the world, lie to their own people. We're all in positions to know that it happens every day." He wanders over to the piano and begins to play. The magic notes of Beethoven's Piano Sonata No. 14 fill the suite. Fletcher is in awe as Watkins plays with the skill of a concert pianist. Present and Merleau look uncomfortable and leave the room.

WATKINS IS DEEP into Rachmaninov's Prelude in C-sharp Minor when he becomes aware that Present is standing beside him. He has no idea how long he has been playing. Present has changed his shirt and appears to have taken a shower. Fletcher, too, looks refreshed. These people, Watkins realizes, must have an apartment next door. What had Merleau said? They control the whole floor. He feels indescribably grimy, as if he had been four days on the road through Samarkand without a bath or a decent meal. They are keeping him in this state for a reason.

He gets up from the piano and, before they can speak, he warns them wearily: "I'm feeling very tired. This can't go on much longer. You must tell me what it is you really want from me so we can get this over with." He turns directly to Fletcher: "Did you have my note delivered to the Prime Minister's Office?"

Fletcher glances warily at the others and hesitates. "Yes, I personally double-checked to see that they have received your note to Mr. Pearson."

Merleau smiles quietly to himself. Fletcher can't bear to look at him. Only Present remains impassive, his eyes blank behind his spectacles. He clears his throat. "Why is it you have never married, Mr. Watkins?"

"Instead of a search for the truth, then, the real shit is about to begin."

"It's because you have a basic antipathy toward women, right?" Merleau intrudes.

"Given the option, I would rather spend an hour in the company of an intelligent woman than with most men I know who think of themselves as worldly."

"But that wouldn't include men like Akhundi or Khamal?" Merleau continues in a hard flat voice.

"I refuse to answer your questions until you have the courage to identify yourself as the CIA representative here."

Watkins watches Merleau's body contort with rage. My God! How could *they* know about Akhundi and Khamal? Of course Alyosha knew, but what would he have to gain from telling the CIA and the RCMP?

He laughs out loud and asks Present, "Do you know the Russian joke about Kennedy getting together with Khrushchev at Yalta? No? The Soviet leader takes Kennedy aside and says, 'This KGB business is going to bankrupt us.' The American president agrees. 'I know! I know! The CIA costs more to run than our own government.' Khrushchev had the solution: 'Well, let's get together and pay the same guys once!'"

Only Fletcher allows the trace of a smile to flicker along her lips.

"Gentlemen," Watkins remonstrates, "you're never going to get through life without a sense of irony."

In the cold silence that follows he watches Present, his head down, flipping through the fat file binder in front of him, the pages marked with different-coloured plastic tabs. He leans forward and, before Present can block his view, reads the code name on the file cover: "Operation Rock Bottom."

"Rock Bottom! That's me?" He chuckles. "Now that, for example, I find extremely ironic. Sixty-two years of a personal and professional life reduced to extracts in a security service folder, read back to me in instalments by secret policemen intent on proving — what? Tell me, Mr. Present, you're an educated man, don't you find that more than a little Kafkaesque?"

Merleau restlessly changes his position in his chair. Present, unperturbed, comes right back at Watkins. "I've been through every one of your dispatches and given special attention to the ones you wrote detailing your unofficial contacts with Russians. Not once do you mention Khamal or Akhundi. Why is that?"

Watkins ignores the question. Present waves documents. "I have here dates and locations of these 'unofficial' meetings with these two Soviet agents, especially with Akhundi, a suspected KGB agent. None of these meetings are recorded in your official dispatches."

Watkins sneers at him. "Anybody could make that up, Mr. Present. Where is your proof? Where does it come from — the hearsay of Russian defectors? Or the KGB itself?" Then he smoothly changes directions and rattles on: "You know, when I consider the predicament I presently find myself in, I think that perhaps this interview is a parallel to the Tibetan Book of the Dead — preparation for the interview I will get at the Pearly Gates. St. Peter will be there to greet me. 'So tell me, Mr. Rock Bottom,' he will ask, 'when —"

"Answer the damn question!" Merleau explodes, slamming his hand down on the table, making Fletcher and Present jump.

In the shocked silence that follows, Watkins smiles in triumph. He is winning this battle, he tells himself. Keep in mind those sun-filled spring mornings in Paris you have to look forward to. He finally breaks the tension by addressing Present: "You realize, by allowing the CIA to call the shots, you have set yourself up like any other Third World policeman who works for them — the next inevitable step is electrical torture."

Present is pained. "Please, Mr. Watkins . . . We're Canadians."

"I dunno," is Merleau's laconic intervention. "I think a few volts from a field battery generator could move this whole business along quite nicely."

"I rest my case," Watkins smiles at Present, "— just when you thought I was becoming overly melodramatic."

Unsettled, Present gets up from the table. It's obvious he feels increasingly uncomfortable with Merleau at the interrogation.

"You see," Watkins keeps relentlessly on, "this is the slippery slope, Mr. Director of Counter-Espionage. You start collaborating with the CIA, and you end up doing things not even lawyers can bring themselves to do." He offers a wry smile to Fletcher, who, despite herself, is secretly admiring Watkins' fight.

"Is it any different from collaborating with the KGB and Comrade Gribanov?" Present asks calmly.

"Your characterization of my years of service in the Soviet Union as 'collaboration' is absurd."

"Ah, you're just another of those left-wing intellectuals who can dish it out, but can't take it," Merleau mocks.

Watkins ignores him and continues with his fix on Present. "While you were focused on hunting down every suspected homosexual in the public service, I was initiating contacts in the Soviet Union that led to the sales of enormous quantities of Canadian grain — surplus wheat and barley that was stored at great cost in silos across the country. The Kremlin paid handsomely — and in cash. That money went directly into the pockets of farm families, who in turn invested in this country by buying all manner of goods and services. At any level you want to examine these transactions, they were an incredible breakthrough in the gridlock of the Cold War. I know the trade deals were instrumental in leading to the recent discussions with the Soviets on a nuclear non-proliferation treaty. I feel profoundly privileged to have been in the diplomatic position to seize this opportunity to serve my country. I'm also very proud that the work I did helped to bring about a redistribution of wealth in our society." As Watkins speech grows in emotional intensity, he stands to face Present directly. "Tell me," he challenges the director, "is there anything in your professional life that remotely justifies your calling my work in the Soviet Union a 'collaboration with the KGB'?"

Red-faced, Present for the moment has no response.

Watkins continues to press his advantage. "Did it ever occur to you and your counterparts in the CIA that the greatest counter-espionage coup of all time would be for the KGB, knowing the puritanical thrust that burdens North American society, to get your organizations, as well as the FBI, to spend all your resources in a time-consuming homophobic witch hunt to purge every homosexual, suspected or real, from all levels of the government, based on information planted with Soviet defectors?"

Present picks up the Rock Bottom file and murmurs to Fletcher, "Let's go next door for a moment."

As they pass, Watkins reaches out to tap the thick file binder with his index finger. "All that information on me and still you have no clue about where my loyalties lie? Shame on you, Mr. Present."

"This is not about political loyalties —"

"Oh yes, it is! As in everything to do with politics. Yet you must know by now that I believe that politics can never save us. Not Canada, not the Soviet Union, not even the United States."

"Then what will?"

"Art, Mr. Present, art is the only endeavour that will ultimately save the human race from itself."

Fletcher and Present stare at Watkins, then leave the room. Although exhausted from this marathon chess game, the old ambassador is able to gather his energy and smile at the deserted Merleau with an impassive mask.

"Art never changed a damn thing," Merleau mutters.

"You're right, but as Picasso said, 'It's the lie that shows the way to the truth.'"

"Shit!" Merleau rises in exasperation and also leaves the room.

Alone, except for the guard sitting behind him in the chair by the door, Watkins relaxes with a deep weary sigh and allows his shoulders to sag. He begins to feel despondent. When would Mike return his message? How much longer must he hold out? No, he must guard against these psychological letdowns. As he tries to anticipate their next move, Fletcher re-enters the room by herself and, with trembling fingers, hands him a teletype dispatch. "Mr. Watkins, I'm sorry, but it is my duty to pass this message on to you. It's an official release from External Affairs. As of yesterday, you have been suspended without pay from your post and from the civil service, pending the results of this investigation."

Watkins reads the note carefully and, with a polite smile, hands the paper back to her. He has the impression that she was sent in to do a job and no longer has the stomach for it. "This is just too clumsy, Inspector Fletcher. Things are not done that way in our department. I prefer to wait for my final interview with the minister of external affairs, an honourable man whom I know well. But, nice try."

"I don't blame you for being suspicious. Unfortunately, it is true."

Watkins is not to be convinced. "Were you named Jane after your mother?"

"Yes," she replies distractedly.

"An interesting coincidence. My mother was also called Jane. Of course, it's a common name. Are you close?" he asks, knowing the answer.

"She died when I was born —"

"Ah yes, that's right, twins, aren't you?'

Murray! She suddenly realizes he is trying to tell her he knows Murray — and immediately she leaves Watkins to himself again.

WATKINS HAD NOT INCLUDED in the memo of his meeting with Alyosha the next hour or so of their conversation in the Coq d'Or. They ordered another carafe of wine and Watkins watched his companion idly taking in the passing throngs of Parisians. He had never seen Alyosha in such a mellow mood.

"What do you see in all these idlers, these poets and painters?" Alyosha asked him.

"I admire artists, especially those whose lives seem to be full of rejection, because failure never seems to defeat them."

"And you would excuse all their bad art simply for that reason?"

"Absolutely."

"Why?"

"It's the antithesis of what is known as success in North America. Let me explain. There's a joke in my country: In America, the only important artist worth talking about is the financially successful one. In France, all artists are important. In Britain, there are no important artists. In Canada, an artist still has to explain to people what he does."

Alyosha grinned appreciatively. "In the Soviet Union we guarantee an artist his living. This is why culture is so important —"

"And so bad," chuckled Watkins. "That's why I prefer to buy 'unofficial' art."

Alyosha was greatly condescending. "Yes, we know all about that — the art you buy through your Greek friend in Moscow. We think it's amusing, all that secret activity he goes through to convince you he's selling subversive art. But if you want to waste your money, my friend, it's your own business."

"Well then, what drives you in your life?" Watkins asked.

Alyosha was startled by the question. "Strange, I was just reflecting along the same lines myself. Perhaps it's because today is my fiftieth birthday."

"A good time to pause," Watkins agreed. But he was disappointed by

Alyosha's answer. It was just too ordinary, although he didn't doubt for a moment it was true.

"What has driven me all my life is to try to even things up for the Soviet Union in its struggle with the rest of the world."

"Do you think you have been successful?"

"Only in some small things. To tell you the truth, in my bleakest moments I think we are doomed."

Watkins was surprised. "You are the other superpower in the world! Leaders in the exploration of space —"

"All true, but our people have paid too high a cost for all these achievements. Our internal economic structures cannot support these colossal expenditures on weapons to defend ourselves against the American threat. Look at their aggression in Vietnam, in NATO —"

"Well," Watkins interjected, "we could talk about Hungary, Czechoslovakia, the Warsaw Pact, Cuba."

Alyosha laid a hand gently on his wrist, "Let's not get into that, my friend. It will only lead to another sterile discussion, and this afternoon I'm trying to speak openly with you. Even though Khrushchev is working to open the way to more private production in agriculture, our past farming policies have been irreparable disasters. In so many areas we cannot provide what the people need for minimum comfort, let alone all the basic consumer products you take for granted in the West. We can successfully put astronauts in space, but we can't give the people what they need to live a decent life. I think deep down most of our leaders know this. For a long time they believed that the only question was who would fall apart first. If we could hold on long enough, it would be the United States. Now everyone who thinks about these things knows that our institutions are too inflexible and that one day the house of cards will collapse."

They sipped their wine in thoughtful silence. Finally Watkins turned to the Russian: "Well, Alyosha, you would surely agree that if I were a true believer, I would choose this moment to recruit you as a spy for the West."

Their uproarious laughter attracted the curious stares of others in the bar. Who were these two men, talking in Russian, laughing uninhibitedly, and slapping each other on the shoulders?

"Tell me, Alyosha," Watkins inquired, suddenly serious. "There's something I must ask you about. You remember Dag Hammarskjöld and I were close friends —"

"We had nothing to do with it."

"Then who killed him?"

"We had people on the ground — military advisers. Che Guevara was also there with his Cuban detachment, fighting with Lumumba's lieutenant, Laurent Kabila. From everything we can piece together, we think the British mercenaries fighting for Tshombe to establish the breakaway province of Katanga fired the missile that brought down Dag Hammerskjöld's plane."

"But why the British?"

"The British mercenaries under . . . what was his name . . . Mad Mike?"

"Colonel Michael Hoare."

"Yes, that's him. He and his white mercenaries were fighting for Katanga and were being supplied by the British MI6 and the CIA. We think that Hoare did it as a favour to the CIA. Or, since Hoare had worked for the CIA before and also as a mercenary for South Africa's intelligence services, he might have done it directly at either of their requests. You know that, at the same time, someone in the U.S. government had described Hammarskjöld as a 'potential communist,' and Hoare might even have done it to obtain favours from the Americans in the future."

"But it wasn't a fight against communism."

"No, of course not. It was all about mining. The Americans, British, and Belgians were all squabbling to get hold of Katanga. The place is so rich in minerals. Purest uranium in the world. The uranium for the atomic bombs the Americans dropped on Hiroshima and Nagasaki came from that part of the Congo."

"I didn't know that. I wonder if Dag knew."

Watkins sat quietly for a few moments, draining his wine glass.

Ten minutes later, they paid the cheque, left the Coq d'Or, and strolled with their arms around each other's shoulders into the fading November afternoon. Watkins asked his companion: "Why did you show me the Dobrynin cable this afternoon? You know that I will have to report back the content of our conversation to External Affairs."

"Of course, of course! Why? Well, because, my friend, we have done some good things together. Look at those grain contracts, for example. Your farmers made money and my people didn't go hungry. This would never have happened if we hadn't pushed our timid ministers to take the political risks to meet and sign trade deals. And . . ."

"And what?" Watkins prompted.

"I know that you are well placed in External Affairs and that your opinions about policy, especially how it affects us vis-à-vis the Americans, are respected. When you return to Ottawa, I want you to see what you can do in the cause of mutual cooperation between our two countries to make life easier for our ambassador, Dmitri Chuvakhin."

So there it was, thought Watkins. Nothing is free in the Cold War. They had reached the Seine. The weather was unseasonably mild for November. Coats open, they leaned their elbows on the parapet and stared down at a young woman in a white racing scull, cutting through the trails of mist that hung above the surface of the dark river. Behind her on the other side of the river were the dim outlines of a barge. Watkins was reminded of a Degas sketch.

"Alyosha, the writing is on the wall. When I go back I will be urged to take early retirement."

He expected Alyosha to be shocked and disappointed, but, if anything, he was surprisingly grave and thoughtful. "Don't tell me it is because of Khamal?"

"Only if you have told them," Watkins chuckled. "No, it's my health. My heart is not what it used to be. I can't put in the hours that the job demands. I have to take sick leave too often."

"I think most of the members of the Politburo are on some sort of heart medication, but still put in the long days."

"Probably so. That's likely true in most governments around the world. But with me it doesn't stop there. I know what has to be done, but for some reason I can no longer bring myself to do it. I think this reaction is some kind of weariness of the soul."

Alyosha solicitously put a hand on his shoulder. "I'm sorry that your career should end so soon and in this way. Together you and I have made a real difference through our diplomatic relationships with the rest of the world. Perhaps in your retirement you will find a new energy for life."

"I hope so." Watkins decided he would never get another chance like this to ask. "What will happen to Khamal? You know he wants to get out?"

Alyosha's face closed. "I will see what I can do."

"It was you who got him out to Oslo that time, wasn't it, Alyosha? I thank you for that."

"Ambassador Watkins, I think of us as friends more than simply diplomatic colleagues. Don't be foolish about Khamal. He is a superficial young man and also an aggressive opportunist."

Watkins smiled sadly. "Yes, I know that. He has all the best and worst qualities you could hope to find, but compressed in one personality. Have you ever known anyone like that?"

"Of course. She's the love of my life."

Watkins laughed, delighted.

"Somehow I don't think you will report this part of our conversation to your ministry," Alyosha observed wryly.

They both chuckled and straightened up from the wall to shake hands in farewell. But Alyosha reached past his hand to give Watkins a bear-like embrace and then kissed him on both cheeks.

Watkins asked innocently. "For more than six years, Alexei Gorbunov, I have known you by your nickname 'Alyosha.' So tell me now, for we will probably never see each other again, what is your true name?"

He held Watkins for a moment and whispered in his ear. "My friend, besides you there is only one other from the West who knows me as Zoltan. If you should ever be in the same room and this person refers to Alexei Gorbunov as Zoltan, be very careful what you say."

Then, giving Watkins one last pat on the shoulders, the Russian energetically turned away. With a spring in his step and his black briefcase swinging playfully at his side, he walked off into the late afternoon gloom. What other state secrets were in that worn leather bag besides the Dobrynin cable? Watkins wondered.

AGAIN IT IS FLETCHER who breaks the silence in his Ritz prison suite. "When did you find out that Alexei Gorbunov was not a diplomat with the Soviet Foreign Ministry who taught occasionally at the Moscow Academy of History, but really Oleg Gribanov, KGB colonel?"

"When Mr. Present informed me. I think it was during the first of our conversations when he came to speak with me in Paris."

Present nods, lost in deep thought. He lifts his head up, his eyes still distant behind the thick lenses of his eyeglasses. "And what is it in detail that Zoltan asked you to do for Ambassador Dmitri Chuvakhin?"

Watkins feels a shiver run down his spine. "Zoltan?" he asks, puzzled. "Who is Zoltan?"

Both Merleau and Fletcher are staring at the seemingly perplexed Present. Fletcher prompts him again, "You referred to Oleg Gribanov as 'Zoltan'?"

"Ah, did I? An unconscious slip. It's just a code name I use for him in my files . . . just a memory aid. Nothing more . . ."

Watkins needs to buy some time. "I feel exhausted. I must lie down for a while."

"Yes, of course. Let's all take a break." Present is quick to release him from the questioning. "What can we get to make you comfortable? It's almost noon. Some lunch? Are you hungry?"

Watkins is dazed. "No, no, I just want to rest quietly for a bit.

SATURDAY, 11:15 A.M. Flat grey taste of exhaustion in his mouth, eyelids dry from lack of sleep, but a twitchy buzz of adrenaline zipping through his mind and body. No turning back now. This could only go two ways, and, with one, there's no possibility ever of rehabilitation in External Affairs. Murray watches the small man in his sixties with the deeply lined face and horn-rimmed glasses, nattily turned out in a very English khaki raincoat, get his coffee and doughnut at the counter and carefully thread his way through the pink and yellow plastic tables until he finds a place away from the few other clients in the Donut Shop — taxi drivers and workmen in overalls. Murray waits as the man settles down to what must be an often practised ritual: first he balances a worn leather briefcase on the chair next to him, then removes his raincoat and tidily folds it on top of the briefcase, and finally opens the *Times Literary Supplement*, which he begins to peruse with the aid of a magnifying loupe attached to a black cord pinned somewhere inside his jacket. Only then does Murray make his move.

"Mr. Banks?"

Startled, the older man glances up at Murray over the top of his glasses. "Yes," he answered in an anxious way, searching Murray's face for a clue of recognition.

"You don't know me, sir. And I apologize that I'm not able to give you my name — at least not immediately —"

"Are you asking for money?" He holds the coffee mug frozen halfway to his lips.

"No, sir." Murray smiles reassuringly. "It's not about money. It's about a very sensitive matter that involves an old friend of yours —" he can see the alarm intensifying in the eyes that are strangely enlarged by the thick lenses "— Ambassador John Watkins."

He watches the apprehension in the magnified eyes turn rapidly into fear. Banks lowers the coffee mug and shakily returns it to the table beside the chocolate doughnut marked by a single bite.

"He's in a very difficult situation and needs your help, sir."

Without a word Banks springs to his feet, grabs nervously for his raincoat, and hurriedly pulls it over his tweed jacket, tangling the sleeves. Murray reaches out to assist the older man, but Banks shrinks away from him, stumbles backward a few steps, and falls up against the plate-glass window, his coat all awry around his shoulders and an expression of sheer panic on his face. Murray glances anxiously around the shop. The other customers are staring at him and the young woman in the orange and pink uniform behind the counter calls out to a man working in the kitchen.

Murray rushes to explain. "I understand you have known John Watkins for a long time and, as a friend —"

But Banks, without a word, pushes his way past Murray and hurries to the door. He is almost at the glass door when he remembers his briefcase and dashes back for it. Murray follows at his heels. "If, at least, you could phone Mr. Pearson and let him know —"

Banks pushes through the door and flags an approaching taxi.

"Someone has to tell the prime minister. He must be informed that your old friend John Watkins is being held by the Mounties in a safe house, a floor they control in the Ritz Hotel in Montreal —"

The taxi pulls up and the still silent Banks, head down, reaches to open the door. Murray realizes that his own hand has moved out to gently restrain the older man's agitated flight. "You must understand, sir. It's a setup and they're using Watkins' homosexuality to try to pin —"

But Banks shakes him off and dives inside the cab, slamming the door behind him. Murray watches the cab pull away in the direction of the Glebe. He hears his father's voice, "Too many men grow old and scared."

5

FLETCHER CLOSES the apartment door behind her, walks ten paces down the hotel corridor, takes a deep breath, and opens the door to the next suite, which has been converted into an office with desks, phones, and filing cabinets.

In the outer office, two uniformed officers are focused on a television screen: news footage of Queen Elizabeth and Premier Jean Lesage leaving the Quebec legislature in a motorcade; separatistes marching up and down, chanting slogans; men in uniform; demonstrators; riot sticks. The police turn their anger on the journalists, beating the reporters with cameras to the ground . . . Startled at the sight of Fletcher, the officers scramble to their feet.

"Turn that off," she says peremptorily. "One of you relieve Fitzpatrick, who is in there with Mr. Watkins. And the other go pick up some food for the gentlemen. Fitzpatrick has the order."

"Right away, Inspector."

Behind them in an inner office that was formerly the bedroom, Present and Merleau break off from a secretive conversation to look at her briefly, then return to their intense discussion. "Mr. Merleau," she interrupts, "I would like to speak alone with Mr. Present."

"Let us finish this, will you?" Merleau responds, annoyed.

"No," says Fletcher, "it can't wait."

Merleau snorts in disgust. "Mickey Mouse warned me there would be days like this. Why can't you —" he breaks off at the mean look in Fletcher's eyes. "Okay, okay, I'll get a breath of fresh air."

"Well, don't go too far, Mr. Merleau. I have a feeling we're going to be able to wrap this up very quickly."

He stares at her, shrugs, and leaves the office. Present sits down wearily in a bizarre apparatus that has been built around a wheelchair.

"What on earth is that?" Fletcher asks.

"Oh, it's . . . it's something close to a lie-detector machine?"

"Don't tell me! I've heard rumours about this monstrosity . . . this is the 'fruit machine,' right? . . . but I just couldn't believe it really exists."

Present squirms. "Thousands of dollars have gone into the research and construction of this machine under one of Canada's leading psychiatrists. We're going to use it."

"Not on Watkins?"

"Certainly!"

"That's insane and depraved."

"It's just an extension of the idea behind the lie-detector machine."

"Then the psychiatrist who designed it used science to degrade men."

"The funds for the research and construction of this machine were signed by the solicitor general himself."

"Present, why have you lied to me at every step of this operation?"

"You were informed only on a need-to-know basis. C'mon, Fletcher, you've been around for a while. You know what the procedures are and how I have to use them. We're not handling break-and-entry cases here."

"What do you want out of this interrogation?"

"A signed confession, that's all."

"That Watkins admits to what?"

"That he acted as an agent of influence for the Soviet government."

"There's no evidence."

"We have evidence that Watkins fell into a homosexual sex trap set by the KGB."

"You and Merleau and the CIA may have evidence, but *we*, the RCMP Security Services, don't have the proof. So if you have it, now is the time to tell me.

"The CIA has shown me testimony from two witnesses."

"Testimony isn't necessarily evidence."

"The information comes from two separate sources whose previous information has led to the identification of several possible moles."

"Several possible moles! This is smoke and mirrors, David —"

"No!"

They both turn to see that Merleau has re-entered the office to get his raincoat, which he takes off the rack behind the inner office doors as he speaks. "These two sources formerly worked in the KGB's Moscow Central. Their information has shown us how intelligence organizations in the West have all become totally paralyzed by KGB infiltration. This case is definitely not smoke and mirrors."

"So we are talking about Soviet defectors?"

"Yes."

"Recent?"

"Within the last eighteen months."

"Are you going to tell me who they are?"

Present glances at Merleau, who shakes his head.

Fletcher smiles mockingly. "So let's take a legal look at this. Here we are detaining a Canadian ambassador against his will — he has asked repeatedly to be allowed to leave — on the basis of information provided by two unidentified Soviet defectors whose testimony comes to us from the CIA, but which we can't verify for ourselves."

"He'll confess," Present asserts.

"And if Watkins denies everything, none of this will stand up legally."

"Your local legal problems are no concern of mine," shrugs Merleau as he pulls on his raincoat.

Fletcher ignores the CIA officer and turns back to Present. "David, did you ever cross-examine these two so-called KGB sources?"

"I went to CIA headquarters in Langley. I went over the information in great detail with the interrogating officers."

"That's not what I asked."

"Did I get to ask question directly of the two defectors? No. The CIA refused to let me have a direct interview."

"Did they identify Watkins directly by name?"

"One couldn't. The other did by implication."

"What does that mean?"

"The second defector is identified as having worked in Moscow Central and knew about the sex traps run by Oleg Gribanov."

"Did he work for Gribanov in his department?"

"No. In some parallel operation."

"Then," demands Fletcher, "we'll have to get him up here to ID Watkins."

Merleau throws up his hands in disgust. "Angleton will never go for it. The logistics would be . . ."

"Why? Are you holding this Soviet defector in irons?"

"This guy is still being debriefed by counter-espionage. They're not going to let him be moved — not at this stage in the game."

Fletcher is fuming. "You guys in intelligence! You couldn't even run a simple B-and-E bust."

"I'm heading over to the consulate," Merleau retorts. "I'll be back in an hour." He turns his back on them and exits the office, leaving the two Canadians staring after him.

"Arrogant little prick!" swears Fletcher, and turns on Present, slumped over in the absurd contraption. She wheels over an office chair and sits opposite him. "Okay, David, come clean."

"THAT'S IT, THAT'S EVERYTHING?" Fletcher asks.

Present nods slowly.

"That's all you have?"

Present nods again.

"Then we're really in trouble."

Present heaves the massive Rock Bottom file against the wall. The binder breaks loose and the pages flutter all over the office. He turns on Fletcher: "This is all your stupid fault!"

"Mine?"

"If you weren't so blinded by your own ambition and didn't have your brother to feed you information, we wouldn't be in this disaster."

"Wait a minute now —"

"I never wanted or intended to act on this CIA information. If you think Merleau is arrogant, then you should meet his boss, James Jesus Angleton, head of counter-espionage. He talks only to God. All their information is contaminated by their prejudices —"

"So why did you even —"

"I did my interviews with Watkins in Europe. I took him over for a briefing with MI5 in England. They cleared him. I talked him into coming back to Canada for the sake of appearances. I wanted to let it go at that. We had a deal with External. They even sent your brother from the security branch to give Watkins a message that if he made a run for it, nobody would stop him. But, instead, your brother tipped you off, and you got the idea that to arrest Watkins would be a huge coup and give you a leg up in your career. And now we're in this mess."

Fletcher rises, engrossed in thought, her hand to her mouth. "No. My brother didn't tip me off that Watkins was making a run for it."

"You expect me to believe that? He was the one who knew."

"Murray warned me to get out of the situation long before Friday night. The tip that Watkins had left the hotel came from the doorman, Bruno. I tried to find you, but you were lying low . . . Now I understand why. So I made phone calls. I had to go over your head — I would never have made the arrest without authority. I was ordered to bring Watkins in."

"You were *ordered* to pick up Watkins?"

"Exactly — but you'll have to figure out who gave the order."

Ashen, Present looks like a trapped man. Then he slowly pulls himself together as a plan shapes up in his mind.

"What are you going to do now?" she asks.

"Just watch —" he threatens, struggling out of the cumbersome chair.

"No!" And she pushes him back down again. "We're both in this mess together. You better put your cards on the table because this time I want to play with a full deck."

"All right . . . I believe the ambassador was caught in a sex trap and was then blackmailed by the KGB to write pro-Soviet reports."

"Good God, man, that's the stupid CIA line. Are still going to stick with that?"

"You saw those dispatches — 'An opportunity to break the icy grip of the Cold War!'"

Fletcher laughs out loud in derision. "You know what? That analysis makes perfect sense to me — and I think we blew it. From just the little bit we know now, nobody wanted the Soviet Union to be allowed to change — especially the Americans."

"Come on, it takes two to tango."

"Of course, and the American military and the CIA kept the pressure on Khrushchev and his group, who were trying to reform communism, until they finally had to backtrack and give in to their own hardliners. Those are the only guys the hawks in the United States wanted to dance with. They wouldn't allow the Soviets to maintain a more flexible position internationally."

"That's too simplistic."

"Sure, there's a lot more to it. Left to themselves, their centralized economy is falling apart anyway, but I'm talking strictly at the level of international diplomacy. If Kennedy hadn't kept stacking missiles in Germany, Turkey, and Greece, right on the Soviets' doorstep, would the Cuban Missile Crisis ever have happened? Would Hungary have happened?"

"Yeah, well, what if my grandmother was a bus?"

Merleau returns to the outer office and, unknown to Present and Fletcher, sits down to hear their heated voices.

"No, David. This is the time to think clearly. You just told me those guys like Angleton and Merleau can't tell the difference between communism and social democracy, so don't fall into the same stupid rigidity. What's more, Watkins knows we blew it. If you read between the lines of the dispatches he sent from Moscow, he's absolutely right in what he implies: the Americans didn't want a change in the status quo and still don't. There are too many powerful people with vested interests, political and financial."

"Perhaps this could lead to an interesting political discussion," Present sulks, "but it's not what we need right now."

"David, let me suggest a simple solution. Why not drive Watkins to the airport, put him on the first plane to Paris, and send him on his way?"

"But you told me you were ordered to stop Watkins and bring him back here."

"Yes, I was. But you weren't — and you have the authority to turn him loose." As Present seems to waver, Fletcher continues: "Think about it. From here on only three things can happen: one, he will sign a confession that he is or was an agent of influence — and that's hardly likely, given the way he's defended himself so far; two, we just let him go; three, he has a heart attack at any moment."

Present gets to his feet and scrounges around the room collecting the scattered papers from the Rock Bottom file. "Thank you, Inspector Fletcher. This discussion was very useful. Now, let's go back in there and try to get that signed confession."

"Oh, so your first priority is to protect your ass with the CIA? What have they got on you?"

Present smiles grimly: "Nothing that I can't handle." He moves to the door, stops, and raises a silencing hand to Fletcher. She misses the cue.

"Okay, David. Have it your own way. But there's one thing you need to know —"

"Ready, Mr. Merleau?" Present interrupts her.

They both consider Merleau impassively. They have no idea how long he has been sitting there or how much he has heard. Fletcher has never seen Present so nervous. She can smell the sweat break out on him — the odour of fear a man gives off just as you are about to arrest him.

Merleau nods without speaking and leads the way out of the office and down the corridor to the apartment that holds Watkins. Fletcher leans over to whisper in Present's ear: "What you need to know is —"

"Not now, Inspector! Not now!" Present stumbles as they enter the apartment, and she can see that his normally pale face is even whiter now. She nods and takes her position at the table.

"How are you, Mr. Watkins?" she asks cheerfully.

Watkins has washed and changed his shirt. He looks confident and refreshed. "Looking forward to getting this over, Inspector."

Present sits down beside her. All eyes are on his shaking hands as he tries to calm himself, fastidiously organizing the files and objects on the table so they are all neatly lined up with each other.

Merelau clears his throat and, with a sly smile, produces a telex file from the inside of his pocket, along with a folded wire photo. "I think I have something that will help us all move along." He lays out the telex in front of Watkins, who watches warily. "While I was at the consulate I took this off the wire. Our SDECE colleagues in France regret to inform us that the young man by the name of Khamal apparently killed himself two hours ago."

"No," Watkins gasps. Merleau folds opens the page in front of the ambassador to show the blurred distorted face of a young man with a cloth wrapped tightly around his neck. "Apparently he hanged himself in his cell with a scarf."

Silently Watkins buries his head down in his arms on the table.

"Fortunately," Merleau continues relentlessly, "before he was taken to his cell, he signed a full confession and —"

"Mr. Merleau! Why didn't you discuss this —" Fletcher tries to interrupt.

"— he admitted that he worked closely for the KGB," Merleau, his voice rising, shouts over her protests. "He agreed to cooperate with them by meeting Ambassador Watkins in several locations for sexual assignations where cameras had been installed so that pictures of the sexual activity between them could be filmed. He also left a suicide note in his cell, saying that he refused to be returned to the Soviet Union."

Merleau jumps to his feet and bellows down at the slumped-over figure: "Mr. Watkins, do you still insist that you were not blackmailed by the KGB officer, Colonel Oleg Gribanov, after he showed you the evidence of these photographs?"

Enraged, Watkins struggles to glare up at Merleau. "No, he wouldn't have commited suicide. He could have returned without problems to the Soviet Union. You and your kind killed him."

Merleau pulls another piece of paper from his pocket and thrusts it in Watkins' face. "This is the phone number that was on the Players pack you tried to throw away. It led SDECE to a Paris hotel where you had booked rooms for you and Khamal."

Fletcher tries to pull Merleau away from the incensed Watkins, but Merleau pushes her off. For a moment it looks as thought they might all come to blows. Present intercedes by laying a calming hand on Merleau's arm. "Come, we must discuss this development in the office."

Merleau pulls his arm away in disgust and continues to yell at Watkins: "We have the photographs with you and your boyfriend, Watkins. We have the evidence. You're cooked. Better start cooperating right now."

"Then show me the photos," Watkins fights back.

Merleau drops his eyes and allows himself to be led from the room by Present.

"You see," Watkins yells after them, "I know you're bluffing."

As soon as they are in the office, Fletcher wants to know: "Well, do you have the photographs?"

Merleau remains silent.

"Mr. Merleau, do you have the photographic evidence that clearly shows Ambassador Watkins having sex with the Soviet citizen Khamal?"

"I'm not dealing with you anymore. I heard you tell Present to throw in the towel."

"Be careful, Mr. Merleau. I'm the ranking RCMP officer on this investigation. I have full responsibility and authority from my DGI and, if you refuse to do business with me, I will have you escorted from this building and demand a more reasonable CIA liaison officer."

Merleau looks at Present, who nods. "She can do it."

Merleau draws a deep breath. "We have a KGB source who has seen the photos."

Fletcher can't keep the sarcasm out of her voice. "He *says* he has seen the photos. But they are not in the CIA's possession, and no ranking CIA officer has seen any evidence?"

"This source has never been wrong about anything."

"But you don't have the smoking gun?"

"Dammit! When do you ever find the smoking gun, Inspector?

Besides," Merleau adds with extreme exasperation, "Watkins is not important in any of this."

"Careful," Present warns him.

Fletcher can feel the river rushing towards her. Focus, she tells herself.
Don't get into that space with Present. He's about to cave in to all the
events that are spinning out of control. One step at a time. Keep asking
all the vital questions.

"Is the man Khamal really dead, or was that a trick to confuse
Watkins?"

"He died in his cell."

"So the confession is worthless."

Merleau shrugs. "Those SDECE guys know how to get the job done."

They hear Present grunting and groaning behind them as he doggedly
manoeuvres the clumsy fruit machine out of the office.

"We have to start at square one," Present explains. "First we have to
prove that Watkins is a homosexual."

"This is barbaric," Fletcher protests.

"You're clutching at straws," scoffs Merleau.

"If you don't want to come along, then stay here," Present replies.

Fletcher shrugs, but before following Present, she asks Merleau: "What
exactly did you mean that the ambassador is not important?"

"Nothing really. Just that his days are over. That's all."

Fletcher knows he is lying and goes after Present, arguing with him
as he pushes the wheelchair along the corridor: "You're trying to use
Watkins as a fall guy — to get yourself off the hook with the CIA."

Present pays no attention as he struggles with the chair. It's difficult
to steer and keeps knocking up against the walls.

"Everybody knows," continues Fletcher, "that your competence is suspect after so many of your cases have gone sour." But Present appears to
have tuned her out. She tries harder to sting him: "Under your supervi-
sion, the RCMP Security Services haven't caught one spy in fifteen years."

"That's not true."

"Name me one spy who wasn't a walk-in?"

"We . . . we've had major problems with a lack of trained personnel.
The Force refuses to accept civilians. All we have is paramilitary people

like you who cannot think outside the tunnel vision created by the RCMP command structure and —"

Present breaks off. The uniformed officer opens the door and takes over the chair to wheel it into the living room.

Music fills the apartment, Watkins is seated at the piano playing a haunting Scarlatti sonata. Fletcher marvels at the man's strength of mind. Even Present hesitates, caught by the music and the ambassador's obvious talent, before he finally calls out, "Mr. Watkins! Please?"

Watkins breaks off and, after a moment, slowly turns on the piano stool to regard them curiously as they stand beside the chair. "Is this your idea of comic relief, Mr. Present?" he asks. "Somehow I think it's poor fare in return for that farewell dinner I treated you to at DeLuca's."

Fletcher clutches Present's sleeve, drags him away from the chair, and guides him into a corner of the apartment. Watkins watches them with sardonic amusement. He could just as well be watching Anatoly and Volodya at the villa in Bolyshevo, fumbling around to keep him occupied while they waited for Alyosha to show up. So much of his life has turned on the indecision of klutzy amateurs. Ah, Khamal, what have I done to you? Did you really hang yourself? No, I can't accept that yet, not in these circumstances. Soon they'll want me to sign something, and this talk of your suicide is only pressure to make me do so. We live and die by the stupidity of others . . . At least, he thought nostalgically, watching Present and Fletcher arguing vehemently in the corner, the Russians had been more amusing company.

"IT WAS UNFORGIVABLE," apologized Alyosha. "We got too drunk and noisy, singing and dancing as if we were out for a weekend at a country dacha."

Watkins was amused. "Well, I am the ambassador and it is my embassy, so I don't think you have much to worry about. Personally, I thought everyone had a good time."

"All the same, I wouldn't let Volodya come this evening —"

"It's true," nodded Anatoly. "Alexei kicked him out of the car on the way over."

"Yes, that was terrible, falling asleep dead drunk in the middle of the carpet after doing his ridiculous folk dance," Alyosha agreed. "He's really a nice man, but when he gets a few vodkas inside him . . ."

"I thought he danced . . . well . . . with a lot of passion," said Watkins.

"No, I must apologize for Volodya. Ambassador Watkins, you are a generous man, but you must never invite him again to the embassy," warned Alyosha.

"It was really all right. He did no harm."

"But I'm worried because we stayed so late and made so much noise. We might have disturbed your staff and embarrassed you."

"Nonsense," laughed Watkins. "If the others hadn't been so busy that evening, I would have asked them to join us. They would have been happy to meet more Russians."

Watkins never ceased to be surprised how close to the surface all the Russians' insecurities lay. "Of course, they could have objected if they had wanted to, but it's no secret. I've never hidden from External Affairs that I made a few Russian friends during my first posting in Moscow, and that I've made several more this time. Why should I? We all welcome the chance to get to know more Soviet intellectuals. My minister encourages the practice."

Alyosha relaxed his shoulders, settled back in his chair, and grinned. "Intellectuals! I'm happy to hear that. You know that we're required to ask that now — it's part of the new program of development and self-criticism."

Watkins was puzzled. "You've lost me."

"Soviet officials must now ask foreigners with whom they come into contact what it is they do not like in the Soviet Union," Anatoly explained.

Watkins chuckled as he recalled a young Red Army officer he had met in Gorky Park a few nights before who wanted to practise his English. "What is it you object to?" the officer had murmured. At the time he had thought it was just stilted English getting in the path of seduction, unaware he was part of a huge political social experiment.

"You see," Alyosha turned to Anatoly, "the ambassador is laughing at us. There is really no need for this Cold War business."

"Ah no, Comrade. The *business* is very important."

Alyosha persisted. "But Mr. Ambassador, for the future you must remember to tell me your criticisms."

"Well, perhaps another time, but right now I'm enjoying this meal you have invited me to. And in the West it's considered extremely bad form to complain to your host."

"I like that," Alyosha grinned. "I think this is a custom all Russians should adopt."

"But if you have any complaints in the future," Anatoly, the officious flunky chimed in, "you must take them to Alexei."

"Why *must* I take them to Alexei?"

"Because, my dear friend, our Alexei can take them all the way to the top."

"The top top?" Watkins teased, remembering their conversation about Peter of the top-top desk in the Kremlin."

"The top-top top!" Anatoly reiterated, without any flicker of a smile.

"To Khrushchev himself?"

"Of course, Mr. Ambassador."

Alyosha told Anatoly to shut up, but he said it good-naturedly, as if he really hadn't minded. On the contrary, he had wanted Watkins to know how much influence he had. And, indeed, Watkins felt a thrill of deep satisfaction.

"Don't do this, David, it will end badly," Fletcher warns. But Present is determined. His thin lips contract into a grim straight line. "You are trying to focus on one ludicrous bureaucratic detail, in the hope it will rescue this operation from disaster."

"Are you after my job, Fletcher?"

"No, most definitely not. But let me remind you again, David, that although officially you are in charge of the interrogation, you're still a civilian employee of the security services, not a career officer like —"

"Yourself? . . . I know, Inspector Fletcher," he snarls, "that you can pull down all the administrative powers from above."

"And I just might do that if you don't back off on using this ridiculous machine."

"No, you're not going to do that." Present is so quietly confident that, despite herself, she is curious.

"Oh no, and why not?"

"Because the only way you can really stop me is to ask the DGI to halt the whole investigation. And you're not going to bring down the big guns for this — at least, not yet."

"What is this, Present, some kind of macho poker game?"

"Perhaps, but you do also know that, for some reason, the DGI wants Watkins here and —"

"Yes, it was Williams who instructed me to detain the ambassador. But did you ever stop to think that he may not give a damn about what finally happens to Watkins? If that's true, then what is it the DGI wants out of all this?"

Present seems to waver for a moment, then asks, politely: "Did you ever get it in writing?"

"What?"

"The DGI's order to hold Watkins?"

Fletcher feels the cold river pulling her under. "You know there wasn't time . . . everything was done over the phone."

"Yes, the DGI did mention that."

"You've already spoken to him about all this?" she gasps.

"Oh, yes."

PRESENT STARED BACK as Williams studied him through the smoke curling into the heavy-lidded eyes. The gravelly voice whispered through vocal cords wrecked by a lifetime of chain smoking: "I don't see what you're so upset about, Present."

"I think this interrogation, under these circumstances, is a mistake."

"So, what do you suggest?"

"I think we should drive the ambassador to the airport — tonight. Let him retire in peace."

"Tell me why?"

"First, because he's a very sick man. I don't think he can take much more of this kind of interrogation. If he dies on us it will —"

"If the ambassador has information, that's not really an excuse. You had no qualms when you interrogated him for a month over in Europe."

"Yes . . . but that was different. We met at two in the afternoon. We strolled around Paris, took leisurely excursions to see cathedrals — the ambassador loves cathedrals."

"No wonder you never got anything out of him. Sounds like it was a bloody vacation. Perhaps the man played you for a fool?"

"Sir, we already know everything there is to know about Ambassador Watkins."

"That's a bold statement from a man with a long line of dud cases on his record."

Present winced at the brutal slap. "There will be serious problems if the ambassador dies on our hands."

The DGI lit another cigarette from the tip of the one he was finishing, examined the glowing butt in the half darkness of his secluded office, and reached across the desk to crush it into an overflowing ashtray that was closer to Present than to him. His eyes watered from the layers of smoke and ash that clouded the claustrophobic room, its drapes permanently drawn against the windows.

"You're confusing me, Present. At first you pestered me to let you go to France to interview Watkins. Then it was your idea to bring him back, and now you want to let him go again."

"I brought him back to meet the demands of the CIA, but —"

"Present, for ten years I've given you a free hand. Your budget has mushroomed exponentially each year. I've allowed you to reorganize the whole counter-espionage operation from top to bottom. I let you personally recruit and build the Watcher Service. You are our man against the KGB — yet in all that time there have been no results. Absolute zero!"

"There are some —"

Williams held up a hand. "When I go to the CIA headquarters I have to listen to shit from that bastard Angleton, telling me that the RCMP has been completely and effectively paralyzed as an intelligence organization."

"That's not true, sir —"

"And that our lack of results make it very difficult for the CIA to justify continuing to share intelligence with us according to the first-country treaties we, as allies, signed after the war. You must acknowledge, Present, that the situation is extremely serious. Angleton has already made a recommendation of non-sharing to the Senate Intelligence Oversight Committee in Washington."

"That's arbitrary for —"

"Angleton's analysis is that we have been penetrated by a mole. You have intimate knowledge of every single operation that has been mounted, am I right?"

"Yes, sir."

Williams hunched his great bulk across the desk, ground out the cigarette butt furiously in the filthy ashtray, and lit yet another in a burst that momentarily illuminated his pock-marked skin. "Could a mole function in the RCMP counter-espionage branch without your knowledge, Present?"

Present coughed to clear his throat, but was seized by a fit of hacking. "As soon as this Watkins business is over," he sputtered, "I will conduct a personal review of all the cases on file. We may find —"

"For his own reasons, Mr. Angleton has decided to give us a last chance. He informs me that, as we speak, a coup that has everyone in Washington very nervous is taking place in the Kremlin."

"A coup?" Present was visibly shaken.

"Yes, all the NATO bases are on red alert. The Pentagon is on emergency readiness. Nobody knows which way this is going to bounce."

"Does Angleton have any details about who is leading the coup?"

"He has chosen to tell us lowly Canadians only that the Central Committee of the Soviet government is trying to force Khrushchev to resign. Khrushchev refuses. Our latest information is that he has barricaded himself in his dacha outside Moscow, where he is fighting a desperate battle to pull together some support from other sectors of the Politburo. He is apparently losing out, and it's only a matter of time before they kill him — probably. They'll call it suicide. We have no idea who is going to replace him, or what their policies towards the Western allies will be."

Williams watched Present very carefully as he absorbed this information.

"Excuse me, sir, fascinating as all this information certainly is, how does it bear on the ambassador's case?"

Williams inhaled deeply and let the smoke drift through the yellow teeth of his half-open mouth. "Wait a couple of days. Keep on at Watkins, but keep him alive."

"Why, sir?"

"Because it seems Watkins' friend Oleg Mikhailovich Gribanov, alias Alexei Gorbunov, formerly Khrushchev's trusted right-hand man and, as you know, the second-highest official in the KGB's Second Directorate, has assisted in Khrushchev's fall from grace. I'm sure the slippery Oleg is now fighting for his life. Depending on who takes over, they may shoot him or they may reward him. If this turns out to his advantage, then Oleg's friendship with Watkins may be very useful to us."

"That's all then, sir?" Present, his chest constricting, got up to leave.

"Present?"

"Yes, sir?"

"The last thing we want, under the circumstances, is for the ambassador to return to Europe and slip back through the Iron Curtain to Moscow to collect a KGB pension like those other fags, Burgess, Maclean, and Philby."

"Ah . . . Philby is a lady's man, sir."

"Whatever. Even if there's a remote possibility of that happening, we don't need it. Especially on top of our dismal record of counter-espionage operations."

"Yes, sir. And if the ambassador should collapse under interrogation?"

"That's your responsibility as chief of the KGB desk. As long as you can establish that he was a homosexual who fell into a KGB trap and was blackmailed, then I'm sure there's nothing that you won't be able to take care of, Mr. Present. You have my complete confidence."

Present winced again at the heavy sarcasm in the DGI's dismissal.

"Well, what did he say about Watkins?" Fletcher wants to know.

"All he said was, 'The ambassador has been delivered into our hands.' And that it was up to me and you to exploit the situation . . . to take it from here."

"I don't believe it! That's all he had to say?"

Present nods sympathetically. "You know something, Fletcher? The only way I've survived for fifteen years in this job is that I always get everything in writing. Now, excuse —" he brushes past her and approaches Watkins.

Watkins looks across at the bizarre wheelchair from his position on the sofa. The armrests have been widened with attached wooden boards, and there's a series of nylon straps slotted through the wood to hold down the individual undergoing the test. Other longer straps with buckles, to immobilize the torso and legs, hang forbiddingly from the back of the chair and the footrest. But the most ominous attachment is a helmet-like metal cage that perches above an adjustable vertical bar above the headrest. Electrodes dangling from the helmet are attached to a heavy power pack fixed to the back of the chair. A rolled-up power cord completes the assembly.

"You see," smiles Watkins, "I warned you about that slippery slope. You start trying to please the CIA, and you end up with some kind of torture apparatus."

"It's simply a variation on a polygraph machine," Present protests.

Watkins glances quickly at Fitzpatrick, the uniformed officer, and Fletcher. "I really think, Mr. Present, you are the only one here who believes that. Me? I sense something ugly in the air."

Fletcher makes a move for the door, but Present will not allow it. "It's necessary for you to stay in the room as a witness, inspector — at least in Mr. Watkins' interests."

Hopelessly manipulated, Fletcher sits down. Fitzpatrick, mid-twenties, scrubbed clean-shaven face, looks embarrassed, but fascinated by the machine.

"As I said, this is a lie-detector test of sorts. The technician is waiting in a room down the hall. But first let me tell you how it works — and then give you an opportunity to make history as the first guinea pig."

"Marvellous," murmurs Watkins, "a scientific breakthrough. I imagine the zealots of the Spanish Inquisition rationalized their use of the rack with similar intellectual delusions."

"You leave me no choice. So far you've denied everything."

"Isn't that my right in a democracy?"

Present appears to have lost his composure. His face looks cold and vicious . . . a dog at the gate about to attack a stranger in the street. He dials a phone number and, while he waits for an answer, stares balefully at Watkins. "I'm going to prove," he mutters through clenched teeth, "that you're a weak homosexual who, to indulge yourself and hide your sexual adventures in Moscow from your own government, allowed yourself to be exploited and blackmailed by the KGB into becoming an agent of influence."

"This is all quite crazy, Mr. Present. But I must admit it is certainly not boring."

"Send in Mr. Cleroux," Present barks into the mouthpiece. He takes out a handkerchief and mops his face. "I want to offer you a chance to clear yourself."

"But I haven't committed a crime," Watkins protests.

"Submit to being tested on this lie-detector machine specially built by a scientist commissioned by the RCMP to evaluate the degree of homosexuality in an individual or —"

A huge belly laugh from Watkins drowns Present out. Cleroux knocks and enters the room, a white smock over his suit. He walks over to the machine, unrolls the power cord, and plugs it into an outlet. The transformer warms up. Blue and red lights flash on a panel. Watkins slaps his thigh and guffaws. Fletcher and Fitzpatrick try nervously to suppress their smiles, but Present is clearly enraged. Only Cleroux remains impassive.

Abruptly, Watkins stops laughing. He stands up to his full height, towering over Present. "I will be very happy to take this test on your machine, Mr. Present."

"You will?" Present can hardly believe his ears.

"Yes — on one condition."

"I know it — you want me to give you permission to leave."

"Not even that. I will gladly take this test, but only if you take it first."

In the silence that follows, only the hum of the transformer on the back of the chair can be heard. Present's mouth drops open.

"I . . . " he begins.

A giggle escapes from Fitzpatrick, who tries to cover it up with a series of coughs. "Excuse me, sir."

"Fitzpatrick," Present regards him coldly, "get in the chair and take the test."

The officer gasps in disbelief.

"That's an order, Fitzpatrick."

The officer walks hesitantly towards the machine. Cleroux holds up the headgear to allow the strongly built constable to sit down. But Fitzpatrick refuses. He turns to Present. "Sir, I know that I'm not a homosexual."

"Yes, yes. Of course. Just get strapped in and let's do a test."

"But what happens if the machine says I am."

"It's only a test, you'll be okay. Just —"

"No, sir! I won't take this test. If this machine says I am, then you'll have to fire me from the Force, right? Those are the rules — no homos on the Force."

Present is stumped. He doesn't know what to say. Watkins begins his chuckling again.

"Give it up, David," Fletcher whispers in Present's ear. "Let it go. You're making us look ludicrous in front of the men."

Present caves in and orders the now grinning Fitzpatrick to help Cleroux remove the wheelchair from the suite.

Watkins feels energized by his success. He strolls around the room, humming a few bars from Shostakovich's Third Symphony and helping himself to sandwiches from the buffet laid out on the food trolley. "Don't you think this calls for a drink, David?" he suggests to Fletcher and Present. "What do you say we return to a civilized level of discourse over a glass of wine?"

Present has collapsed morosely into a chair and ignores Watkins' suggestion. Fletcher fetches a bottle of wine from the office and hands it to Watkins to open. Still humming cheerfully, Watkins makes a fuss over the bottle, an ordinary French white. He finds three wine glasses in the sideboard and sets them out on the table. Fitzpatrick returns with a smile on his face. Fletcher can imagine the laughter his fellow constables have shared at the story of the fruit-machine. She orders him to stay outside the door.

"Lovely, you can always count on the Ritz, real professionals," Watkins murmurs as he fills up the glasses. "Inspector Fletcher?" He hands her a glass with a slight bow. She takes the other glass and puts it down beside the brooding Present.

Watkins raises his glass with a smile and an unspoken "Cheers" to the other two. Fletcher returns the gesture and takes a sip. Secretly she's full of admiration for the ambassador.

"Mr. Watkins," she asks with a smile, "are you a homosexual?"

"Yes," Watkins replies calmly. "That's the way I've been all my life."

Present's head snaps up to watch the exchange.

Fletcher continues quietly. "Were you sexually active during your diplomatic posting in Moscow?"

Watkins is equally grave in his responses. "Yes, and everywhere else I was posted — Oslo, Copenhagen."

"Did you ever have a sexual relationship with a Russian poet, a man you knew by the name of Khamal Stoikov?"

"Yes, on several occasions."

"Were you ever approached by a Soviet citizen you knew as a history professor, Alexei Gorbunov, who alleged that the KGB held photographs and film of you in sexual activity with Khamal?"

"No. Never."

"Did he ever offer, either directly or by implication, to use his influence and connections with the KGB to prevent the release of the alleged photos of you and Khamal in sexual activity together, and to protect you from the resulting public scandal, on the condition that you become an agent of influence for the Soviet Union?"

"No. Never."

"Thank you for your honesty, Mr. Watkins. I have one more question. In retrospect, how do you look upon your sexual activities with other men in the Soviet Union?"

Watkins cannot suppress an avuncular chuckle. "My dear Inspector Fletcher, why would I feel ashamed of being what you and I both know is a perfectly natural occurrence?"

Flethcer flashes him a quick and wary glance. "Weren't you ever afraid of blackmail?"

"From whom?"

"The KGB might have thought to make you a possible target of sexual blackmail."

"You people are unhealthily obsessed with sex."

"So you never believed you were vulnerable."

"Inspector Fletcher! How could I be? I never made it a secret, so I really couldn't ever be exposed. My minsiter was aware of my homosexuality and so was the DGI."

Fletcher cannot keep the awe out of her voice. "The Director General of Intelligence, Williams, knew?"

"Of course, he even recognized that it probably gave me an advantage of penetrating, if you'll forgive the unintended pun, the ranks of Soviet officialdom. You could say the DGI tacitly encouraged me to indulge myself. I must remind you, I developed better contacts than anyone in the U.S. embassy."

Once again, Fletcher feels unnerved. To compose herself, she asks: "Mr. Watkins, would you like me to play back the tape recording of this conversation, in case you want to change your mind about anything you have said?"

"No, it's not necessary, but I think another glass of wine might be a good idea."

Fletcher brings the bottle of wine and hands it to Watkins.

"Am I free to go now?"

"It's not up to me."

They both turn to look at Present, who is rapidly writing notes on his yellow pad beside the battered Operation Rock Bottom file. He answers without looking up. "No, it's not up to Fletcher."

"I thought so," Watkins sighs. "Now I know for sure it's not me you're after."

Fletcher waits for the revelation, but both men stay silent. Finally she asks, "Who are we after?" But the only sound is the friction of Present's pen moving quickly across the paper.

PRESENT FLIPS OPEN the Rock Bottom file and quickly scans the pages he withdraws. "I have here one of your dispatches written to the prime minister when he was minister of external affairs," he says. "Why were you so intent on his having direct contact with a senior officer of the KGB? And why did you mark this dispatch for his eyes only?"

Dispatch R591
For the Minister's Eyes Only
An Important Breakthrough

Success! Alexei has dropped all pretence of being a history professor with "connections" at the Moscow Institute. Last night I was invited to his house for dinner. A grand place, indeed, and almost as big as our embassy. After dinner he took me away from the other guests for coffee in his discreetly lighted study and immediately got down to business.

Although he kept the tone light and casual, I could see this was an important discussion for him. He is obviously a right-hand man to Khrushchev. Off the top, he informed me that the Soviet government is now ready to agree to my request and to extend a formal invitation for you to visit the Soviet Union. And, as everything in this dispatch has to do with your forthcoming visit to Moscow, I urge you to give these matters careful thought. This way we can get a head start on what we have to discuss when I come to Ottawa next month.

Alexei wanted to make plans for your visit so there would be no unpleasant surprises. Did I know, for example, about any particular questions of international political importance you would raise while you were here?

I mentioned that an exchange of parliamentary delegations had been suggested as a way to break the ice between our countries, and that a decision might be made after your visit to Moscow. Otherwise, I had no information about any questions you might wish to discuss.

I would have a better idea after I had talked with you in Ottawa.

Alexei said that the Soviet government regards your visit as extremely important and hopes it will result in improved relations and closer connections between Canada and the Soviet Union, as well as contribute to the relaxations of international tension in general. Since it will be the first official visit of a Canadian foreign minister since the Gouzenko defection, it is clear that the Soviets are quite nervous and want things to go well. "We hope to discuss practical problems and produce concrete results that would benefit both countries," he said. In other words, let's not get bogged down in past recriminations.

I replied that we had not yet had a chance to discuss the trip in detail, but it was obvious that you had accepted Molotov's invitation in the hope that your visit would lead to better relations between our two countries. I was sure that the prime minister, the Cabinet, and the Canadian people shared that hope. He seemed reassured by this response.

Alexei said he had been asked by somebody high in authority (read Khrushchev) to inform me, in confidence, before I departed for Ottawa, of several topics that the Soviet government wished to raise during your visit. You could then be prepared to discuss them and perhaps take concrete action on some of them. From the attached list you can see that they all have to do with improving relations between our two countries and, more important, helping to relax international tensions over nuclear warfare. Obviously this sets the stage for Canada to pull off a diplomatic coup of considerable international consequence.

Alexei is trying to confirm a date early in October that suits both Bulganin and Molotov, and I suggest you leave that period free. Most of all, Alexei said, the Soviet leaders want to convey their hope that you will enjoy your visit to the Soviet Union and that Mrs. Pearson will accompany you. If you advise them which places you would most like to visit, they will do their best to plan accordingly.

They regard our embassy as a bit primitive, and want to put a private house and a dacha outside Moscow at your disposal, or, if you prefer, a luxury suite in a hotel. It is for you to decide.

Once again, I think you will see that this visit represents probably the biggest diplomatic breakthrough in East-West relations since the

Second World War. I do not need to urge you to plan with the utmost care how, exactly, we can reap the benefits from this opportunity.

Present peers up with exasperation from the Rock Bottom file. "Why all this attention to extraneous detail, why all these pretensions to a literary style in your dispatches?"

Watkins smiles benignly. "Did you know that when the sky was overcast by storm clouds, the early Polynesian sailors could tell by their balls where they were heading?"

"What on earth does that have to do with what we're talking about?"

"It's all about being centred. Surely you must know, Present. Bureaucrats are by definition exogenous, existing inside a shell of rigidity. If they have any balls at all, they're soft and withdrawn deep inside somewhere."

Fletcher allows a flicker of a smile.

Present responds, "Then you should know — as a lifelong diplomat, you are the quintessential bureaucrat."

"Then tell me, why am I here listing to your ridiculous questions about completely open dispatches written from Moscow to my minister?"

Present coldly turns to the next dispatch.

Dispatch T119
For the Minister
Copy: Internal Security Branch

I should have commented before now on Mr. R.A.D. Ford's very interesting and comprehensive paper on the destruction of the Stalin myth, with whose conclusions I generally agree.

Many Russians say that one of the reasons for using the 20th Congress to criticize Stalin so severely is the need to encourage individual initiative and responsibility so as to advance industrial and agricultural production more rapidly.

Under Stalin, they say, the country was paralyzed. Many people with valuable ideas were afraid to put them forward because of what happened to persons accused of "propagating erroneous views."

One senses in Russia of the 20th Congress a consciousness that the Soviet Union is emerging from a long, hard period of struggle and is now facing up to the consequences as well as the opportunities.

Among the responsibilities is the very real problem of dealing, for the first time in Russian history, with a largely literate population and an increasingly important elite in the bureaucracy, universities, institutes, and research organizations who could hardly be expected to pay more than cynical lip-service in the long run to the more obvious distortions and omissions of the official version of Soviet history.

To retain their respect and loyalty, the party no doubt realizes that a more objective (in the Western sense) approach has to be introduced, and this could hardly be done without dismantling a large part of the intellectual scaffolding erected by Stalin. The degree of objectivity must have been, and must still be, a delicate question for the party leaders to resolve. To appear genuinely objective, the attack on Stalin himself must be kept within bounds, and not become a personal vendetta as irrational as the myth itself . . .

One of the things that has impressed me most during my stay here has been the evidence of extreme social mobility resulting from the Soviet educational system, and the way it is taken for granted by, say, a taxi driver that his sons will become members of the scientific or artistic middle class, and may even join the elite if they can qualify for this status. This in turn reflects the increasing importance in the political economy of Russia . . .

Cutting Stalin down to size may pay incidental dividends in making communism more respectable abroad. I agree that, generally speaking, a post-revolutionary hankering after respectability is increasingly important, but this is balanced, in the short run at least, by confusion in the party ranks and by the ridiculous posture in which the more ardent foreign Stalinists are now left. Some responsible foreign observers here think that even Khrushchev may have lost some stature in the eyes of many Russians by revealing the abject servility of the top party figures during the last dark days in the Kremlin. I doubt myself whether, given the Russian mentality and tradition, this is really the case; but even if it is, they at least had a very good excuse.

Merleau is aggressive, trying to make up for Present's fading energy. "Why didn't you prepare your foreign affairs ministry more properly for the export of revolution from the Soviet Union to South America?"

"Export! You don't think the Cubans and the South Americans have minds of their own? Besides, my responsibility was the Soviet Union and Europe."

Dispatch T114

For the Minister
Copy: Internal Security Branch

Although censorship has been lifted on stories going abroad regarding Mr. Khrushchev's speech to the special session of the 20th Congress (see dispatch T103), and the account published by the *London Daily Worker* substantially confirms the rumours that have been flying about Moscow for the last fortnight, the Soviet press continues to make no mention of this even. The speech indicates a sea change in the Soviet Union's relationship with the rest of the world. The challenge is for the rest of us in the West, particularly the United States, to seize upon this opportunity and prevent us all slipping back into the icy grip of the Cold War — which I sometimes fear many Americans prefer as a means of maintaining political control.

Meanwhile, it seems evident that indoctrination of party members is in progress. I managed to obtain a circular sent out shortly after the conclusion of the Congress giving four examples of what had been meant by the references in the speeches to the harm caused by the Stalin "cult of personality." They are identified as:

a) The brutality of the collectivization program. Collectivization itself was necessary, but the methods employed were not and were Stalin's responsibility.
b) The purges. Not only did Stalin frequently act without the advice or knowledge of his colleagues, but the form taken by the charges was frequently false. Furthermore, the purges of the army left Russia in a weakened position to face the German invasion.

c) Poor military leadership. The example cited is said to be the unnecessary losses incurred in the Kharkov campaign.

d) The "Doctors' Plot," which is revealed as a pure fabrication of Stalin.

So far as the general Soviet public is concerned, the demystification of Stalin is being handled fairly cautiously, and there has been no wholesale purging of images. The main physical indiction recently of what is going on was the taking down of most of Stalin's portraits from the Tretyakov Gallery.

The change is reflected in other subtle ways. When I visited the Revolutionary Museum, I found Stalin is certainly still very much in evidence there, although for the most part in paintings showing him at Lenin's side. Where the change comes is in the lectures by the guide. I noticed that references to Stalin seemed to be deliberately avoided. One guide pointed out that there was a slight historical inaccuracy in the picture of Lenin addressing the crowd at the Finland Station with Stalin close by. "Stalin," said the guide, "had not really been there."

Present extracts another dispatch from the file. "You had, I take it, many secret meetings with Oleg Gribanov?"

"You mean unofficial, surely?" retorts Watkins.

"Did you report all of them?"

"Even the spontaneous occasions."

Dispatch S281
Att: Minister of External Affairs
Copy: Internal Security Branch

Alexei sent for me late tonight in one of the state cars he seems to have at his constant disposal. How far we have come since the days at the Crimean dacha when everybody pretended to be impecunious college instructors!

After a glass of wine in his office, he said he wanted to inform me of a sensitive issue. The Soviet government is going to send a note to the United States government to protest against balloons equipped with photographic apparatus being sent over Soviet territory.

The Russian have quite a collection of these balloons that they have brought down. They are equipped with apparatus weighing about half a ton, including special cameras that operate automatically and carry enough film to photograph about 4000 kilometres of Soviet territory. Alexei reluctantly admitted that they take very good pictures, showing roads, railroads, buildings, and houses quite clearly.

He said the balloons are being launched from various countries around the perimeter of the Soviet Union — Greece, Turkey, Sweden, Finland — and are constructed to fly on currents in the upper atmosphere, which should carry them to Alaska. They are equipped with signal devices that come into operation when they fall on land or in the Pacific Ocean, so they can be found and picked up by U.S. military support units.

I asked how Soviet officials could be certain the balloons were American. Alexei laughed and said there would be no question about their identity if the case were brought before the United Nations. The balloons had "U.S.A." in huge print on their sides.

Were they going to take the matter to the U.N.? I asked. But I was really wondering why he had sent for me so late at night for this interesting, but, for Canada, not crucial piece of information.

He did not know if they would go to the United Nations. They had not yet decided. He invited my opinion, but I remained silent.

Realizing I wasn't going to offer advice, he went into a tirade against the United States. Why should the Americans want to send such balloons over Soviet territory? Why should they want to photograph the Soviet Union so intensively? Was this preparation for a military attack of some kind? What would the Americans think if the Soviet Union were to retaliate by sending balloons to photograph U.S. territory? He was sure there would be panic in the United States if they did. But, of course, they had no intention of doing so.

I noted that it was still open to the Soviets to accept the U.S. president's offer to photograph all they wanted in the United States.

Alexei made no comment, and switched to what turned out to be the subject that was really on his mind. The Soviet government, he said, was pleased with Mr. Pearson's remarks about China and asked if this meant Canada will soon formally recognize the new China.

I replied that it was well known we had been close to recognizing Communist China for some time. When public opinion in Canada was in favour of recognition, we would do so. When that would be, I had no idea, but would certainly inquire of my minister.

Alexei thought it must be clear to everyone by now that Chiang Kai-shek had no hope of taking over the mainland and that the present government was firmly established.

As he walked me down to the waiting car, he remarked sardonically that the United States had waited something like fifteen years to recognize the Soviet government and would probably take just as long to recognize the new Chinese government.

What, Mr. Minister, are your instructions on how to handle further solicitations for Canadian advice? I have the feeling they will begin again soon.

Present leans back in his chair and asks, in what Watkins hears as a forced conversational tone: "You've never really explained how this special friendship of yours with Oleg Gribanov first got off the ground."

WHEN WATKINS WOKE at ten on Sunday morning, he found the Russians at the back of the dacha, quietly nursing hangovers by taking dips in the Klyasma River and sunning themselves on the riverbank. Only Alyosha was still sound asleep in the sunroom.

Nobody dared wake him. They sat around in the garden talking in hushed voices. There was no doubt who called the shots around here. They had to wait for Alyosha to wake up before they could eat, and it was well after eleven when they sat down to breakfast — Russian style — ham, sausage meats, cucumbers, cheese, and even cold fish. The others started with Watkins' bottle of French wine, which they pronounced excellent, but he contented himself with toast, tea, and a little ham.

Alyosha led the good-humoured banter at the table about the evening before, mostly at the expense of short, stout Anatoly, who had been seen wandering in the garden with strings of bottles hanging around his neck. "The three of us were known as the three musketeers in our student days," he explained.

After breakfast the conversation turned to more serious subjects. Watkins began to suspect why they had brought him here. They wanted to isolate him from his diplomatic coterie and make him part of their group. He was both charmed and disconcerted at their transparent behaviour.

Alyosha was surprisingly blunt: "Through us you have an advantage over all the other foreign diplomats in this country to observe and report on the real conditions in the Soviet Union."

Watkins agreed. It was true, the contacts opening up for him had already made him the object of malicious envy. "Heard you've gone native, old chap," murmured the British ambassador in his ear at a Swedish Embassy reception. "Be careful. Next thing they'll foist one of their official translators on you as a bride."

Volodya was curious. "How do the other foreign diplomats in Moscow report to their governments on Soviet conditions and opinions? It's a mystery to us, since they don't seem to associate much with Russians."

"They have to scalp the local press," Watkins explained.

"But newspaper articles can often be interpreted in different ways, and it would surely be useful to discuss them with Russian intellectuals," Anatoly suggested.

"Of course discussion with Soviet intellectuals would be more useful," Watkins agreed, "but I don't think the diplomats can be blamed entirely. For the most part, Russian intellectuals are afraid to have anything to do with them."

"No, no," they all objected. "There are no restrictions, official or otherwise — never have been."

"But before you met us, you already had many friends here," Alyosha said.

"Oh yes. I was lucky on my first posting here. I made a few Russian friends, and I spent many pleasant hours with them." How had Alyosha known about his previous friends? Watkins wondered. Through information collected by the police guards on duty at the embassy gates? "There was no secrecy in my friendships. I visited them in their apartments, and always went openly in the embassy car with the Canadian pennants flying. But, you know," he pointed out, "they never visited me at the embassy. There was one man who rejected my invitation to dinner several times. When I pressed him, he told me he was so afraid of being kidnapped that he would not even take 30,000 rubles to venture inside a foreign embassy."

"Is the offer still on?" Volodya wanted to know. "We'll be on your doorstep tomorrow!"

Watkins knew the discussion must be leading up to something. Finally Anatoly embarked on a long-winded explanation of a conversation about fraternizing with foreigners that he and Alyosha had recently had with a mutual friend, Peter. "Peter is on a very high desk in the Ministry of Culture," he explained. "He told us it has now been agreed at the top — at the very top executive level of the Politburo — that it was a great mistake to cut off the foreign representatives in Moscow from contacts with the Soviet intelligentsia."

Watkins smiled to himself. The Russians had never admitted there were restrictions in the first place. "It has also been decided," Anatoly continued, "that the officers in the Foreign Ministry should be permitted to associate with foreign diplomats on a social and unofficial basis."

Yes, thought Watkins, the thaw is definitely on. There had been signs of this in recent weeks. The Soviet head of the section dealing with the Netherlands had invited the Dutch ambassador and his wife to a luncheon at the new Prague restaurant on Arbat Square. And at a concert in the Bolshoi about a week ago, Mme. Teplova, the wife of the former Soviet chargé d'affaires in Ottawa, had approached him and asked in a rather pointed way what the inside of his embassy was like. He had immediately invited her to the July 1 reception.

"Will this mean," Watkins asked Anatoly and Alyosha, "that the police guards will now be removed from the gates of my embassy?"

Stunned, not even Alyosha had a comeback to that remark, so Watkins pressed his point. "It is only the Soviet block countries that post guards at embassy doors to keep local citizens from coming in to do business."

"No, no," Anatoly countered quickly, "those policemen are there for your own protection." Returning to his earlier theme, he continued. "They have also decided that it is wrong to be ashamed of our inadequacies. We know there are still a great many things that are not as they should be in the Soviet Union, but considering the destruction we suffered in the last war and the terrible hardships the whole population has endured, we Russians have not done too badly."

Watkins was touched. Something else was changing. He had never heard such an artless plea for understanding. Previously the Russians had always maintained a stoic face to foreigners about the war years and their aftermath. They had become so conditioned during the Stalin years that even to admit to the devastation and defeats suffered at the hands of the Germans was to admit to a failure, to a flaw in the Russian character. Worse, it would also be a condemnation of Stalin.

"We think," Alyosha added, "that many of the diplomats — the Americans, for instance — are prejudiced against us and critical of everything in this country. I cannot imagine they would want to have Russian friends."

"On the contrary," Watkins replied, "many of them would welcome the chance. There might be officers with certain prejudices on any staff, but the Americans I've talked to seem eager to get as accurate a picture of Soviet life as they can."

Alyosha finally brought up the big request the whole weekend had obviously been build around. "Would you," he asked with a nervous smile, "consider passing on the content of this conversation to your fellow diplomats in Moscow?"

"Of course. I will be happy to do so," Watkins replied.

Both Russians heaved sighs of relief. Mission accomplished. They could now relax and were giddy with boyish questions.

"Do you think that the U.S. ambassador, Charles Bohlen, is a bright guy?"

"Yes, indeed. He speaks Russian fairly well and appears acquainted with Russian culture."

"We don't understand the Commonwealth."

"Dear God, can we leave that to another time?"

They laughed good-naturedly.

"How much do you pay your chauffeur?"

"Maxim? You mean you don't know?" Watkins teased them.

"We just want to know if he's telling us the truth," laughed Alyosha. "How much do they pay you?" he suddenly asked Watkins, smiling innocently.

Russians, Watkins had long ago learned, had no inhibitions about asking such questions. "You know, I'm not really sure, but I think it's somewhere around $10,000 a year."

They looked at him in amazement. "That's not very much for a man with your responsibilities."

"In my next dispatch to my minister I will certainly pass on your observation."

Alyosha walked Watkins to his car and quietly murmured: "Thank you for all your help. I feel today we have become real friends. To Russians, friendship is more important even than family bonds."

"Then what about some travel permits to the interior?" Watkins asked. "It takes months to get those passes, and I am desperate to see more of your country."

"Don't give it a thought," Alyosha said with a dismissive wave of his hand as he closed the car door behind Watkins. "Leave it to me."

That's really how it all began, Watkins says, and he looks Present straight in the eye.

NOON, SUNDAY: Fletcher stops beside Watkins, who is once again trying to take the weight off his back by leaning forward with his hands on the window sill.

"Montreal in mid-October," she murmurs, at a loss for something reassuring to say. "You and my boss, DGI Williams, have a lot in common — bad backs, chain smokers, like to drink —"

"— and loyal patriotic citizens," Watkins interrupts with a grimace as he straightens up to massage his lower back.

"I'm sure once we get the story straightened out —"

"Don't patronize me Inspector Fletcher —"

"I was only trying to . . ." Her voice trails off as she, too, stares out at the gloomy cityscape. Although the apartments across the street are veiled by a steady drizzle of rain, she can make out some figures in the dimly lit apartments. Watkins feels as if he is inside an Edward Hopper painting.

"I suppose you've got the cover-up all worked out," says Watkins, without a trace of bitterness and still staring at the rain.

"Cover-up?"

Watkins can see she is genuinely mystified. "Then I suppose Present is taking care of it. Yes, I can see it now, a small short notice in the press: 'Ambassador Watkins died suddenly of a heart attack while dining with friends at a farewell dinner before a planned return to Europe, where he was to retire. He had been ill for some time.'"

"Mr. Watkins, you're not going to die, especially not here. And why on earth would we need a cover-up story?"

"Ah, Inspector Fletcher, you of all people must know. All Canadian citizens who die during the course of a police interrogation are automatically entitled to a full inquest to determine the circumstances that led to their deaths, and their relatives have the right to the results of an official autopsy."

"I will not let you die, Mr. Watkins. Please stop being so paranoid. You must trust me."

Why, he wonders, has she come over to me? Is she trying to tell me through her body language that she is really on my side? "Never trust the ones who choose you," Ahkundi smiled. They'll be the first to betray you." She is standing so close he can smell her perfume. Something subtle, a pale whiff of desert flowers. A cop with perfume! Well, why not? Alyosha was a cop and he always reeked of that Soviet-made cologne. Now, though, he better keep all options open. Fletcher, he believes, is his only hope. "That's a nice perfume you're wearing."

"Oh, thank you." She's a little taken aback. "You know, I don't think in all my years on the Force another Mountie has ever said anything about my perfume. I think the men I work with find it hard to acknowledge that I'm a woman officer, let alone an officer who wears perfume."

"What's it called?"

"Something Italian . . . Sotto voce."

"Appropriate brand name for an intelligence officer."

"It's good to see you haven't lost your sense of humour."

They turn as Merleau opens the door and sidles up to Present. Why, she wonders, does she always manage to sound so bloody humourless herself?

"I'm desperate, Fletcher. You must get me out of here," he pleads in a hoarse whisper as he turns his back on the men opposite.

"I . . . I can't."

"Things are only going to get uglier."

"You know I can't — at least right now."

"What is it? You still believe this trumped-up stupidity about an agent of influence?"

"No, but —"

"Then what, for God's sake?"

He watches her unconsciously bring her hand to her mouth and gnaw thoughtfully on her knuckle. She looks up, catches his eye, and hurriedly drops her hand with an embarrassed smile. "I thought you were going to tell me not to."

"Not to what?"

"Oh, nothing . . ." God, what is happening to her? For a moment she heard her father's voice: "You have to find other ways to relax, Jane. Chewing your knuckles off is not the best way." But Watkins is expecting a response. "There are still some questions that have to be answered," she says.

"Like what? Why didn't I phone the minister every time I needed to have sex?"

"No. But it seems there were meetings with the KGB officers Oleg Gribanov and Anatoly Gorsky that you didn't report as you were required to do, and that looks bad —"

"How am I supposed to prove something that didn't happen?"

"We are waiting for a witness."

"A witness, really! From where?"

"I don't know exactly, he's a CIA source. Merleau say he might even arrive tonight. They're flying him up from Washington."

"That may be too late."

"Too late for what?"

Watkins ignores her question. "Tell me the truth about Khamal. Is he really dead?"

"I don't know, I'll try to find out for sure."

Watkins knows she is lying. As Akhundi said: Even when people know, why is it so difficult for them to tell the truth? Alyosha used to lie in the same way."

"No, THIS IS NOT TRUE. I cannot tell you how important this is to us Russians: the Soviet Union does not interfere in the internal affairs of other countries. Nobody can accuse the Soviet Union of advising any Communist Party anywhere to try to overthrow its government."

"Oh, c'mon Alyosha, that's plain silly — Hungary, Czechoslovakia —"

"That was the old Comintern under Stalin. It was guilty of cruel interference, but for that reason it was disbanded. Communist parties in other countries now are completely autonomous."

"And their newspapers?"

"Yes, of course."

"Alyosha! The Communist papers like *Humanité* in France make themselves ridiculous by pretending that everything in the Soviet Union is perfect — even when your own Soviet papers are constantly criticizing all sorts of defects in your system."

Alyosha lost his customary aplomb and shouted: "The Soviet Union cannot interfere with the way Communist parties in other countries run their papers!"

"While Moscow subsidizes them? That's just not credible, Alyosha. Why do you treat all Westerners, even ones like me who have considerable understanding of your problems, as if we are fools?" For a moment he thought the Russian was going to explode. He had never seen him this way before. "Alyosha?" he insisted firmly, "there's not a great deal at stake here. No audience. No critics. Just you and me — alone."

The strain went out of the Russian's drawn face. He grimaced and poured Watkins another vodka. "Who said 'the real tragedy of this life is that one is never really alone'? Camus, or was it Sartre?"

"Could be. It also might be an anguished and overworked intelligence officer."

Alyosha studied Watkins with a new respect. "Forgive my bad manners, please?" And nervously shifted to another topic. "The Soviet citizens are the most literate population in the world, but we are starving for books. We will very soon get the government to recognize the international copyright system, and be able to import more books from the West."

"Yes," agreed Watkins with a smile, playing by the rules is always a good idea."

HE WATCHES FLETCHER cross over to Present and Merleau. She's a head taller than either of them and keeps her back to him. Watkins returns to the piano, quietly playing once again the Scarlatti sonata, like a man looking for an answer in the music.

"Did you tell him about the witness?" asks Merleau.

"Yes, just now."

"How did he take it?'

"Hard to say. He wanted to know where the witness was from."

"You didn't tell him?"

"No."

"Good. What else?"

"He wanted to know if you were bluffing about Khamal. I said I would try to find out."

"Good work. Keep up the animosity between us —"

"It's not hard."

"Even better, you come across as really sincere — doesn't she, Mr. Present?"

"Very effective. Let's move to the next stage, can we? Excellent. Oh, Mr. Watkins," he calls across the suite, "could we get back to business?" He gestures to the open chair on the other side of the table.

Watkins lumbers over to the others, but refuses to sit down with them. "I want to know — Is Khamal really dead?"

Present and Fletcher look to Merleau to answer the question. He stares impassively back at the ambassador. "That is what I told you."

"Yes, but your telling me in these circumstances does not necessarily make it true."

They are interrupted by the suite door opening. Another officer hands an envelope to Fitzpatrick, who is seated by the door. Fitzpatrick reads the envelope, brings it over to Fletcher, and whispers something in her ear. Without opening the envelope, she passes it over to Watkins. "Your reply from the prime minister."

Excited, Watkins rips open the envelope to take a single sheet covered by two or three sentences in a written hand. He reads it quickly, then slumps back in his seat. In disbelief he holds the sheet of paper for a moment between the fingers of his left hand, then lets it float away with a flick of despair. Fletcher picks it off the carpet and reads out loud: "Dear John. Good to hear from you. Once you get this awkward but necessary piece of bureaucracy out of the way, we must have dinner together. Maryon sends her best wishes and also looks forward to seeing you soon."

Watkins is vividly aware of the complete silence at the interrogation table. The three faces hang there in the stillness, each with its own agenda, awaiting the right moment. Somewhere in the suite a clock ticks. A slight hush of rain can be heard beyond the windows, and, in the far distance, the faint wail of a police siren. That's it, Watkins thinks, there goes my last chance. But I'm damned if I'm going to let them know it. "I'm sure that you've misinformed the prime minister. I doubt whether you made sure he got my original note."

"No," says Fletcher, "I double-checked with his personal secretary that he got your note. She even read it back to me. I can remember the words: 'Dear Mike, I need your help to extricate me from this overzealous questioning by the security services. Would you please be kind enough to give it your immediate attention. All it will take is one phone call from you.' Isn't that more or less it, Mr. Watkins?"

"Yes, but again, your saying it's so doesn't make it true."

"Why do you think the prime minister refuses to rescue you?" Fletcher inquires.

Watkins, head down, lurches from side to side, a wounded bull. He remembers Gromyko's warning: "When a leader takes your loyalty for granted, he is ready to abandon you." He must not let them defeat them.

Once again he refuses to sit down, and moves around the room with the air of an executive cajoling a group of peers to be more constructive in their search for solutions. "I think it's time, don't you, that we all got down to the . . . well . . . let's just call them 'the masked intentions of this interrogation' of Ambassador John Watkins." He turns to confront them with a questioning smile. But they give him nothing. "Ah, I see I will have to do all the work, at least to get the subtext of this activity out in the open. If you won't help me, I will have to risk boring you with a brief but important preface."

Present looks to the others. "Mr. Watkins, please sit down —"

"Oh, I will. I will. But I'm not doing badly for an old man with a heart condition whom you insist on harassing . . . although you did allow me a couple of naps."

"Can we get to the point you were trying to make?"

"Gladly. The premise —" he turns a beaming smile on Present "— is that the history of your department, sir, is a joke. I can assure you that they snicker about us in the halls of the United Nations, London, Berlin, Paris, and many other cities of Europe, not to mention Moscow."

He pauses for a moment to examine Present's sober face. "There's nothing personal in all of this, I assure you."

Merleau is smiling, enjoying Present's discomfort. Fletcher is not far behind.

"You and your lot couldn't ever offend me," Present retorts.

"Aha, and there's the slip that allows me to go back to where I started from — 'my lot,' indeed. Now, what does that mean exactly — my modest origins? But we both know, Mr. Present — remember those long, lazy dinners we had in Paris? — we know —"

Present nods, but is becoming increasingly restless.

"— that you come from the hard-scrabble background of a bleak coal-mining valley somewhere in the Maritimes, so when you talk about 'my lot' you're not referring to my class origins. I must therefore con-clude that your use of this English working-class derogatory term is some sort of attack on my homosexuality?"

"You know full well that it is a criminal offence to be a practising homosexual. And, at the very least, grounds for declassification of the security status you hold as an ambassador."

Watkins behaves as if he doesn't even hear Present's comments. "Not one spy," he says thoughtfully and with great emphasis as he walks slowly back and forth in front of the interrogation table. "Not one Soviet spy ever caught in how many years . . . fourteen, sixteen years?"

Present's pale face is now beginning to colour.

"How come the security services have never caught a *real* spy? Oh, you've had walk-ins, agents who have surrendered, ballet dancers who wanted to further their careers. Is the security service so inept it can't catch a real spy? Or is Canada the only country in the world in which the KGB does not operate? Or is the rumour that circulates through every Western intelligence service and diplomatic corps true: Canadian intelligence services are paralyzed by a mole deep inside their operations?"

"Can you get on with it?" demands Merleau. "Because I hope you have answers to all these rhetorical questions."

"Very well. Back to the main thread. Suddenly, after you've known for many years that I was, as you put it, a 'practising homosexual,' I am pursued through Europe, carted off to England to visit your colleagues in MI5, arrested on the way to the airport —"

"No, you agreed to come of your own free will," Fletcher chides.

"Really, Inspector Fletcher, you will have to do better than that . . . anyway, detained and held as an unwilling guest at the Ritz hotel — by the way, will I be expected to pay for my room?"

"No, of course not," mutters Fletcher.

"— all under the laughable charge of being an agent of influence. I can only come to the conlusion that this charge is an excuse. I am not that important. The man who you really want to bring down is —"

Present jumps to his feet, knocking his own chair backwards. "No! A very serious charge," Present shouts, "one you refuse to answer."

Merleau waves a conciliatory hand. "Let him finish his point."

"I am in charge here," Present answers impatiently. I will determine the nature of this interrogation." He pulls a document from his briefcase.

"Sit down, Mr. Watkins, and read this immediately. We have no more time to waste."

Watkins takes the sheets of paper Present holds out to him and sits down quietly to read the typewritten pages. He finishes, gets up, struggles to regain control of himself, and comes back to confront Present. His voice trembles in anger and desperation. "You want me to sign a confession that incriminates me as a traitor to my own country and my own government?"

"Sign it and you can be on your way to an immediate and comfortable retirement at full pension."

"I don't believe you for one moment."

"Why not? I give you my word on it."

"Because your objective is to destroy me in order to get at —"

"Be careful, Mr. Watkins."

"Why do you force me to play Anthony to your Brutus?"

"Oh, spare us this academic indulgence," Present jeers. "You really are a has-been. It's over for you, Mr. Watkins. Can't you understand? Your time has come and gone. I'm offering you an easy way out of the mess your personal weaknesses left you in . . . Brutus indeed, what nonsense!"

"And who is Caesar?" Merleau asks dryly.

"Why, the prime minister, of course," Watkins replies.

A strange silence settles over the room. But in Fletcher's ears the river is roaring . . .

SHE SAW THE SMALL GREEN CAR under the streetlight. Murray, haggard, reached across to open the door for her.

"Quick, Murray. I have to get back."

"Okay. I told you Angleton was in Britain a few months ago, attempting to convince MI5 they should arrest British Prime Minister Wilson for being a Soviet spy."

"Yes, yes," she fretted, looking at her watch.

"Also seems on his list of suspects is our own prime minister."

Fletcher laughed to hide her rising panic. She reached out for the thwart of the canoe, but it was the door handle of Murray's Volvo that unlatched. Murray reached out to grab her arm.

"Jane, can't you see what's happening."

"This is crazy."

"No! You're in the middle of an attempted coup engineered by the CIA, and especially James Jesus Angleton."

"What do you want me to do — resign?"

"Yes. Resign tonight. Walk away from it. Don't have anything more to do with it."

"All right for you to say with your good-time life."

"No, Jane. I've quit. Today."

"My God! Murray, what are you going to do?"

"I've got a job teaching English at Beijing University."

Fletcher was horrified. "I can't handle this. We'll talk about it later. I have to go." And she slammed the door closed behind her.

Murray watched the figure of his sister fleeing down the dark street. "There won't be time, Jane. I'm leaving tomorrow."

"YOU'RE BEING MELODRAMATIC. Sign it, and I can get home to have Thanksgiving dinner with my family."

"That's all you get, Mr. Present? That's all you get for betraying your country, selling out your prime minister, doing the dirty work for an American intelligence service —"

Merleau tears the document from Watkins' hands, reads it over quickly, and fixes Present with an ugly glare. This is not the damned confession we agreed upon."

"Not one spy in sixteen years, so now you have to do the dirty work for the CIA," taunts Watkins. Cackling, he takes another shot at Present: "Alyosha warned me. He told me to expect this sort of thing from you."

Merleau nods his head to indicate they should talk outside. Watkins flops down on the sofa and waves an arm at Fletcher. "You're excused, too, my dear Fletcher. I wouldn't miss this discussion if I were you, Inspector. Your whole career may well rest upon it."

Embarrassed, Fletcher rises to hurry after her colleagues, but pauses to tell Watkins in an undertone: "It's true. I'm sorry."

"What's true . . . what?" Watkins feels a mounting horror.

"Khamal. He's dead."

Devastated, Watkins slumps back in grief on the couch. But his terrible sense of loneliness is almost immediately interrupted by a stabbing pain in his chest. He calls out after Fletcher, "Please, I need my pills," but she doesn't hear him. He remembers the pair she slipped him earlier, fumbles in his pocket, and swallows them.

SOMEWHAT RESTORED, he stares at the sky as rain from yet another storm lashes the windows. Watkins focuses on the door leading to the balcony. He awaits his chance. Unshaven, slumped on the sofa, he looks slovenly and ill. He is ignored by Fitzpatrick, who regards him as a beaten man.

Fitzpatrick opens the door into the corridor, but can't find anybody on duty to relieve him. He glances at Watkins, eyes half-closed, breathing heavily on the couch. He shrugs and goes quickly to the washroom, leaving the door ajar as he urinates noisily into the toilet. He comes out, drying his hands on a paper towel, and — Panic. Watkins has disappeared. The outer door is open. Fitzpatrick dashes through, but the balcony to the corner of the building is empty. He looks down over the edge, shielding his eyes from the pouring rain, to see if Watkins has jumped, then sprints past the windows to the other end of the balcony, where it continues at a right angle around the outside of the apartment, and lets out a yell of relief. He can see Watkins crouched on a chair at the other end. Fitzpatrick starts towards him, smiling, and in his soft Irish accent asks politely, "Please come inside, sir. You'll only catch your death of cold."

"Come any farther and I'll jump," Watkins screams. He stands up, one leg on the chair, and throws the other over the railing. The chair teeters and Watkins almost goes over. Fitzpatrick stops, terrified, then dashes back into the apartment and out the front door into the corridor.

Fletcher rushes out onto the adjoining balcony, separated by two feet of space from Watkins. He grins at her. In seconds she too is soaked from the downpour. Fitzpatrick also reappears and begins slowly to move towards Watkins.

"That's it, no closer!" Watkins shouts, and lurches farther over the rail. Fletcher holds up a restraining hand and Fitzpatrick stops.

"Order him back inside the apartment!" Watkins commands.

Fletcher waves Fitzpatrick inside. The young officer leaves reluctantly, and Watkins can see him hovering behind the windows.

The pain in his chest returns, but Watkins is cocky. He knows that, for the first time, he is in control. "Where are Present and Merleau."

"They've gone to sort some things out. They'll be away at least an hour."

"That's okay with me. I can wait." He waves to a couple at their apartment window across the street.

"Please come back inside, Mr. Watkins," she implores.

"What for, I've had enough of this farce. It's your job that's on the line now," he taunts her. "If I jump on your watch — it will be an incredible public scandal. 'Why was a Canadian ambassador trying to get away from an apartment full of the secret police officers of the RCMP?'"

"We would deal with it."

"I don't think so, Inspector Fletcher. The Mounties are already trying to live down poor Herbert Norman's supposed suicide off a Cairo apartment rooftop. Weren't the RCMP questioning him then? Two diplomats in a row. Probably you and Present were in on it back then."

Fletcher shakes her head. "Your death by suicide won't be important. Besides, the press will be easy to deal with —"

Watkins agrees, wiping the rain away from his face with one hand while clinging to the balcony railing with the other. "You're probably right. The media will say anything you tell them, they're so terrified of you. But it will be the end of your career."

"The last thing I'm worried about at this point is my job."

"What then?" he asks, caught off guard.

"I don't want you to die. You remind me too much of my father."

Watkins wants to believe her and remembers Akhundi: men kill themselves only when they come to believe there is no one who cares. "Yes," he says, "your father was lucky — he didn't die among strangers."

"What do you really want, Mr. Watkins?"

"To spend the rest of my life in a tiny village I know in the south of France. Every morning I will go to the café, sit at a table in the sun, and write the poetry I have been thinking about all my life."

"You will," she tells him. "More important, I want you to know that I believe you are innocent of all these charges."

"Then give me my pills," he demands.

"I can't do that — Merleau has them.

Watkins lurches ever more precariously over the edge of the rail. Fletcher screams at him through the rain. "I don't want you to fall. I know you're not a Soviet agent."

"Then why this," he asks her, indicating the apartment behind her and all the mental torture it has meant for him.

"I'm just doing my job. It's not personal."

"But it is now," he replies. "I've made it so. My medication, please?"

Fletcher pauses for a long moment. "I know you didn't come out here only to get your heart pills."

He remains silent.

"I believe you're out here to get away from the microphone bugs inside the apartment. You want to tell me something you know about Present."

Police sirens sound and emergency vehicles arrive below. Two men in raincoats move out to talk to the crews. Watkins can see them cluster around, listening, then move back to their vehicles.

"You must get me my pills. There must be a doctor in the hotel — nitroglycerin, fifty milligrams. Get me the pills, then I will tell you."

Fletcher asks him to wait and goes back inside.

Watkins holds on to the rail with both hands. The rain continues to come down heavily. He sees a boy's hands clutching at a barbed-wire fence-puller while the powerful forearms of a man nail the wire into a fence post — all in the pouring rain. "Luc," he yells in a rage, "Luc, where are you now when I need you, you Dutch bastard?"

Fletcher reappears with the container of pills. He needs two immediately, he tells her. She shakes out two pills and, reaching out across the space that separates them, carefully puts them in the palm of his hand. But when Watkins attempts to take them to his mouth, his hand is shaking so badly that they tumble out, bouncing off the balconies below.

Watkins looks at her imploringly. After a long pause, Fletcher shakes out two more pills. This time, she wraps his fingers around them, and he desperately stuffs them into his mouth.

The medication has an immediate effect. "And now the container," he demands.

She pauses. "We have some unfinished business," she reminds him.

"The pills."

"It's against orders."

"You said you believed in me. I'm not going back inside until you give me the container."

More sirens and more emergency vehicles arrive below. Fletcher rattles the vial of pills, then reluctantly gives it to him— again wrapping his fingers around the container so he won't drop it. Watkins triumphantly shoves it into his pocket, takes his leg off the rail, and collapses back into the balcony chair.

In a minute, Fletcher reappears on his side of the balcony and helps him back towards the apartment door. As he leans on her, Watkins warns: "Present will be furious with you for giving up the medication."

"It's not important," Fletcher replies. "Simply sign the confession. Everything will be hushed up. You can go and live quietly in that village in the south of France."

"No," he tells her, it doesn't matter what I sign. They have to kill me now."

"Why? Tell me quickly."

Just as Watkins is about to answer, Present appears through the balcony door, accompanied by Merleau. Momentarily, Present returns to his former amiable self. "A real diplomat would have jumped," he chides Watkins, and orders Fitzpatrick to help Fletcher get Watkins inside.

They lay him on the sofa. By way of response, Watkins triumphantly shakes the vial of pills in Present's face. But before Present can turn on Fletcher, Merleau calmly whispers something in Present's ear and they both stare at Watkins in a strange way. Watkins realizes he has been tricked. He pulls a small wad of paper out of the top of the container and empties a mound of aspirins onto the coffee table. He can't believe it. How could Fletcher betray him? But she appears as surprised as he. She glances at Merleau, realizing that he must have fixed it. Watkins begins to giggle hysterically, finally roaring in uncontrollable laughter. Fletcher can't look at him.

Wearily, Watkins pulls himself together. "It doesn't matter anyway, because now I know you can't afford to let me die," he bluffs.

Merleau smirks, a man about to crush a bug. With grim humour he reminds Watkins, "When Anthony defended Caesar, he eventually had to pay with his life."

BEFORE DAWN ON MONDAY, Fletcher knocks gently and enters the bedroom, lit only by moonlight filtered through the partially opened vertical blinds, to find Watkins on his hands and knees beside the bed, writing the final lines of a poem on the wall with a marker. He turns to see her, a black shape backlit by the light from the suite. He sees her arm reaching for the light switch.

"Please don't turn on the light."

As he finishes writing the last line on the wall, her eyes adjust and she can make out the title and the first few lines. She softly reads them out loud:

The Gift of Harun Al-Rashid by W.B. Yeats

I am falling into years
But such as you and I do not seem old
Like men who live by habit . . .

She trails off, unable to continue, deeply affected by the pathos of the moment.

Finished, Watkins wearily sinks to the carpet beside the bed. She shuts the door and crosses over to lie on the bed, close, but above him. Clouds at times pass across the face of the moon, casting moving shadows over the still figures in the room.

"How are you feeling?" she murmurs.

"Weary beyond all previous experience of fatigue."

Fletcher takes the blood pressure kit from the night table and rolls up his shirt sleeve. She is gentle, almost tender in her movements as she works in the half light, wrapping the cuff of the apparatus around his upper arm. She takes a small flashlight from the drawer of the night table and gives it to Watkins to hold.

"Did your father first teach you how to do this?"

"When I was a little girl and still wanted very much to be a doctor."

"What changed your mind?"

"I'm not sure now. I think I just wanted to experience the world in my own way . . . something like that."

She puts the listening prongs to her ears and continues to talk quietly. "I have disabled the microphones in the bedroom. You can speak freely."

He remains silent, intently watching her face.

"Why did you hide your contacts with your lovers Akhundi and Khamal? It makes things look very bad for you."

He chuckles and asks, "And I suppose you report every encounter you have with another woman to your superiors?"

When she doesn't respond, he adds with resignation, "I was told to."

"Who told you to?"

"The resident security officer in Moscow."

"In writing?"

"Of course not. Akhundi is a poet; he never could be an agent. We both loved music. We would drink vodka and play everything from Uzbek folk songs to Shostakovich deep into the night. Mostly it was a meeting of minds. Haven't you ever had a simple love affair, Fletcher, in which the mutual interest you shared with another woman was far more important than the sex?"

Fletcher has a fleeting image of galloping on horseback, another woman racing a horse beside her. The other woman is laughing joyously, her hair flowing out behind her in the wind.

"But if you reported it to the resident security officer, did he tell you on whose orders not to report it formally?"

"Yes, he told me they came from the director of B Operations."

"Why do you think Present would want to do that?"

"C'mon, you people are always looking for ways to use people. Present obviously had this pipe dream that he could somehow manipulate

Akhundi through me, use him down the road as some sort of agent for Western intelligence. But that was ludicrous. Akhundi was too pure of heart to ever let himself be used as an agent by anyone . . . Are you really going to do anything with that?"

She finally hand pumps the air pressure into the cuff with the little rubber bulb. "Shine the light on the gauge. You loved him?"

"Yes, that's all it was — something between two men. But you could never really understand that."

She loosens the valve and listens to the noise in her ear give way to the ragged beat of his heart — 190, and then, too soon, silence at 120. "You're right — I've never loved a man. I just don't care for them that way."

She unwraps the pressure band. "Not to worry, your numbers are fine."

"I don't believe you. I feel too ill."

She replaces the equipment on the night table. "What about Khamal?"

"Different, completely different."

"Do you think he ever decided to work for the KGB?"

"Who knows . . . if he did, I wouldn't look upon it as betrayal."

"Why not?"

"He had a hard life in a society of which you have no real comprehension. And now . . . well, he's dead."

"Have you ever been truly happy?" she asks.

"No, I've been desperate for love all my life," he answers, and she can hear the searing sadness in his voice.

"Just like my father," she says, tenderly reaching out to stroke the hair on his temple into place.

"Then be careful, you may just turn out to be your father's daughter."

"My twin brother Murray never told my father he loved him."

"Why not?"

"Because he knew that's what my father so desperately wanted to hear."

Watkins has a sudden understanding of why this woman wanted to be a police officer. But before he can speak, she is ready with her next question. "Did KGB Colonel Oleg Gribanov ever give you a code name if you had to contact him in an emergency?"

"Yes," Watkins replies, "the code name is 'Zoltan.' When he gave it to me he told me that he worked under other code names, but only two people in the Western world knew him by the name 'Zoltan.'"

"Did you ever have occasion to use it?"

"No," he laughs. "I always thought all those code names and boy scout secret signs were ludicrous."

What is she here for, he wonders, where is this all going? Then he is answered by her next question: "Why don't you just sign the confession to your unofficial meetings with Akhundi and Khamal?"

"Why?"

"It's your only hope."

"No, the prime minister will certainly call when he understands the true —"

"No!" she interrupts. "All your friends, including the prime minister, have abandoned you. They are all afraid for themselves. Sign, and Present will give you the medication. You will be able to leave, live quietly in retirement — in the south of France or wherever — and write in peace."

"What happened to the CIA special witness? I want to see him face to face."

"It's not going to happen. The CIA have changed their minds about letting him come. They don't think we can adequately protect him."

She can see he still hesitates. "Mr. Watkins, Khamal is dead. Nothing can bring him back. There is nobody to protect."

Watkins caves in, "All right. I'll sign the confession. When do you want me to do it?"

She gets up from the bed. "There's no hurry. I'll write it up and we'll all sit down together later in the day. Try to get some rest now."

She leaves, not quite closing the door. Watkins climbs awkwardly onto the bed and immediately falls asleep, as the early grey light of dawn fills the room.

MONDAY, OCTOBER 12, NOON. Watkins notices that the sky is continuing to clear, as patches of blue show through the grey clouds. They have even let him have a shower, though Fitzpatrick watched him the whole time. He felt shy, unnerved, and apologized again to Fitzpatrick for giving him the banged-up nose. "It's nothing, sir. I've taken many a harder knock than that in a rugby game." The young constable helped him on with the suit jacket, smoothing out the back of his coat with the palm of his hand. "Nice piece of cloth that, sir," he murmured.

Now he comes out of the bedroom to find Merleau and Present watching the football game on television. The Winnipeg Blue Bombers against the Montreal Alouettes. Fletcher is on the phone in a soft murmuring conversation — with Williams, the DGI, he would guess.

They all glance up at him as if he is a stranger they must now reluctantly deal with. They gather at the table and sit once again in their respective places. Watkins feels as if he is moving through a strange, heavy calm. When they speak to him, the words come from a long way away, as if through water.

It is Merleau who pushes the confession across the table for Watkins to sign. Fletcher and Present watch him closely. Merleau, suddenly in charge, nods at the guards by the door: "I think we should have privacy. Would you gentlemen leave?"

Fitzpatrick and the other officer on guard glance at Fletcher, who nods, and they leave reluctantly.

Watkins looks up from his reading and asks Merleau: "What is your rank in the CIA?"

Merleau ignores his question. Present and Fletcher pretend to stare out at the cityscape.

Watkins struggles to read the confession. He is having difficulty focusing. It is the same nonsense: he allowed himself to be blackmailed through his homosexual liaisons to become an agent of influence. He feels exhausted, defeated. Signing his name to the confession brings him no relief. "May I have my medication now?" he asks humbly.

"Yes, of course, as soon as you sign this other document," Present promises, and places a second confession, to Fletcher's astonishment, in front of Watkins.

Watkins struggles through this new document. Then he abruptly tears it up and throws it back. "This is disgusting. You want me to sign a confession that states that I met with Oleg Gribanov with the full knowledge and secret consent of the prime minister. And that we both knew we were dealing with a senior KGB agent. I won't sign that rubbish."

Merleau is enraged. "Sign it, or we stay here until you do." He takes from his pocket Watkins' original container of pills and puts it on the table in front of him.

Watkins turns his anger on Present and Fletcher: "What are you trying to do, carry out a bloodless coup d'état? Bring down Pearson and his government and replace them with — what? Somebody already picked out? A former executive of the United Fruit Company, perhaps.

"We are allies," yells Merleau.

"An ally that can't understand that people want to think for themselves? You must have known that such a clumsy attempt to compromise the prime minister could never have succeeded —"

Fletcher comes out of her paralyzed state. "Just sign it," she implores, "nobody will ever know."

"Yes," replies Watkins with simple dignity, "but I will."

"I'm contacting the DGI," Fletcher tells the others, and runs from the room.

"Wait, Inspector Fletcher!" Present calls after her. But she ignores his feeble attempt at command.

His voice growing hoarser by the second, Watkins attacks Present: "This is just a card you are willing to play in order to save yourself."

Present ignores the remark and turns to Merleau: "I must stop her from talking to the DGI," and he leaves in pursuit.

Watkins turns to look over his shoulder, to try to call out to Present as he leaves. But the pain explodes, this time deep inside his chest. No words come out of his mouth. He knows now this is probably the end. What a bad joke. First Dag, now me. Is Mike next? He hears himself asking Merleau for the pills that sit in the container just out of reach on the table. But Merleau is fixated on another time, another place. He is driving through the dark Congolese night. The car sweeps past small makeshift bars lit with kerosene lamps and surrounded by clumps of armed men in combat fatigues drinking litre cans of beer. The terrified black man beside him crouches down under the dashboard of the U.S. Embassy's Buick, raising his head only to give occasional instructions. A rutted sideroad leads to the edge of the swamp. Even when caught in the headlights, the massive bodies of the crocodiles on the mud flats do not move. Merleau helps the man remove the body from the trunk and they drag the corpse as close to the mud flats as they dare. The man stoops to strip the body of a silver medal and Merleau executes him with one shot from his revolver. The small figure falls over the body of Lumumba, the medal still clutched in his hand.

Present and Fletcher, angry and pale, return to the suite. The phone rings insistently, but nobody answers. They gather around the body of Watkins on the sofa.

"He went fast," Merleau says . . . "Aah, the old guy's better out of it all. Now he won't have to live through the humiliation of a destroyed reputation."

Fletcher sinks to her knees beside Watkins to feel for a pulse. Present finally picks up the ringing phone. It's the prime minister. He wants to talk to Watkins. President apologizes, staring at the body of Watkins as he speaks: "The Ambassador has just left, sir. Yes, to go out for lunch, but I will get him to call you back, sir."

IN THE BEDROOM of the other apartment Fletcher takes a plastic garment bag from the closet and changes from her civilian clothes into her officer's dress uniform. When she is fully dressed, she makes a brief phone call to DGI Williams. For the first time since her father died she can't hear the roar of the river in her head. As she goes back into the adjoining apartment, she has to stand aside as the ambulance attendants take Watkins' body out on a gurney. The coroner's assistant, a woman with a heavy Eastern European accent, asks her to sign her name as a witness to his death. Instead of her own name, Fletcher writes in George Merleau's.

In the suite, Present and Merleau are having a whisky, watching the last few minutes of the football game. They glance up at her. She nods to Merleau, who stands to one side. He knows what is coming.

Present is apprehensive, eyeing the uniform. He makes a motion to leave. Fletcher holds up a hand. Behind her a change of guards enter.

"Mr. Present, on the order of DGI Williams, I am commanded to detain you in this place. And to inform you that you have been suspended from all duties and responsibilities until this inquiry is satisfied."

"What are the charges?"

"DGI Williams will elaborate. He is on his way, but he has asked me to begin the interview. Mr. Merleau will assist. Will you please sit down?"

Present is ashen but calm. "Be assured that I will cooperate completely and promise to answer fully and truthfully any questions you may have."

Fletcher sits down, takes out a form. "Your name, rank, and date of birth?"

Author's Note

To TELL THIS STORY, I have at times drawn heavily upon Ambassador John Watkins' official dispatches from his years of service in Moscow. To fold these dispatches into the style and structure I have created for this novel, I have had to change tenses, work in my own characters, and refigure time and place. But I did this only where necessary, because, as Mark Twain said, "It's no wonder that truth is stranger than fiction. Fiction has to make sense." Watkins was a fine writer with a good eye for detail, and in those places in the novel where I set him up to speak in a stream of consciousness, I did it because I felt I really had to know the man. I tried not to tamper with his views of the people he wrote about.

Inevitably, there will be those who will disagree with what I've done. So be it. If they wish, they can read his dispatches in their original form — most are available on request from the National Archives in Ottawa.

Or they can turn to the excellent collection of John Watkins' documents in the book edited by Dean Beeby and William Kaplan, *Moscow Despatches: Inside Cold War Russia.*

But, because I started out as a visual artist and because painting is still a big part of my life, I like to think that Watkins would have been pleased, perhaps even delighted, to see his official dispatches used in the expressionistic way I have shaped them. He was, after all, an avid and iconoclastic art collector who, in his collecting as in the other passions that drove him, went against convention: he especially sought out and purchased "forbidden" Soviet art. And we know now he was also a generous man: he gave away his collection of paintings to friends, for safe-keeping.

I would have liked to have met John Watkins. A well-travelled man who spoke many languages, he told a good story. He believed in friendship, liked and admired beautiful women and was comfortable in their company. He was also an excellent pianist and an unpretentious bonvivant who treasured a good meal and a decent glass of wine. He lived in a fascinating period and was good at his work, though in a difficult posting in a dreadful city. Moscow, during the 1950s and early 1960s, was designated by External Affairs as a "hardship posting." In Moscow he quickly learned to speak Russian fluently, a unique quality among Western diplomats even in those most intense days of the Cold War.

Because Watkins developed high-level contacts in the Soviet Politburo that were the envy of most other diplomats, especially the Americans, he was able to bring Prime Minister Lester Pearson and Nikita Khrushchev together during 1955 in what must have been one of the most extraordinary meetings ever held between two heads of state from East and West during those Cold War years. The two leaders had absolutely nothing in common: Khrushchev, son of a coal miner in the Donbass region of the Ukraine, a revolutionary rifleman whose first wife died of starvation during the horrendous famine of 1921 while he was at the front, was then living under threat of assassination from his Politburo colleagues; and Pearson, the urbane intellectual and internationally acclaimed luminary from the United Nations, was soon to be awarded the Nobel Peace Prize. According to Watkins' account and those of others present, the two leaders did not exactly connect. Nevertheless, it was during these meetings that Ambassador Watkins played an unsung but key role in finessing what would become the massive grain deals that, beginning in 1955, sold millions of tons of Canadian wheat to the Soviet Union. Paid for in gold bullion, these sales, right through the 1960s, brought wealth to western farmers and their families. They were also an irritant to the U.S. government, which saw them as "trading with the enemy" — despite the fact that its own western grain farmers were clamouring to be allowed to do the same. Ironically, Watkins' success, his contacts in the Politburo, his diplomatic skill, his fluency in the language, and his genuine love for all things Russian were used against him in those paranoid times, and no doubt became another reason for the CIA to justify their labelling Watkins an "agent of influence."

Watkins went against convention in that he lived as a homosexual when it was an extremely dangerous time to be one. Surrounded by manipulative and homophobic intelligence officers — on both sides of the Iron Curtain — and in a career that made it even more perilous to follow his true emotions, his homosexuality would in the end cost him his reputation, at least in the eyes of conventional diplomatic and government society. Finally, it certainly cost him his life.

For me, the Watkins story began almost twenty years ago when, during the research I did for an earlier novel, S. Portrait of a Spy, I kept hearing whispers suggesting that the "official story" of Watkins' death did not reflect what had really happened. Since his death on October 12, 1964, this story maintained that Watkins had died suddenly of a heart attack during a farewell dinner with some friends in a Montreal restaurant the night before a planned return to live in retirement in France.

The official story held up until 1980, when, through a lawyer, I dug up Watkins' death certificate in the Montreal archives and immediately recognized the name of an RCMP security services officer, Harry Brandes, who was described as a "friend" who had witnessed the death. I phoned the attending Montreal coroner who had signed the death certificate, Dr. Ilona Kerner, to ask if Brandes had been identified to her as an RCMP officer. No, he had not, she replied. Why had she written death due to "coronary thrombosis"? Had she carried out an autopsy? No, she admitted, she had not. Would she have done so if she had known Watkins was in some form of police custody? "Yes, of course," was her reply. It was immediately obvious that John Watkins had not died among friends.

Still more incredible to me was that this shabby fiction had been allowed to persist for so many years, even though Watkins had been a friend of Prime Minister Lester Pearson, External Affairs Minister Paul Martin, and many high-level bureaucrats in that department. Watkins had, after all, been one of the core group of new diplomats who, after the Second World War, built External Affairs into a modern diplomatic corps that quickly found a powerful international presence on the world's stage. Indeed, the multilingual Watkins was brilliant, and his career was carefully nurtured and fast-tracked by Pearson himself.

In life, as a professional diplomat, Watkins did much for Lester Pearson, and in death, I think, probably even more. But, strangely, you will find only the odd one-line reference to Watkins in Pearson's official autobiography. How could such a brilliant and distinguished Canadian have become overnight a "non-person" in the truest Stalinist sense? It couldn't simply be because Watkins was gay — a reality that Watkins had apparently not gone to any great pains to hide. As I dug more deeply into the story, the answer turned out to be much more complicated.

With a paperback reissue of *S. Portrait of a Spy*, I published Watkins' death certificate and all the now obvious contradictions to the official story. The media, especially in Quebec, immediately took a great interest in these revelations. And, under political pressure from the Parti Québécois government, the RCMP was soon forced to admit that John Watkins had died under police interrogation while being kept in a "safe house" — a suite in the Holiday Inn on the Côte de Liesse in Montreal — and to admit tacitly that he had been denied a basic right for all Canadian citizens: when an individual dies under such circumstances, an autopsy and inquest are mandatory. Quebec Minister of Justice Marc-André Bedard quickly called an inquest into John Watkins' death, some seventeen years after the event, and on September 1, 1980, ordered senior coroner Stanislas Dery to begin the inquiry.

In my opinion, the inquest was bizarre, misleading, and simply became the stage for a fallback position confirming the official story. The media was fed, and seized upon, the salacious and sensational information that John Watkins had been caught in a "homosexual trap" masterminded by the KGB. Allegedly, he had been photographed having sex with men supplied by the Russians, and the KGB had attempted to blackmail him into becoming an agent of influence — a diplomat who would surrender his country's own best interests to shape policies that would favour the economic and political interests of the Soviet Union.

Watkins' perceived betrayal was that he had never reported this blackmail attempt to the government or to the RCMP Security Services. But no real evidence was ever presented. No photographs of the so-called trap were ever offered. At the inquest, the RCMP consistently refused to release the full report of the interrogation that led to Watkins' death — the questions asked by the RCMP and Watkins' own answers — giving reasons that it would be damaging to the security of the state.

Further, although Coroner Dery gave a verbal finding that Watkins had died of natural causes, and referred to the original death certificate, his official written report has mysteriously disappeared from the archives of the Quebec Ministry of Justice. The current explanation is that it "may have burned in a warehouse fire in Quebec City."

To my mind, the RCMP officers who testified at the inquest left the eerie impression that the tragic consequences of Watkins' interrogation had actually been a benign form of state euthanasia. There was no recognition that the intelligence services had in all likelihood hounded the ambassador to an untimely end; rather, the implication was that the poor old ambassador, with his bad heart, had escaped both his misery and the ignominy of having to live with a destroyed reputation as an unmasked homosexual.

Nobody asked the RCMP any really tough questions. It was very hard to, for the real information was hidden behind the defensive "security" position — the Official Secrets Act. And, after the inquest, there were many newspaper exclusives — in reality, selected journalists being briefed by high-ranking RCMP executives such as the director general of intelligence, John Starnes. I've always found it fascinating, given the extremely limited range of political discussion and perspective available in our country's media, that so many conservative reporters could build reputations as "investigative journalists" simply by reporting what the RCMP wanted them to know.

These journalists faithfully reported a truly misleading spin — that External Affairs had tried to protect John Watkins from RCMP interrogation — which turns out to be another layer of the official story. A close examination of declassified files reveals that Canada's ambassador to France, Jules Léger, was at first reluctant to participate in a "trap" that was to be sprung on Watkins. After a few phone calls and coded messages back and forth between the Solicitor General's Office, the Department of External Affairs in Ottawa, and the RCMP officers in Paris, however, Léger was quickly brought in line and from then on cooperated fully with the RCMP Security Services. The RCMP, it seems, was afraid of only two things once Watkins was confronted with the charge that he had become an agent of influence — that he would commit suicide or attempt to escape to Moscow.

Watkins, of course, did neither, and somehow he was pressured into going to Britain, where he was interrogated by MI5 and cleared, and then convinced to return to Canada for further interrogations by the RCMP and the CIA. At the time, he was still recovering from a serious heart attack.

In the end, the inquest into Watkins' death and the subsequent commerce between the press and the secret police reinforced the fallback position of the official story: that John Watkins was a weak and pathetic homosexual whose self-indulgence had somehow made his government, his country, and the whole free world vulnerable to the masterminds of the KGB, and that, sadly, it was simply better that he should be forgotten. Hidden under this cover was the somewhat reluctant admission by the RCMP that Watkins had not succumbed to any Soviet blackmail — real or imagined — and that he was totally innocent of any treasonable acts.

I think now, given the documents I have more recently been able to obtain through the Freedom of Information Act, both in Canada and the United States, and through interviews, reports, and conversations I have had over twenty years, that it is possible to arrive at a much more sober and plausible conclusion regarding the events that led up to John Watkins' death. I have used my deductions as the premise for writing this book.

In early 1964, shortly after the assassination of U.S. President John Kennedy, James Jesus Angleton, the head of the CIA's counter-intelligence branch, made a special visit to the British intelligence organizations of MI5 and MI6. There he tried to convince the heads of the British secret police that he had new and substantial proof that the recently elected prime minister, Harold Wilson of the Labour Party, was an active agent for the KGB. Unfortunately, he explained, he could only reveal his sources if MI5 promised to act against Wilson.

Even the most eager-to-believe right wingers in MI5 balked at these conditions. A year earlier, Angleton had supplied his prize Soviet defector, Anatoli Golitsin, to the British for debriefing. Golitsin, Angleton claimed, could prove that Wilson, a committed socialist, had, on instructions from the KGB, killed his predecessor, Hugh Gaitskell (who had died suddenly and mysteriously in January 1963). Gaitskell had been the quintessential pro-American middle-roader, the kind of leader U.S. foreign policy planners lavish with money and support, and love to put in power in countries all over the world. Wilson was just the beginning, Angleton assured his MI5 colleagues. He showed them a long list of names that included many members of Wilson's Cabinet and leading supporters of the Labour Party who came from the private sector. In all, Golitsin supplied more than sixty "serials" — leads that in the end went nowhere, and were what the then head of MI5, Peter Wright, later described as "rotten harvest."

It was not that the extreme right-wing warriors that headed up MI5 and MI6 in 1964 were averse to hearing Angleton's accusations against Harold Wilson. For years they had been running their own dirty-tricks campaign in an attempt to destroy Wilson, who, as a socialist leader, was anathema to the extreme right-wing ideology of British intelligence executives. But the timing of Angleton's visit was terrible, for it coincided with an extreme state of panic in both MI5 and MI6. So severe was their predicament that, British journalist Anthony Leigh writes in his book *The Wilson Plot*, if the real truth had come out at the time, the two intelligence organizations would have been discredited and immediately dismantled by Wilson's government.

The crisis centred around the escape to Moscow of British Intelligence's now notorious double agent Kim Philby and the revelation of the "fourth man," Anthony Blunt, in the spy group of Burgess, Maclean, and Philby. Worse, before Philby had been allowed to slip away to Moscow, he had confessed to an MI6 officer in Beirut that he had been working for the KGB for many years. Blunt, it turned out, had been employed by the Russians equally as long as Philby, and, even more incredible, MI5 had known about him for years but had done nothing publicly to unmask Blunt as he continued in his role as official arts adviser to the queen. These facts were effectively hidden from Harold Wilson when he was leader of the parliamentary opposition, and he didn't realize until he came to power a few months later how profoundly he had been manipulated by the intelligence services of his own country.

So the ironic reality was that, in 1964, British Intelligence needed Prime Minister Harold Wilson more than he needed them. They could not really afford to antagonize him openly and risk their own dismantling. (Nevertheless, over the next ten years they kept up a campaign of smears and misinformation, often planted in the tabloid British press, to undermine their prime minister.) And, finally, British intelligence executives were loath to act on Angleton's information because they suspected that behind Angleton's ploy was a serious attempt to seize control of their organizations.

Rebuffed by his British counterparts, Angleton returned to CIA headquarters in Langley, Virginia, where he continued to work on his long-held belief, apparently verified again by Soviet defector Golitsin, that the Canadian prime minister, Lester Pearson, was also a KGB agent. The CIA took great personal offence at Pearson's independent stands in foreign policy, his grain trades with the Soviet Union, his anti-war positions on Vietnam, and especially his friendly stance on Cuba.

The obsession of Angleton with Pearson as a KGB agent now sounds completely bizarre, even mad — and there is good evidence to suggest that the head of CIA counter-intelligence was no longer of sound mind. Philby's defection to Moscow had left Angleton a shattered and embittered man. He had known Philby since 1948 and they had developed a close friendship. From information that is now surfacing from CIA files, there is much to suggest that Angleton had revealed to Philby sensitive information that had seriously damaged U.S. counter-intelligence efforts.

On his return to Langley, Angleton invited Canada's head of counter-espionage, Leslie James Bennett, who ran the KGB desk for the RCMP, to a high-level meeting. Bennett, a British-trained intelligence officer, had a less than successful career. His inability to catch any Soviet spies of real stature during the fifteen or more years that he ran the KGB desk at RCMP headquarters in Ottawa, and his failure to lure Soviet intelligence officers into becoming double agents, triggered suspicions as to his loyalty — not only from some of his own colleagues but also from the CIA. (It is reported, however, that he wrote a really good memo).

Bennett went to Langley and, after business and over drinks, Angleton launched into a tirade against the British intelligence services, followed by a virulent attack on Prime Minister Wilson and his Labour government, denouncing them all as communists. Bennett, who came from a bleak British coal-mining valley, made the mistake of attempting to defend his colleagues. He reportedly told Angleton that he and his CIA cronies didn't know the difference between a socialist and a communist. For his pains, he was suddenly physically assaulted by one of Angleton's aides. He paid dearly for his outburst: Angleton mounted an attack on Bennett that eventually drove him out of his job in the RCMP under the suspicion that he was a KGB mole. (Bennett's secret dismissal was at the heart of my book, *S. Portrait of a Spy*.) Many years later, the RCMP belatedly exonerated Bennett from any suspicion of being a communist agent.

But before Bennett's dismissal, Angleton somehow succeeded in pressuring the RCMP into the persecution of John Watkins. Ironically, it was Bennett himself who went to France and convinced Watkins to submit to an MI5 interrogation and, later, to return to Canada. Again, the evidence that set this tragic train of events in motion was reportedly based on information that came from Angleton's Soviet KGB defectors. It was fuelled by Angleton's knowledge that Watkins and Herbert Norman had been good friends.

Norman was the Canadian diplomat who had allegedly committed suicide in 1958 by jumping off a building in Cairo while being hounded by Angleton and the U.S. Committee on Un-American Activities. Lester Pearson had been caught out in a careless if well-intentioned public misstatement in his initial defence of Norman. (This sorry episode has been meticulously documented in the recent NFB film directed by John Kramer, *The Man Who Might Have Been: An Enquiry into the Life and Death of Herbert Norman*.) Pearson's incautious explanation gave more fuel to Angleton's conviction that Pearson was a KGB spy. Angleton wanted to bring down Pearson, and this time he was going to use John Watkins as a stalking horse to get at the prime minister. I have no doubt that Angleton believed he would somehow find vindication in extracting a confession from Watkins that would fatally compromise Pearson and bring down the Canadian government.

My conclusion is, that in this context and after being badly burned by the Norman affair, Pearson did not act to save his former friend and colleague John Watkins. Of course, even if he had done so, I am sure Angleton would have seen it as one more attempt by Pearson to block an investigation that would inevitably lead to himself.

Angleton was not alone in his pursuit of the Canadian prime minister. The FBI's Edgar Hoover was also taken with the idea that Pearson was a KGB agent. There are voluminous FBI files on Pearson, mostly built on poisonous and uncorroborated evidence flowing from the infamous Elizabeth Bentley. But, interestingly enough, the FBI files completely cleared John Watkins — until the summer of 1964, when the FBI got wind that Angleton was on the hunt for Pearson and a hold was put on Watkins' files.

Angleton's obsessions might now seem laughable, but the CIA's pursuit of leaders it didn't like is well known and chilling: Lumumba in the Congo, Allende in Chile, and Diem in South Vietnam all died violently. Others were simply undermined: Gough Whitlam in Australia, for daring to demand a different deal in the sharing of secrets; and Willi Brandt in West Germany, the target of a STASI sting that was gleefully observed and leaked to the press by the CIA.

In the end, for all his own political and personal reasons, Pearson abandoned Watkins to the RCMP and the CIA. Thereafter, Watkins was forsaken by the only man who could have saved him. As prime minister, Pearson must have been briefed on the interrogation; to stop it, all he had to do was pick up the phone. Evil triumphs, as the philosophical observation goes, when good men do nothing. To me, the great unanswered question that still remains in this many-layered story of political paranoia, corruption of power by intelligence agencies, and personal betrayal of long-time friends is why the RCMP so willingly went along with the CIA in the persecution of John Watkins, in what was, really, an attempted coup to bring down the prime minister and the government of Canada.

I hope this book in some modest way begins to resurrect the spirit of a decent and honourable man who served his country well. I believe he deserved better, a lot better, than what he got.

If the reader finds merit in this book, a large part of that must go the extraordinary group of professionals I had the great good fortune to work beside. First to my editor, Rosemary Shipton, whose indefatigable intelligence and wit kept prodding me to try harder. Then to managing editor Don Bastian and vice-president Nelson Doucet at Stoddart, whose patience I have sorely tried but whose support for the project has never faltered. And last, but not least, to two expert researchers, Elizabeth Klink and Virginia Clark, who put up with my nagging and impossible demands and always came up with the goods. As for any faults the reader may find in the writing, I take full responsibility.

IAN ADAMS
Toronto
February 1999

11 e 09/10